Forge Books by Anthony Bruno

Devil's Food
Double Espresso
Hot Fudge

HOT FUDGE

ANTHONY BRUNO

FORGE®

A TOM DOHERTY ASSOCIATES BOOK / NEW YORK

HOT FUDGE

Copyright © 2000 by Anthony Bruno

A Forge Book
Published by Tom Doherty Associates, LLC
175 Fifth Avenue
New York, NY 10010

www.tor.com

Forge® is a registered trademark of Tom Doherty Associates, LLC.

Library of Congress Cataloging-in-Publication Data

Bruno, Anthony.
    Hot fudge / Anthony Bruno.—1st ed.
      p. cm.
    "A Tom Doherty Associates book."
    ISBN 0-312-86651-8 (alk. paper)
    1. Parole officers—Fiction. 2. San Francisco (Calif.)—Fiction. I. Title

PS3552.R82 H68 2000
813'.54—dc21

                                             00-026421

First Edition: August 2000

Printed in the United States of America

0 9 8 7 6 5 4 3 2 1

For my in-house sex yenta
whose healing powers are legend

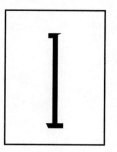

1

"I don't think this is a good idea," Loretta Kovacs said.

"I do," Frank Marvelli said, and he kissed her again.

She didn't object. In fact, she might have been holding him a little tighter than he was holding her, but it was hard to tell. They were sitting on the lone hard bench inside one of the holding cells at the rear of the offices of the Parole Violators Search Unit—better known as the Jump Squad—where they both worked as parole officers. The Jump Squad picked up parolees who had violated the conditions of their parole and stopped reporting to their assigned POs. The walls of the cell were Pepto-Bismol pink, and the bars weren't bars at all. It was cyclone fencing. But the decor didn't matter to either of them. *They* were what mattered.

"Marvelli," Loretta mumbled, her lips mashed against his, "it's getting late. People will be getting here soon."

Marvelli brought his wristwatch to his face without disengaging from Loretta's lips. "It's ten to eight," he said. "We've got time."

"Julius usually gets here early," she said. Julius was their boss, Julius Monroe.

"Not this early," he said.

"Okay. You're right."

Loretta felt like a shaken-up can of Coke. She couldn't believe they were doing this. She couldn't believe she was here with Marvelli, necking. But she was, and it was pretty freakin' wonderful.

Despite some of her best fantasies, she'd never in a million years thought they would get this far. The cards were stacked against them: First of all, they worked in the same office. Second, Marvelli was not her type because he was a greaser—not the trendy retro kind but the real item, like a *T. rex* that had somehow survived the Ice Age on some uncharted tropical island. And last of all, Loretta had been absolutely convinced that Marvelli would never get over his late wife, Rene, who had lost her battle with breast cancer a little over a year ago. But finally Marvelli made his peace with it and decided it was time to move on. And Loretta had been there waiting for him at the side of life's highway, her thumb out, praying that he'd give her a lift.

Not that she was desperate. Not at all. She'd gotten used to celibacy . . . so used to it, it was scary. But she could've managed just fine without a man. Not happily, but she could have done it. Fortunately she was now out of the running for a *Guinness Book of World Records* citation.

Marvelli squeezed her closer to him, and she held the back of his neck, feeling the goop he put in his hair between her fingers. That didn't bother her anymore. But as their tongues wrestled, she had to admit that the constant taste of chocolate was beginning to bother her. It had been nice at first, but here it was—eight o'clock in the morning—and he was already eating ice cream. He seemed to be eating ice cream all the time. This couldn't be good for his health, she thought. And if he dropped dead and left her all alone, that would be disastrous for *her* health, too.

She glanced down at the empty pint of Arnie and Barry's Elmer Fudge Whirl sitting on the floor next to Marvelli's pointy, black, imitation-alligator shoe, and she just couldn't contain herself.

"Marvelli," she said, pulling away from his lips, "we have to talk."

He looked startled. "About what?"

"Your eating."

He shrugged, puzzled. "What about it?"

"Ice cream in the morning? What is it? Are you pregnant or PMSing?"

"Loretta," he said. "You know I have a problem with low blood sugar."

"But you eat constantly." *And you don't gain an ounce,* she thought jealously.

"This isn't news, Loretta. I've always eaten like this."

"I realize that, but this ice-cream obsession is something new. I don't want you keeling over with a heart attack before you're forty."

Marvelli looked a little embarrassed. "C'mon, I wouldn't call it an obsession."

"No? What *would* you call it?"

"I just love the taste. I mean, this Elmer Fudge Whirl stuff is out of this world. Arnie and Barry's has Ben and Jerry's beat by a mile, at least with this flavor. Their other flavors aren't nearly as good, but this stuff . . ." Marvelli kissed the tips of his fingers like a French gourmet.

Loretta just gave him a look. "Shut up and kiss me," she said.

"Isn't that a song?"

She grabbed his lapels and pulled him closer, grinding her lips into his. Their tongues said hi, and it was like live wires touching. *Bam!* She was back in heaven.

●   ●   ●

Marvelli moved Loretta's hair away from her cheek as he tilted his head the other way, rubbing noses with her as he continued to kiss her. He just couldn't get enough of her these days, and he'd be perfectly happy to stay right here, locked up in this cell, the two of them making out like teenagers for a long, long time. Just the two of them . . .

And maybe a freezer full of Elmer Fudge Whirl, in case they got hungry.

He strained an eyeball to catch a glimpse of the empty pint container on the floor, and suddenly he felt guilty for thinking about ice cream when he was kissing Loretta. Maybe she was right. Maybe he was getting a little obsessed with this stuff.

He glanced down at the carton again, remembering the fudgy taste. *Nah*, he thought. *I'm not obsessed. It's just good stuff, that's all. She's just a little upset because of her weight, maybe.*

Of course, Loretta hadn't been as crazy about her weight lately, not since they'd started going out. It used to be her number-one hot button, but she'd calmed down about it . . . a little. She didn't exactly welcome the topic if it came up, but she didn't go ballistic either. He'd noticed that the little markers on her bathroom scale hadn't moved in quite a while. When he'd first started staying at her place, the sliding plastic markers were always set back to zero, even after he'd set one for himself. Then one day while he was brushing his teeth, he looked down and saw that one of the markers was on 178 pounds. She had to have put it there because that wasn't his weight, but she hadn't bothered to set it back. He didn't say anything, of course—he wasn't that stupid— but he kept checking it whenever he was in the bathroom, and it stayed there. He figured she'd forgotten about it because she wasn't weighing herself anymore. The old Loretta would never have left evidence like that behind.

He was glad that she'd come to terms with her looks. She still had a bit of a self-image problem, but for the life of him he couldn't understand why. He thought she looked great. Thick, wavy, naturally dirty-blond hair that hung just below her shoulders. Peachy skin. Green eyes that sparkled like jewels. And a body that made him feel like Columbus sailing the seven seas, discovering new worlds all the time. In fact, at this very moment he had an incredible urge to unbutton her jade silk blouse and go exploring. Maybe he'd discover America.

His hands slowly slid up the satiny material along her sides as they continued to kiss. He was heading for land, his main mast at full sail.

Suddenly he thought back to their first time, which wasn't all that long ago. Five and a half weeks, to be exact. She'd been wearing this same blouse that night. They were on a stakeout, sitting in an unmarked Department of Parole Chevy Cavalier, watching a two-family brownstone on a quiet street in Hoboken. They'd gotten a tip that a seventy-three-year-old minor-league wiseguy named Carlo Carlucci was visiting his longtime *goomah* who lived in that house. Carlucci hadn't reported to his PO in over eight months, and Loretta and Marvelli had been assigned to his case. Even though Carlucci was relatively harmless, he was still a made man, which made him a priority. But Marvelli sort of knew the old guy, and he didn't want to embarrass him in front of his lady friend. Instead of banging on the door to make the arrest, Marvelli had convinced Loretta to wait until Carlucci came out of the house and went to his burgundy red Lincoln Continental so they could take him quietly out on the street. It was after one A.M., and they had already been waiting in the Cavalier for three and a half hours.

Marvelli had been going crazy, trying to keep his eyes on the building when the only thing his little pupils wanted to do was look at Loretta. He'd been thinking about nothing but her for months. He was going *wacky* thinking about her. But he hadn't dared do anything about it. He didn't know exactly what was stopping him, but he was afraid it wouldn't work out—afraid that it hadn't been long enough since Rene had died, afraid of what his mother-in-law would say, afraid that he'd wouldn't know what to do with a woman who wasn't Rene, afraid that he'd blow it with Loretta and just end up humiliating himself. But sitting in that car with Loretta right next to him—their shoulders practically touching—he was going out of his mind. The sexual tension in the car was so thick, he could have made sandwiches.

Finally at 1:21 A.M.—he knew because he'd been checking his watch all night for want of something better to do—he turned to her and said, "Loretta—?"

"Yes," she said immediately. It wasn't a "Yes, what is it, Marvelli?" kind of yes. It was more like a "Yes, of course, definitely" yes.

"Yes, what?" he said, playing dumb. "You don't know what I'm gonna ask."

"You're right. That's why I'm answering in case you don't ask the question I want you to ask." Her eyes glimmered in the moonlight. She was leaning toward him. He could smell her shampoo, they were so close.

"Oh . . ." he said, wondering if he should keep going. "And what is it you want me to ask?"

"I want you to ask me what I've been dying to ask you."

"And what's that?" He leaned closer to her.

"Don't play dumb, Marvelli." She took his hand.

He felt as if he were going to burst. His heart was thumping like mad, and he felt light-headed. Somehow his other hand had found its way to her thigh, and when he realized it was there, his palm started to tingle. "Loretta"—he cleared his throat—"Loretta? Can I—?"

"Yes!"

But his hand was already on the back of her neck before he'd even started to ask if he could kiss her. He pulled her closer and put his lips to hers, and pretty soon their hands were everywhere, and their tongues were doing a slow tango, and one thing led to another and then another and then something else, and it was almost four o'clock before he realized that they were in the backseat and his pants were down around his knees and Carlo Carlucci's burgundy Lincoln was gone. Carlucci had gotten away. But neither of them cared.

Oh, Loretta, Loretta, Marvelli thought in a dizzy haze. Physically he was in the Pepto-Bismol cell, but in his head he was in the backseat of that Cavalier. His hands were sliding under Loretta's blouse, heading north along her ribs. *I want you so bad,* he thought. *Right here, right now—*

Suddenly her elbows clamped down on his hands like twin rattraps.

"What?" he said, breathing hard, blinking his eyes, not entirely sure where he was.

"Not here," she whispered urgently. "What if Julius catches us? He—"

"And what if I do catch you?"

"Jesus!" Marvelli flinched, snatching his hands back. He looked through the cyclone fence and saw his boss staring in at them, clucking his tongue and shaking his head. Julius Monroe was short and stout with a pointed goatee and penetrating eyes. His dark skin reflected the dim light of the naked forty-watt lightbulb inside the cell. He was wearing black slacks, a gray dress shirt, a black-and-white silk tie with piano keys running down the length of it, and his ever-present skullcap.

"Must be mating season at the zoo," Julius said, stepping into the open doorway.

Loretta was blushing through her scalp. Marvelli felt plain stupid for getting caught like this. Loretta was right. A cell wasn't the place for this.

"Julius," she said, as she quickly checked the buttons of her blouse, "this isn't what you think."

"Oh, yes, it is!" His belly laugh bounced off the cinder-block walls as he looked from one parole officer to the other. "Mizz Kovacs! Marvelli the marvelous! You two are fooling no one."

Marvelli caught Loretta's eye, looking for some help. Should he fess up or deny, deny, deny?

"Let me explain," Loretta said.

"No need, my dear," Julius said, cutting her off. "It's plain as day and as dark as night. You two have been skulking around here for weeks, thinking no one knows. But love is blind, and you two need radar if you think people haven't figured it out yet."

"What do you mean?" Marvelli said, trying to sound indignant.

"Please, Marvelli, spare the DeNiro routine. It's not your trip."

Marvelli looked at Loretta. There was no explaining their way out of it now, and they both knew it. "So now what?" he said to Julius. "You want one of us to quit?"

Loretta sighed. "No one has to quit. I'll put in for a transfer if that's what you want, Julius."

But Julius just scowled at them both. "Are you out of your minds? It's hard enough getting people to work in the Jump Squad. I don't want either of you going anywhere."

"But you don't mind that we're—?" Marvelli didn't exactly know how to phrase it.

Julius cocked an eyebrow, and lines appeared on his forehead like venetian blinds. "Yes, I very much do mind, Marvelli. Take the slap-and-tickle act somewhere else. You can be in love on your own time, not the state's."

"I'm sorry," Loretta said, frowning. "We'll try to control ourselves in the future."

"How about controlling yourselves right now?" Julius said. "Look, people, I don't want to be the love cop, but this goo-goo eyes stuff is bad for morale. The other POs have been talking. It looks like I'm running a sloppy operation around here. That ain't good, people. Not for *vous* or *moi*."

"I hear what you're saying," Marvelli said. A sinkhole was opening up in the pit of his stomach. This was just what he didn't want to happen.

"I hope you hear what I'm saying," Julius said, "because I'm not so sure your ears are tuned in to my melody. We haven't been playing in the same key lately."

Marvelli got defensive. "What do you mean? I've been getting my work done."

Julius pointed at the empty Arnie and Barry's container on the floor. "It's things like this that make me go atonal, Marvelli. What's a jumper supposed to think when he gets locked up with your designer ice-cream trash? Our clients already have an acute sense of the have/have-not scene. They don't need us rubbing their noses in it."

"I wasn't going to leave it in here," Marvelli said.

"Doesn't matter," Julius shot back. "This stuff's all over the office. In the refrigerator, the wastepaper baskets, on the windowsills, on top of your desk. If you're gonna OD on ice cream, can't you do it just as well with the store brand?"

Marvelli's face started to get hot. He hadn't been eating *that* much Arnie and Barry's.

"Look, you know I don't like being the finger-wagger," Julius said. "I'm a man of peace and beauty. This authority stuff goes against my grain. All I'm saying is shape up and do your jobs the way you used to so that we don't have to have this little chat again. You picking up on what I'm putting down?"

Marvelli and Loretta nodded glumly.

"Now don't go acting like Adam and Eve getting the big eviction notice. I'm not mad at either of you. I'm just giving you a heads up before I *have* to get mad."

"Got'cha," Marvelli said.

"We'll behave," Loretta said.

"Amen then," Julius said. "No more needs to be said."

A woman's voice gradually drifted into the holding cells from the next room. She was singing, but there were no words, just *do-dos* and *dah-dahs*. Still, Marvelli recognized the song right away— "Viva Las Vegas." But when he suddenly realized who the husky mezzo was, his face sagged.

"Julius!" the woman called out. "You back there, my man?"

"I'm here."

"I got a jumper for you, J. A good one. And that ain't all I got."

"*Who's that?*" Loretta mouthed to Marvelli.

"You don't want to know," he muttered.

"Where are you, Julius? I got a lot to tell you."

Julius rolled his eyes. "I'm coming, Vissa, my sweet."

"Thankyouverymuch," the woman said, drawling it out to make it sound like one word. It was actually a pretty good Elvis imitation.

Too good, Marvelli thought.

Marvelli, Loretta, and Julius filed out of the holding pens and into the bright fluorescent lights of the main office like moles coming out of the ground. This was where the POs' desks were lined up in two straight rows surrounded by dozens of file cabinets pushed up against the walls, each one bulging with case files. No one else had arrived for work yet. The only people in the office were this woman, who had just called out for Julius, and a tall skinny guy with his wrists cuffed in front of him. Loretta didn't recognize either of them, though it was clear that the woman had appre- hended the man. But the woman didn't look like she was in law enforcement. She looked more like a lounge act.

Loretta tried not to stare at her, but it was hard not to. The woman's hair was jet black and voluminous—gravity-defying mounds of it encased her head and shoulders like whipped cream. Her lipstick was a shimmery pale pink, and it looked like she'd used a felt-tip pen for eyeliner. Her fingernails matched her lipstick, and the extensive collection of bracelets on both wrists jingled whenever she made the slightest movement. She was wearing black patent leather boots, skintight bell-bottom jeans, a hip-length black leather jacket, and a red velveteen scoop-neck top that showed off some considerable cleavage. But the odd thing about her was that the sum was greater than the garish parts. Somehow it all fell together and produced a very attractive person—even if she was a bit on the slutty side.

"How do, Jul'?" she said to Monroe. "And Marvelli! Goodness gracious, it's been a long time." Marvelli extended his hand, but she ignored it and threw her arms around him, giving him a big hug.

"How's it going, Vissa?" he said.

"Not bad, not bad at all," she said. "Say, how's that little girl of yours? Nina, right?"

Marvelli nodded. "Nina's not so little anymore. She'll be fourteen in a couple of months."

"Good golly, Miss Molly! I remember her when she was just a little bitty thing."

Loretta couldn't quite place the woman's accent. She had the distinctive delivery of a Jersey girl, but her phrasing was down-home Southern.

"And who might this be?" the woman said, peering at Loretta with her chin on Marvelli's shoulder.

"This is Loretta Kovacs," Julius said. "She joined us about a year ago. Loretta, meet Vissa Mylowe."

"Nice to meet you," Vissa said, reaching past Marvelli to shake Loretta's hand. "Vissa is short for *Elvissa*. See, I was named after my daddy, sort of. His name was actually Dexter, but he worked most of his life as an Elvis impersonator. He was born and raised in Tupelo, Mississippi, just like the King, so he sounded just like him, singing *and* talking. My mom—Doris was her name—was a do-do girl in a girl-group sound-alike band called the Sha-la-las. They met in Atlantic City, fell in love at first sight, and never left. The two of them melded together like a great big hunk-a-hunk-a burning love."

"Really," Loretta said. Vissa was still pumping her hand.

"You may think I'm forward, Loretta, but I always tell people my whole story up front because I know they're just dying to know how I got my unusual name."

"Of course." Loretta nodded, her hand still getting pumped. She really wasn't *that* curious about Vissa's name.

"Vissa's a PO, too," Marvelli explained. "She works down the shore, out of the Toms River office."

"Yeah, it's teeny compared to this one," Vissa said. She had a cute way of wrinkling her nose. It was hard to tell what she really looked like under all the mascara and eyeliner, but her style kind of reminded Loretta of Rene Marvelli.

"So what brings you back to the mother ship?" Julius asked, as he eyed the tall, skinny jumper who was just standing there, showing attitude. The handcuffed man was in his early thirties, but he looked like hell. His complexion was sallow, and what hair he had left was dirty, greasy, and unkempt. He had too many teeth for his small mouth, and the pencil-thin mustache just highlighted that fact. He was wearing a stylish three-button black suit with an open-collar white shirt, but it looked like he'd slept in that outfit several nights running. Julius tried to look him in the eye, but the man had his head tilted straight back. He was staring at the ceiling, showing a very pointy Adam's apple.

"This is Freddy Maxwell," Vissa said to Julius, "but he's no big deal."

"Oh, really?" Freddy muttered under his breath, still looking at the ceiling.

"Hasn't reported to his regular PO in a year," Vissa said. "I spotted him coming out of some no-tell motel in Seaside Heights. He got in his car before I could get to him, so I had to follow him all the way up here to East Orange. The guy's a pimp."

"I beg your pardon," Freddy mumbled. His voice was so nasal it sounded like he had cotton jammed up both nostrils.

"I decided to bring him here 'cause it was closer," Vissa said.

"Could've killed me in that friggin' thing you call a car," Freddy droned. He didn't try to hide his contempt for her.

Vissa stopped smiling and got in his face. "Your attitude leaves something to be desired, sonny boy. And unless you want me to hand you that pitiful little thing you got between your legs in a doggie bag, you'd better shut your mouth."

Loretta couldn't hold back her grin. Vissa had as much attitude as Loretta had.

Freddy mumbled something, but no one could understand what he was saying.

Marvelli jerked his thumb at the pimp. "So if this isn't the catch of the day, what's your big news, Vissa?"

"Brace yourselves." Vissa extended all ten fingers, looking from Marvelli to Julius. "I think I've found him." She waited for their explosive reaction, but when it didn't come, she frowned, looking like an unhappy raccoon.

Marvelli looked at Loretta as he stuck out his lower lip and shrugged.

Julius was still waiting for the punch line. "Who, dear Vissa? Who did you find?"

Vissa shook her fists. "Who the hell have I been looking for the past eight years, for God's sake? *Ira Krupnick!* Who else?"

Marvelli's eyes rolled toward his boss, who simultaneously rolled his eyes back at Marvelli. They wanted to be impressed, but it was clear that they were both skeptical.

"Are you two deaf or what?" Vissa said, raising her voice. "Didn't you hear me? I think I found Ira Krupnick. *Ira Krupnick!*"

When the two men didn't say anything, Loretta jumped in. "Excuse my ignorance, Vissa, but who's Ira Krupnick!"

Vissa threw up her hands, totally annoyed. "You mean these guys never told you about him? Ira Krupnick is only the worst case this office has ever seen. He is the most recidivist criminal this state has ever incarcerated. And the most low-down. And the most dangerous. And the slipperiest. When it comes to bad characters, Krupnick is the king." After a moment Vissa blinked, surprised by her own unwitting reference to *the* King. It was obvious from the sour look on her face that the misguided allusion had left a bad taste in her mouth.

Julius rubbed his chin. "Well, yes, Krupnick is a bad cat, but I don't know if I'd exactly put it that strongly."

"I would." Vissa turned to Marvelli. "Don't *you* think so?"

Marvelli pressed his lips together as if he were thinking about it. "Well, yeah, he is bad, but, you know, it's not like he's the only one like that in the world."

Loretta noticed Marvelli's gaze wandering back toward the old refrigerator in the hallway. He was thinking about food. He was *always* thinking about food. Especially fudge-whirl ice cream. It was amazing he wasn't a blimp.

Freddy the pimp mumbled something.

"What?" Vissa snapped at him impatiently. "Speak up. No one can understand you."

"I said, what'd this Krupnick guy do? Why's he so bad?"

"It's none of your g.d. business," she said.

"Well, actually I'm kind of curious myself," Loretta said. "What *did* he do?"

Vissa sighed loudly and tossed her head. Her big hair didn't move. She was clearly exasperated with the men, so she addressed her remarks to Loretta. "My friends here seem to have forgotten. Ira Krupnick was convicted of selling guns and silencers in quantity. He was also connected with the kidnapping of an executive in Philadelphia, but he was never charged with anything in that case. He's what the shrinks call a criminal opportunist, which means he'll get into anything he thinks he can get away with—you name it—theft, drugs, burglary, extortion, anything. But what makes Krupnick different is that he's also very smart. Except for the guns, he's never gotten caught on any of the other things he's been involved with. He always seems to slip away, leaving someone else holding the bag."

"Tell me to shut up if I'm out of line," Loretta said, "but it sounds like there's something personal here."

Marvelli, Julius, and Freddy all nodded simultaneously.

Vissa glowered through her mascara at the three of them. "Yes, of course, it's personal," she said. "Eight years ago, back when Krupnick had first violated his parole, I was the one who caught him. All by myself. He was sleeping off a bender at one of his girlfriends' houses. He had quite a few girlfriends at the time. This was down in Cape May. I cuffed him, got him in leg shackles, and paid a couple of truck drivers to help me get him into my car. I filled up the tank and brought him straight to this office. I didn't want to fool around handing him over to the hicks downstate. I figured Krupnick was too important." As she said this, she was staring accusingly at Marvelli.

"Now wait a minute," Marvelli said. "That was not my fault."

"I'm not saying it was. Krupnick is a superior intellect. I'm not surprised he tricked you."

Loretta glared at Vissa. What the hell did she mean by that? Loretta thought. That Marvelli was an *inferior* intellect?

Marvelli raised one finger. "No, no, no, no, Vissa. It was *your* fault. Superior intellect had nothing to do with it."

"For cryin' out loud, Marvelli, I had been driving for three hours straight. I had to pee. I asked you to watch him for *one* minute."

"No, you said *stay* with him for one minute. You had taken his leg irons off—"

"I had to. It was a long walk from where I'd parked."

Marvelli continued, "He wasn't wearing leg irons or hand-cuffs—"

"He must've picked the lock on the cuffs in the car when I wasn't looking. He must've pretended that they were locked, then took them off when I handed him to you."

"You did not *hand* him to me. You said *stay* with him. The guy was dressed pretty nice. He sounded intelligent. He didn't look like the kind of mutts we haul in here every day—"

"Hey, I resent that." Freddy said, raising his voice.

"You shut up," Vissa snarled.

Marvelli ignored the pimp. "From the way Ira Krupnick looked that day, I thought he was a friend of yours, maybe another PO. How was I supposed to know he was a jumper? You never actually told me."

Vissa pointed down at the floor by the entrance to the holding cells. "He was standing right there—*right there!*—and you just let him walk out the door. *Poof!* He was gone!" She looked at Loretta, eyes wide. "And I only went out to pee. Can you believe it? Men!"

Loretta didn't say anything, but she didn't appreciate Vissa running down Marvelli like this. Maybe there was a reason she worked out of the field office down the shore. Maybe nobody here could stand to work with her.

"Calm down, Vissa," Julius said. "You're messing up the energy in here. Now tell me. Where's Krupnick, and why didn't you apprehend him?"

"It was a fluke," she said. "I was down in Atlantic City in one of the casinos, looking for another jumper, when I spotted this guy playing blackjack. He looked familiar, but I wasn't sure because he has a full beard and he's a lot heavier than Krupnick was eight years ago. He was with a bunch of other guys, a few of them bruisers, so I kept my distance. But the more I watched him, the more I was convinced it was him. Luckily he has an account at that casino, so I was able to get an address. He's living in Southport, Connecticut, using the name Arnie Farber. I think Marvelli and I should go up there and check him out."

Marvelli stuck out his hands, palm up. "What do you need me for?"

Vissa gave him a withering look. "For a second opinion, Marvelli. You're the only other PO we've got who's ever seen Krupnick up close."

"Gimme a break, will ya, Vissa? I've got my own cases to take care of."

Vissa looked pleadingly at Loretta. "You can stand to be without him for a day, can't you?"

Loretta's face turned red. "What do you mean?" she said defensively. *How the hell does this woman know about us?* she thought.

"Well, you two work as a team, don't you? I mean, that's what I heard?"

Loretta was embarrassed for having jumped to conclusions. Sneaking around with Marvelli was making her paranoid. "It's up to him," she said quickly, trying to cover her tracks.

"C'mon, Marvelli," Vissa pleaded. "Southport's not that far. We can do it today. Soon as I get Freddy here squared away."

Freddy gave her a drop-dead look.

"I've got a lot to do today," Marvelli protested. "I can't just take off."

Vissa let loose like a steam whistle. "This is Ira Krupnick we're talking about, for chrissake! He was on the state's most wanted list at one time. What do you have to do that's more important than this?"

Vissa looked to Loretta with pleading eyes. Loretta stiffened. *I'm not his keeper,* she thought. *He can do what he wants.*

"I told you," Marvelli said. "I'm too busy."

"Don't be a jerk, Marvelli," Vissa said. "This is important. Tell him, Julius. He *has* to help me with this."

But Marvelli's back was up now. "I don't have to do *anything*, Vissa."

She raised her index finger and stuck a frosty pink fingernail in his face. "Don't take that tone with me, pal."

"Oh, yeah? And what're you gonna do about it?"

She smirked at him. "Don't make me embarrass you, Marvelli. You know I can."

Loretta furrowed her brows. What the hell did *that* mean? she wanted to know.

Julius stepped between Marvelli and Vissa. "Cease and desist, you two. You're destroying my good-morning aura. Let's take this into my office. Now."

"Fine," Vissa said.

Marvelli just scowled.

"Loretta," Julius said, "will you process Mr. Freddy here while I play Solomon and cut these two brats in half?"

"Sure, no problem," Loretta said.

Vissa pulled the handcuff keys out of her pocket and started to toss them to Loretta. The two women exchanged wary glances just before the keys flew through the air between them.

As Vissa followed Julius to his office, Marvelli dashed back down the hallway to the refrigerator out back. "I'll be right with you," he said.

Julius rolled his eyes and glanced at Loretta. "Again?" he said.

A few minutes later Marvelli returned with a Styrofoam coffee cup filled with ice cream and a white plastic spoon.

Vissa started to laugh. "Ice cream for breakfast? I always knew you were a garbage truck, Marvelli, but now you've reached a new low."

"Have you tried this Elmer Fudge Whirl stuff?" he asked her. "Man, it's out of this world." He dug into his cup.

Vissa reached for his midsection and pinched his stomach through his shirt. "You better lay off the sweets, Marvelli," she said in a breathy whisper. "I don't want you getting fat on me now." Her lips went from a shimmery pout to a flirty grin, her eyes holding his.

Loretta couldn't believe this. Just a minute ago they'd been fighting like cats and dogs, and now Vissa was flirting with him. What was with this woman?

"Come, come, children," Julius said, as he corralled Vissa and Marvelli.

Loretta watched them file into Julius's office, not sure what to make of all this.

Freddy the pimp was staring at her, his eyes mopey, his lower lip hanging open. "So, can I go now?"

She just looked at him. "Sit down." She pointed to the wooden straight-back chair next to her desk. "We're gonna be here for a while."

"Then I can go home?"

"Eventually," she said, clearing paper off her desk.

Maybe in a few years, she thought.

Loretta pulled out a Violator Reentry form from the bottom drawer of her desk and slammed it shut with a loud boom. She found a pen in the middle drawer and wrote down the date at the top of the sheet: April 16.

"Did you file your taxes?" Freddy the pimp asked, an unlit cigarette bobbing between his lips. He was sitting next to Loretta's desk, his long gangly legs crossed as he tried to get to the lighter in his side pocket despite the handcuffs.

Loretta cocked an eyebrow at him. "Did you file *your* taxes?" she asked.

"Just trying to make conversation," he said. He flicked the lighter a few times until he got a flame and held it to his cigarette. She glared at him before he exhaled any smoke, and he picked up on the hint, blowing it out the side of his mouth and away from her.

"Got an ashtray?" he asked.

She looked around and spotted an empty Arnie and Barry's

pint on Marvelli's desk. She reached over and grabbed it, plunking it down next to Freddy's elbow. "Use this."

Freddy tapped his ash into the empty container. "Your friend ought to lay off this stuff," he said. "It's really addictive."

Loretta ignored him and continued filling out the form.

"For real," he said. "I had one girl I had to let go because of this stuff. She couldn't stop eating it. I mean, fat girls aren't really a problem in my business. A lot of guys go for that. But there's fat and then there's *fat*."

She gave him a dead-eyed stare. "Are you *trying* to piss me off?" she asked.

"Oh, no. Don't get the wrong idea. I'm just saying there's something about this particular ice cream that's hazardous to your health." He sucked on his cigarette, tipped his head back, and sent a geyser of smoke toward the ceiling.

Neither of them said anything. The only sound in the room was the soft scratch of her pen as she filled out the form.

"I'll bet he only eats this flavor," Freddy suddenly said. "The fudge whirl. That was the one that got my girl Linda into trouble. She always said the other flavors weren't nearly as good." He shook his head with regret. "She used to be so pretty. It's a shame."

Such a pretty face, Loretta thought bitterly. She must've heard that about a billion times.

"A damn shame," Freddy mumbled to himself.

Loretta kept her eyes on her work. "You're getting on my nerves, Freddy."

"Sorry." He drew on his cigarette and made his lips pop.

Loretta continued to work on the form, checking off boxes and filling in lines. She was stumped, though, when the form asked for the arresting officer's name. She couldn't remember Vissa's last name.

"Mylowe," Freddy said, reading over her shoulder. He spelled it for her.

"Thank you," she said. This guy was really beginning to bug her.

The early-morning quiet was gradually invaded by a rising din coming from Julius's office. Loretta stopped to listen. Vissa and Marvelli were going at it again.

"C'mon, Julius," Marvelli was saying. "This is ridiculous. She doesn't need me for this. Anybody in the office can go with her."

Vissa started whining. "You're the only other PO who knows what he looks like, Marvelli. How many times do I have to say it?"

"Case closed," Julius overrode them both. "Vissa, you can have Marvelli for the day. But that's it. I want to see you back here tomorrow morning as usual, O Marvelous One. And at your desk—not out back in the holding cells with . . . you know."

"But—"

"No buts. Just go."

Vissa's loud hooting laughter drowned out whatever argument Marvelli was making.

"Go," Julius ordered. "I have made my decision, and there are no appeals. Get out of here. *Andale, andele, pronto.*"

Freddy was shaking his head. "Poor bastard," he said. "I feel sorry for him."

Loretta looked up from the form. "Why?"

"I only had to spend three hours with Vissa. Your buddy's stuck with her for the whole day."

"So? What's wrong with that?"

Freddy didn't answer right away. He studied the ash on his cigarette. "Let's just say Vissa Mylowe is a lot of woman."

"Meaning what?"

He took another drag as he considered his answer. "Lemme put it this way. If Vissa worked for me, she's be my biggest earner *and* my biggest headache."

Loretta put the pen down. "The headache part I can understand, but what do you mean she'd be your biggest earner?"

Freddy laughed with the cigarette wedged in the corner of his
mouth. "It always amazes me how dense broads can be about
other broads. Let me clue you in. Vissa Mylowe is one sexy babe.
And not bombshell sexy—I mean *genuine* sexy. The kind of broad
guys get cuckoo over."

"I'm not following you." Loretta wasn't sure she wanted to.

"There's just something about her that's unbelievably sexy.
The way she says things, the way she looks at you, the way she
can change gears in the middle of a conversation and then change
right back again. I mean, look what she did with your friend. She
was bitching at him like crazy, ready to scratch his eyes out, then
just like that she turns around and gets all playful with him, melts
him right down to nothing."

"She did not melt him down to nothing," Loretta objected.

"You don't think so because you're a woman," Freddy said.
"You didn't see it the way a guy would."

Loretta picked up her pen. This mutt was full of crap, she
thought. Right up to his brown eyeballs.

"I'm telling you, though," he said. "If I had her working for
me, it would be like money in the bank. Johns pay big for girls
like her. She'd be the kind guys fall in love with and pay through
the nose to be with. She'd be a freakin' gold mine."

"Right . . ." Loretta shifted her attention back to the form.
Freddy was a jerk, she decided. She shouldn't even bother listening
to him.

But as the pimp fished another cigarette out of his pocket and
lit it with the end of his last one, Loretta glanced back toward
Julius's office. Sure, the woman was sexy and flirty, but Marvelli's
not that shallow, she thought.

Besides, he doesn't seem to like her at all. And they're only going to be together for a day. What could possibly happen in one day? Nothing, she told herself. *Absolutely nothing.*

Freddy was blowing smoke rings, tracking them with his eyes. "You think she's good in the sack?"

"How the hell would I know?"

"I'll bet she's something else," he said admiringly.

"If I ever sleep with her, I'll let you know," Loretta said sarcastically.

Freddy stopped blowing rings and stared at her. "You go that way?"

"What way?"

"With other women."

Loretta scowled at him. "No."

"You go both ways? Boys *and* girls?"

"Keep it up, Freddy. You're doing a great job getting on my good side."

Freddy shrugged, pulling an innocent face. "I'm just asking. That's all. Personally I don't think there's anything wrong with that kind of stuff."

"Did I say there was?" Loretta heard herself getting loud. "Did I?" she said, toning it down.

"Hey, you know what I say? I say, whatever gets you through the night. Long as you don't hurt nobody else. What people do behind closed doors is their business. That's my motto."

"Just as long as you get your cut," Loretta pointed out.

"Only if they're doing it with one of my employees. It's a free country. Amateurs can get laid, too. I don't mind."

"That's big of you, Freddy."

"Don't mention it."

Loretta scrunched her lips to one side of her face as she stared at the form. "I don't have your file here, Freddy. Where did you last serve time?"

"Leesburg."

"Where were you arrested?"

"Wildwood."

"Do you remember the name of the presiding judge at your trial?"

Freddy exhaled his disgust. "Do I remember? How could I ever forget that big mo? Stanislaw Z. Kopinsky. Gave me the maximum and said he would've given me more if he could've. They call that guy the Time Machine."

Loretta couldn't help but laugh. "Freddy, every court in the country's got a judge they call the Time Machine, and every con I've ever met says he's been screwed by the Time Machine."

"Hey, I don't know nothing about the rest of the country, but in my case it's true. That old bastard Stanislaw is the *original* Time Machine."

"Sure, Freddy, whatever you say."

Freddy took a long drag off his cigarette, the smoke slowly filtering out through his nose. "You mind if I ask you something?"

"What?"

"How much do you people make?"

"Parole officers?"

"Yeah."

"None of your business."

"Can't be much," Freddy said, scratching the underside of his chin. "It's a state job, right?"

Loretta looked at him. "You thinking of applying?"

He laughed, hissing through his nose. "Not me, man. I'm just thinking about Vissa. I bet she don't make more than thirty-five, forty grand a year. I could triple her salary easy if she came to work for me."

Loretta just shook her head in disbelief. "You are incredible, Freddy. You just got caught violating the terms of your parole, and here you are discussing future illegal activities with an officer of the court. Are you brain-dead or what?"

Freddy's mouth formed a deep frown as he shook his head. "No way, no how," he said. "I never said *what* I wanted her to do for me. How do you know I'm not looking for a cleaning lady?"

"Yeah, right," Loretta said. She went back to the form. "You'll have to find out if she does windows, though. I have a feeling she doesn't."

"She can do my windows anytime," he said with a lascivious grin. "You, too."

Loretta dropped the pen and reared back to slap him silly when she suddenly realized that he was still handcuffed. POs are not supposed to use excessive force, and they are definitely not supposed to strike a parolee when he or she is in restraints.

Freddy puckered his lips and closed his eyes. "Ooooh, baby," he moaned. "Hurt me. Hurt me good."

"That can be arranged, Freddy. And you won't like it."

He grinned. "You never know."

Just then Marvelli and Vissa emerged from Julius's office. They were both laughing about something.

"This mutt giving you a hard time, Loretta?" Vissa asked.

"No more than any other mutt I've ever had to deal with."

Freddy rotated his shoulders like a stripper. "Ooooh, ladies," he growled in his throat. "I love it when you talk about me."

"Ignore him," Vissa said. "He's been doing this crap ever since I picked him up. I think he turns himself on."

"Not like you do," Freddy said under his breath.

Vissa struck like a cobra, grabbing him by the throat and digging her nails into his flesh. She tipped his chair so far back he was on the verge of toppling over. "Behave," she grunted. Her thumb was on his trachea, cutting off his air supply. When she finally let him go, he wheezed and coughed, sucking in as much air as he could get.

Loretta raised an eyebrow. "He's still in cuffs," she reminded Vissa.

"I know," she said, keeping her gaze on Freddy. She didn't seem to care.

Loretta looked to Marvelli. He didn't seem to approve either, but he held his tongue.

"Here," Vissa said, picking up the Violator Reentry form, "let me finish this up. Mind if I use your desk, Loretta?"

"No problem. Take your time." She wandered toward the coffee machine where Marvelli had gone to fix himself a cup. "A little on the rough side, don't you think?" she said in his ear.

"That's her style," he said, shaking out two packets of sugar. "She believes in the iron-fist approach."

"You gonna be able to deal with that?"

"Oh, yeah. Don't worry about that. Anyway I don't expect anything to come of this Krupnick thing."

I hope not, she thought. She didn't want Marvelli spending any more time with Vissa Mylowe than he absolutely had to. Freddy's assessment of her lingered in Loretta's mind.

Marvelli was stirring his coffee with a wooden stick. "You don't mind me partnering with her today, do you?" His eyes had that pathetic backslant that she adored. But why was he asking for her permission? she wondered, a little peeved that he'd asked.

"I don't mind if you go with her. Why should I?"

"No reason," he said with a shrug. "I'll call you tonight. Unless we find Krupnick, which I doubt that we will. Nothing's gonna happen." He took a sip of his coffee. "Either way, I'll call you."

"Fine. I'll be home."

Loretta glanced at Vissa sitting at her desk, filling out the rest of the form, and wondered why Marvelli was going out of his way to assure her that nothing was going to happen. She watched him drinking his coffee at his desk.

Vissa's complexion was green in the dim glow of the parking lot lights. There were no stars in the sky, but the moon was bright, turning the passing clouds silver. Marvelli sat in the passenger seat of Vissa's 1986 white Cadillac Seville, Vissa behind the wheel. She was staring intently through the windshield at the plate-glass windows of the Dunkin Donuts shop across the parking lot, focusing on a fat man with a full gray beard waiting in line at the take-out counter. Marvelli was staring just as intently at the pay phone out front.

"It'll take two seconds," Marvelli said. "I just want to call Loretta and let her know I'll be late."

"No way," Vissa said, her eyes glued to the Dunkin Donuts. "Krupnick is right there. What if he remembers your face? You'll spook him."

"That was eight years ago, Vissa. And I was with him for only a minute or two. I really doubt that he'll remember me."

"You never know. And Krupnick's not just anybody. He's very smart."

"C'mon. Loretta's gonna be wondering what happened to us."

Vissa turned her head and looked at him straight on, most of her face embedded in shadows. "I'm gonna give you some advice, Marvelli, even though I know you don't want it. Office romances are just plain stupid. I don't care if Julius is looking the other way. One of you two is gonna get hurt."

"What the hell are you talking about?"

"Now don't get all defensive on me, Marvelli. I'm just looking out for you." She reached over and stroked his cheek with the back of her hand.

He froze, wanting to recoil but not wanting to overreact. Vissa didn't mean anything by this, he told himself. That's just the way she was. She liked to touch.

When she put her hand down, Marvelli turned his head and stared out at the doughnut shop. Three customers were ahead of the fat man, and there was only one waitress working the counter. Plenty of time to run over and make a quick call to Loretta.

"Will you calm down, Marvelli? Loretta can manage without you for one night. Trust me."

Vissa flashed what could have been a flirty grin at him, but he wasn't sure because of the shadows.

He reached for the door handle. "I'm gonna go call Loretta. I'll make sure Krupnick doesn't see me—"

"Wait." She grabbed his hand and held it tight. Hers was very warm, but Marvelli felt chills running up his arm. He stared down at their linked fingers as if their hands were a couple of crabs getting fresh on his thigh, as if they had absolutely nothing to do with him.

He pulled his hand away. "Vissa, you're not trying to—? You know."

"Me?" She laughed, and her eyes sparkled. "Why do you think that?"

Marvelli didn't answer. This line of conversation could end up someplace he didn't want to go.

"Well, you are cute," she said. Her mouth was hidden in the shadows, and her husky voice came out of the darkness, like a ghost's. "I've always thought you were cute. You know that."

Marvelli looked at her sideways. "Now I know you're playing with me."

"Sure. I'd like to play with you."

"C'mon, Vissa. Stop fooling around."

"You mean, stop fooling around so we can *start* fooling around?"

He laughed nervously, hoping to keep things light. "You haven't changed a bit, Vissa. You're still a big tease."

"You're afraid of me, aren't you?"

"No. I'm not afraid of you. Why do you say that?"

"Then you're afraid of Loretta."

"I'm not afraid of her, either."

"Then why are you so nervous?"

"Because I don't know what I'm doing here. I mean, do you really think that's Ira Krupnick in there buying doughnuts? Or was this just some elaborate excuse to get me out here alone with you?"

She stared at him for a long moment. "Maybe both," the ghostly voice said.

"I don't think so." He reached for the door handle again, ready to go, but she grabbed his hand.

"I'm kidding, I'm kidding," she said. "You used to have a sense of humor, Marvelli. What happened?"

"I still have a sense of humor."

"Not like before." She circled his kneecap with her frosty pink fingernail. "Remember?"

He closed his eyes and heaved an annoyed sigh. "I knew you were gonna bring that up again."

"How can I not?"

"It was one time, Vissa. It was a moment of weakness."

"Whatever it was, it was great. You are one hell of a lover, Marvelli. That's why I hate to see you wasting yourself on someone like Loretta."

Marvelli's face was burning. He resented Vissa for putting Loretta down when she didn't even know her, and he resented even more her proprietary attitude with him. Yes, they had slept together, but it was only once, and it was a big mistake. He'd regretted it before it was even over. It had happened a long time ago, when Vissa worked at the Newark office, long before his wife had gotten sick. He and Rene had been having marital problems, and she'd thrown him out of the house. He'd complained to Vissa about it, and she offered him her couch. Vissa was just someone he worked with, so he thought it was no big deal to accept her offer. But that night they were on the couch watching TV, and one thing led to another, and by the time the *Seinfeld* credits were rolling, they were down on the carpet, tearing each other's clothes off. He'd never told his wife about it, but part of him wished he had. To this day, he still felt guilty.

"All right, all right," Vissa said, taking her finger off his knee. "I'll behave . . . if that's what you want."

"Yes, Vissa, that is what I want." His face felt hot. He wished to hell he didn't find her so damned attractive.

"Look," Vissa said, suddenly sounding serious as she nodded toward the doughnut shop. "Krupnick's at the counter."

Marvelli focused on the fat man pointing at the trays of doughnuts, telling the waitress which ones he wanted. He must've been buying a dozen because she was using a box instead of a bag. Marvelli narrowed his eyes and spotted the tray of chocolate glazed doughnuts—the only dark tray he could see—and suddenly he felt hunger pains.

A few of those would be nice right about now, he thought.

With a jumbo cup of coffee. Coffee and doughnuts were made for
stakeouts. Or maybe ice cream. Arnie and Barry's Elmer Fudge
Whirl. That would be even better, he thought.

His stomach rumbled loud enough for Vissa to hear.

She reached over and patted his belly. "You miss me, baby?"
she asked his stomach. "Loretta's not feeding you well enough?"

"Enough, Vissa." He removed her hand. "Pay attention to
your man over there. He's paying for his doughnuts now."

The fat man handed a few dollar bills to the waitress, who
opened the register and counted out his change. He picked up the
box of doughnuts from the counter and headed for the door. Vissa
turned the ignition key and started the engine before the fat man
came outside.

"Here we go," she said. The idling engine filled the silence.
Her eyes were keen as she watched the fat man cross the parking
lot, her face all business now.

Marvelli tried to get a better look at the man's face, comparing
it to his eight-year-old memory of Ira Krupnick's face, but from
this distance it was hard to tell if it was the same person.

The man got into a pearl gray Jeep Grand Cherokee. He
started his engine and switched on his headlights. When his white
backup lights went on, Vissa put her car in gear, ready to follow.

Marvelli arched his stiff back, hoping they could finally make
an approach this time. When they'd arrived at the man's address
earlier that afternoon, the man was just pulling out of the driveway. They'd followed him to a crowded mall, where he went to a
movie. Vissa and Marvelli had no choice but to wait in the parking
lot and watch his Jeep until the movie was over. As they waited,
they spent a lot of time speculating on which movie at the omni-
plex he'd gone to see. Vissa was sure Krupnick's choice would be
the new Al Pacino cop drama, but Marvelli was split between the
Steve Martin comedy and the Bruce Willis let's-blow-up-
everything-in-creation thriller. Marvelli remembered Krupnick as

being sort of a wiseass, so he'd probably relate to Willis and Martin more than to Pacino.

It was dark by the time Krupnick returned to his Jeep. From the mall, he drove directly to the Dunkin Donuts. Since they weren't sure this was really Krupnick, Marvelli had insisted that they approach him when he was alone. If Vissa was wrong and this guy was just some average Joe Blow, they could be looking at a mondo lawsuit if they embarrassed the guy in public.

The Jeep pulled out of its space and headed across the parking lot. Vissa waited until he had turned onto the road before she started following. Vissa had always been pretty good at trailing jumpers, Marvelli remembered. She had a lot of patience. That was one thing Loretta didn't have.

Vissa stayed two cars behind the fat man as he picked up speed, passing a series of strip malls and shopping centers with all the usual stores and restaurants—Home Depot, Staples, Applebee's, Einstein Brothers Bagels, Kmart, Circuit City, Chili's, CompUSA, Fuddrucker's.

"I'll bet he stops at Blockbuster Video," Marvelli said when he spotted the blue-and-yellow sign in the distance.

"Why?" Vissa sounded dubious.

"Because he's got doughnuts. What goes better with doughnuts than a movie?"

Vissa shook her head. "It's amazing you're not as big as a house, Marvelli. I've never met anyone who thinks about food as much as you do."

"I have a problem with low blood sugar. I *have* to eat more often than most people. Why is this so hard for people to understand?"

"Because people know it's bull." Vissa was grinning at the windshield, her face lit from below by the dashboard lights.

"Well, it's true. And I don't care what you believe."

"Does Loretta believe it?" she asked.

"Of course she does." But then he thought about the question. "Why do you care what Loretta believes?" he asked.

"I would imagine food is a touchy issue with her."

Marvelli didn't like the implication. "Lay off Loretta. Okay?"

"You don't have to get mad."

"Can we change the subject?"

"Fine with me. How about them Mets?"

He ignored her attempt at humor. Neither of them said anything for a while. The sound of the tires rolling along the pavement filled the silence. Marvelli stared at the Jeep's taillights. He was thinking hard.

Why was Vissa so interested in Loretta, he wanted to know. Was Vissa just being her usual flirtatious self, or was she angling for something else? Or was he just being paranoid?

"Wrong again, Marvelli," she suddenly said.

He whipped his head toward her. "About what?" he said quickly. He thought she was reading his mind.

"Krupnick renting a movie." She pointed at the Blockbuster Video store as the Jeep sailed on by. "I think he's going home."

"You mean you *hope* he's going home."

"Yeah, that, too," she said.

They continued on that road until the stores and strip malls gave way to long stretches of open salt marsh. The pungent smell was unmistakable. In the distance Marvelli could see lights reflecting off the dark water, boats floating on Long Island Sound.

The Jeep stopped at a red light, signaled for a turn, then turned right on red. Vissa did the same but slowed down, keeping a good distance between them. Marvelli noticed the name of the road as they turned, Cutters Mill Road. Arnie Farber's house was on this road.

"You got your gun?" Vissa asked.

Marvelli glared at her. "Yes, I have my gun." He opened his jacket to show her the .38 clipped to his belt.

"Don't bite my head off," she said. "I'm only asking because I know you don't like to carry your weapon."

"I always have it for an arrest," he said, which was a lie. He never liked carrying a weapon because, for one thing, he was a lousy shot. He also felt that when trying to reason with a desperate criminal, the presence of a weapon only made things worse. As soon as a man sees a gun, he stops listening, and that's when trouble starts.

The road curved around a rocky point that jutted into the sound. Marvelli thought it must be pretty out here during the day. Modern-looking houses on both sides of the road were built far apart from one another. Almost every one had large picture windows that faced the water. The people who lived out here had to have money. If this guy wasn't Krupnick, he'd probably have the resources to sue their pants off.

They lost sight of the Jeep for a moment as the road curved sharply to the left, but as soon as it straightened out again, the Jeep was right there in front of them, about fifty yards ahead. It slowed down as it passed a house that looked like a big barn. The Jeep's right-hand signal started blinking. Marvelli recognized the fat man's house, the plain-looking boxy thing that stood on stilts to protect it from flooding. The timbers were as thick as telephone poles. If this was Krupnick, this kind of house sort of made sense, Marvelli thought. The place was like a fortress—easy to defend, hard to invade.

As soon as the Jeep made the turn, Vissa floored the accelerator and raced up to Krupnick's driveway. They didn't want him getting into the house. They wanted to take him outside.

"Here we go," she said, as she spun the wheel and screeched into the driveway, loose gravel pelting the wheel wells.

The fat man was just coming out of his car, the box of doughnuts in his left hand. He looked up, startled by the sound of the approaching car. Vissa's high beams blinded him, so he shielded his eyes with the box.

Vissa skidded to a stop, angling her car across the driveway so that the Jeep couldn't get out. She threw her door open and stood behind it. "Sir," she called out, "we'd like to talk to you." Her gun was in her hand down by her side. A Smith & Wesson long-barrel .44.

"About what?" the fat man said. "Who the hell are you?" His voice seemed shaky. He was backstepping toward the stairway that led up to his house.

Marvelli got out of the car and moved toward him, keeping his hands where the fat man could see them. "We're from the State of New Jersey Bureau of Parole, sir. We'd like to ask you some questions."

The fat man started shaking his head. His mouth was open, fear flashing in his eyes. He turned to run—but only halfway. He was afraid to turn his back on them completely.

"Stop!" Vissa yelled. She had her gun propped on the door frame, pointed at the fat man. "Put your hands above your shoulders, and don't move."

But the fat man did just the opposite, turning around the rest of the way and running. But he was obviously unused to running. He stumbled and tripped over his own feet, falling flat on his face, his arms splayed out in a useless attempt to break the fall. The doughnut box went down with him, skidding upside down along the blacktop until it collided with one of the support timbers.

"I'm not Ira!" the man cried out, flailing his arms. "I swear to God! I'm not him!"

Vissa and Marvelli were standing over him, both wearing the same puzzled look.

"You're not Ira who?" Vissa asked.

"Ira Krupnick!" the man screamed.

She whispered to Marvelli, "Did you mention Krupnick's name?"

He shook his head. "No. You?"

She shook her head.

"I'm telling you," the man yelled, "I'm not Ira Krupnick. You gotta believe me. I can prove it."

Marvelli got down on one knee and patted the man down while he was prone, then helped him to his feet. "Why don't we go inside and make some coffee?" Marvelli suggested. "You can tell us all about it."

Vissa took the fat man by the elbow and guided him toward the staircase while Marvelli retrieved the box of doughnuts. He weighed the box in his hand as he walked.

Hope he bought some chocolate glazed, Marvelli thought.

When Loretta arrived at the office the next morning, she was happy to see Marvelli's black-and-white houndstooth sport jacket hanging over the back of his desk chair. He was back. But when she noticed the black leather car coat with the leopard skin collar draped on top of Marvelli's desk, her mood turned sour. Vissa Mylowe was still around. Loretta went over to Marvelli's desk, picked up Vissa's coat, and hung it on the coatrack.

"Hey, Loretta."

"How's it going, Loretta?"

Two other Jump Squad POs, Bobby McManus and Lionel Williams, were standing outside Julius Monroe's office holding Styrofoam cups of coffee. Loretta was surprised to see these two because they were always out in the field and almost never hung around the office.

"What's going on?" she said, walking up to them.

Lionel nodded toward the interrogation room down the hallway. "Marvelli and Vissa picked up Ira Krupnick last night."

"But he's saying he's not Krupnick," McManus said, stroking

the ends of his bandito mustache with his thumb and forefinger. "He called his lawyer. The guy just got here."

"Yeah," Lionel said, grinning with all his teeth. "Now when was the last time a jumper asked for a lawyer?"

McManus shrugged. "Must've been before my time because I can't think of one. Can you, Loretta?"

Loretta shrugged and shook her head.

Lionel leaned toward her and lowered his voice. "Julius is getting a little weirded out by all this. He doesn't like all those people in the interrogation room. They're invading his space."

Loretta knew exactly what Lionel was talking about. The interrogation room was where Julius liked to practice his flute. He said the acoustics were good in there, and the room was cluttered with his stuff—sheet music, music stand, and posters of some of his favorite jazz musicians. Julius's dream was to become a full-time musician after he retired from the Bureau of Parole.

The door to the interrogation room banged open, and Julius struggled out with a huge reel-to-reel tape deck. He looked like a mad little ant forced to abandon his hill.

"You need help, boss?" McManus asked.

"No," Julius snapped. His tie was askew, and he was wearing the navy-blue suit jacket that had been hanging behind his door, unworn, for God knows how long.

"You sure?" Lionel asked with a sly grin.

Julius glared at the three of them. "What? Did we run out of jumpers?"

The two men snickered. The office was bulging with stacks of files, each one representing a parolee who had skipped out on his or her parole. There had to be at least a couple of thousand.

"Go!" Julius snapped. "Disperse! Work!"

"But it's not eight-thirty yet," Lionel pointed out. "We're still finishing our coffee."

"Finish it somewhere else. Vamoose!" Julius banged the tape deck into the doorjamb as he hauled it into his office.

"Guess we're not wanted here," Lionel said to his partner.

McManus frowned. "Guess not. Guess you gotta haul in an Ira Krupnick to get appreciated around here."

Julius's voice boomed into the hallway from inside his office. "Go away!"

The two POs were grinning as they shuffled back to their desks. Loretta, however, was curious. She slipped past Julius's office and sneaked into the tiny viewing room that was next to the interrogation room. It was dark and musty from lack of use, and crowded with an assortment of broken desk chairs and battered file cabinets.

Loretta quietly closed the door behind her and tiptoed around the clutter to get to the one-way window that took up most of one wall. She wiped away the dust with the sleeve of her blue chambray shirt, making a porthole for herself. A dusty brown and beige speaker hung over the window. Loretta followed the wire coming out of it to a painted-over wall switch. She flipped it on, and to her surprise the speaker still worked.

Inside the interrogation room Marvelli and Vissa were seated at one end of a long conference table. A middle-aged fat man with a mostly gray beard and a pasty-faced man in his early sixties with longish, yellow white hair were huddled at the other end of the table. The pasty-faced man was wearing a pressed, charcoal gray suit and a crisp white shirt while the fat man, who was wearing khakis and a dark green polo shirt, looked like he'd slept in his clothes. Loretta assumed that this was Krupnick. The suit had to be his lawyer.

Understandably Krupnick looked nervous. As he huddled with his lawyer, he kept glancing over at the pint of Arnie and Barry's Elmer Fudge Whirl that was sitting on the table in front of Marvelli. Loretta wondered if Krupnick was hungry.

At the other end of the table, Vissa was whispering something to Marvelli, who nodded attentively as he shoveled ice cream into his mouth with a plastic spoon. Vissa's hand was flat on the table, her gaze locked on Marvelli's face, demanding eye contact. Loretta didn't like the woman's body language. She was crowding Marvelli, encroaching on his space as if she deserved to be there. But what bothered Loretta more was that Marvelli wasn't backing away from Vissa. Had the ice cream frozen his brain? Or did he want to be taken over?

Loretta wondered what Marvelli really thought about Vissa. Stylewise they were perfectly compatible. They'd make a good greaser couple. But how did he really feel about her? Loretta had no reason to be jealous, but she couldn't help but wonder if Marvelli was attracted, especially after what Freddy the pimp had said about Vissa being "*genuine* sexy." Maybe what Vissa had was something that other women couldn't recognize. Maybe it was a guy thing.

Julius Monroe came back into the room and took a seat at the middle of the table between the two camps. "Okay," he said, "so where were we?"

"Nowhere," Vissa said with disgust. "Mr. Krupnick here continues to deny that he is who he is. And his counsel, Mr. Garrett, is supporting him in this charade."

Garrett the lawyer pushed a hank of his white-blond hair off his brow. "I take exception to your characterization of the situation, Ms. Mylowe. My client's legal name is Arthur Berman, not Ira Krupnick. You have the wrong man."

"I don't care what you say his name is," Vissa said. "You can change your name legally for three bucks. That's no big deal."

Garrett exchanged glances with his client. "We will concede that Arthur Berman was not *born* Arthur Berman. He did change his name, yes."

The fat man mopped his brow with the back of his hand. He

did not look comfortable. And he kept looking at Marvelli's ice cream.

"Then we'll have to fingerprint him," Marvelli said with his mouth full. "That'll tell us who he is."

The fat man gripped his lawyer's forearm and started shaking his head violently. "No fingerprints," he whispered.

Julius was silently playing bongos on the tabletop. "Sir," he said, staring at the fat man, "if you are indeed not Ira Krupnick, why won't you let us clear this up with a fingerprint analysis? Or could it be that you have something else to hide?"

The lawyer started to answer, but the fat man cut him off. "Yes," he blurted, his chest heaving. "I do have something to hide, but it's not what you think. I'm not Ira."

"Then pray tell, who are you?" Julius asked.

"Arthur, you don't have to answer that," Garrett said.

But the fat man ignored his lawyer. "I'm not Ira," he repeated. "That's Ira." He pointed at Marvelli, whose eyes shot open just as he was about to take another bite from the pint of Elmer Fudge Whirl.

"Are you crazy?" Vissa said, rushing to Marvelli's defense. "This is definitely *not* Ira Krupnick."

Julius was chortling into his fist, and Marvelli couldn't suppress a grin of his own.

"No, not *him*," the fat man said excitedly. "On the ice cream container. *That* guy!"

Marvelli held out the pint of Arnie and Barry's and furrowed his brows at it. The cardboard container had black-and-white pictures of Arnie and Barry on the label. Arnie had a scruffy beard while Barry was clean-shaven. They were both sort of pudgy and round-faced.

The fat man reached out for the pint, and reluctantly Marvelli relinquished it. "Him," the fat man said, pointing to the picture of the man with the scruffy beard. "*That's* Ira Krupnick."

"No way," Marvelli said, shaking his head with absolute certainty.

"Trust me," the fat man said. "That's not Arnie. *I'm* Arnie."

"Hold it, hold it, hold it," Marvelli said. "You're saying you're Arnie of Arnie and Barry, and this guy in the picture is Ira Krupnick?"

"That's right."

Vissa was drumming her fingernails on the table. "I can't wait to hear this," she groaned.

Julius flipped his palms up. "You've got the floor, my friend," he said to the fat man. "Take your solo."

"I don't know if I can advise this—" the lawyer said, but again the fat man ignored him.

"Okay," the fat man said. "This is the God's honest truth. Okay? My real name is Arnie Bloomfield." He was pointing to the pint in his hand. "I'm the original Arnie of Arnie and Barry."

Marvelli just rolled his eyes and reached for the pint. He wanted his Fudge Whirl back.

"No, wait!" Arnie pulled the pint out of Marvelli's reach. "You can see from this picture that Ira Krupnick and I look pretty similar. We could almost be doubles. See, it used to be *my* picture that was on the cartons. Ira saw it there, and that's how he got the idea of switching."

"Switching?" Vissa asked skeptically.

"Yeah. He became me, and I became someone else, Arthur Berman."

Marvelli and Vissa exchanged knowing glances. "Why?" Marvelli asked the fat man. "What was in it for you?"

Arnie Bloomfield shook his head wearily. "You don't wanna know. My life was crap, and it was just getting worse. I didn't know what to do. I was stuck in a rut. Then when Ira showed up at my office one day, it was like God sending me an angel."

"So what was so wrong with your life that you needed to bail out?" Julius asked.

"Everything," Arnie said glumly. "At the time, believe it or not, our business was doing terribly. Ben and Jerry's was killing us in every major market. And Barry had turned into a real SOB. It got to the point where I couldn't stand the sight of him. On top of that, physically I felt miserable. See, I was the one who used to develop all the new flavors, and my health was suffering because of it. My doctor told me I'd drop dead within a year if I didn't stop eating ice cream."

"But we saw you buying doughnuts last night," Marvelli pointed out.

"It was a splurge," Arnie said. "I hardly ever eat junk food. Not really."

"This is why you switched identities with Krupnick?" Vissa said. "Because of your health? You could've just gotten out of the business if it was killing you."

Berman looked down at the tabletop, suddenly sheepish. "Well, there was one other thing."

Everyone in the room leaned forward, waiting to hear.

"Margot," he said, heaving a deep sigh. "She and I had lived together for twelve years, but that was falling apart, too. I wanted to split up, but she threatened to sue me if I ever left her."

"But you weren't married," Marvelli said.

"Palimony!" Berman said as if it should be self-evident. "And remember, we were living in California. They have a looser interpretation of the law out there, which is not always good for the man, if you know what I mean."

Garrett nodded emphatically.

"Ira Krupnick was having the same sort of problem here in Jersey," Berman said. "Except on a grander scale because he was worth millions. At least that's what he told me. He said he had an ex-wife who was trying to suck him dry, and he just couldn't sit back and let that happen. When he saw how much we looked alike, he came to me and asked if I'd consider doing a switcheroo. Since I was at the end of my own rope, I jumped at the idea."

"Just like that?" Vissa seemed doubtful.

"Well . . ." Berman hesitated, then lowered his voice. "Krupnick did offer certain incentives."

"What kind of incentives?" Vissa asked.

"Well, basically . . . cash."

"How much cash?" Marvelli asked.

Berman looked to his lawyer, but before Garrett could speak for his client, Julius cut in. "Cooperation is the name of the game here. You help us find Krupnick, we don't call the IRS. *Comprende?*"

Garrett nodded for his client to answer the question.

Berman took a deep breath. "Two hundred thousand," he exhaled.

"He actually gave you that much money?" Vissa asked.

Berman nodded guiltily. "In two suitcases."

"Did he tell you where the money came from?" Vissa continued. "Did he say anything about his prior involvement in drug dealing, arms dealing, armed robbery? Anything like that?"

Berman's eyes widened. "No. He told me he was trying to hold on to his money because he had six kids from a first marriage. He said the witch was trying to take him for everything he had. He was worried about his kids."

Loretta studied Berman's face, trying to see if he was lying. He seemed sincere. She studied Vissa's and Marvelli's faces, too. Vissa seemed to be totally focused on Berman, but her body language was directed entirely toward Marvelli, as if she were trying to suck him in. Marvelli seemed oblivious, though. He was more worried about his pint of Arnie and Barry's, which was still on the other side of the table in front of Berman.

"Do you know where we can find Krupnick?" Julius asked Berman.

The fat man glanced at his lawyer.

"Will my client get total immunity from prosecution in exchange for his cooperation in your investigation?" Garrett asked.

"He doesn't need it," Julius said. "As far as I can tell, he hasn't committed any crimes. I'm just gonna assume he paid his taxes on that money he got from Krupnick."

The lawyer took Julius's meaning, but he still wasn't satisfied. "How about aiding and abetting in any crimes Krupnick has committed since the switch or is currently committing?"

Julius stroked his goatee. "I'll have to talk to someone from the prosecutor's office. Granting immunity is not my thing. But let's put it this way. If your client agrees to provide us with useful information regarding Krupnick, and if there's no indication that he profited in any way from Krupnick's subsequent scams, then I see no reason why your client won't get immunity."

"I just don't want this getting to the press," Berman said. "I don't want Margot to find me."

Julius and Marvelli nodded in agreement. Vissa gave them both a raised eyebrow. Loretta tended to agree with Vissa—Margot *should* find the bum.

"So tell us. Where is Krupnick?" Julius asked.

Berman hesitated for a moment, thinking it over one last time before he spoke. "He's living in San Francisco," he finally said. "In the Haight-Ashbury district."

"Isn't that where all the hippies used to live in the sixties?" Marvelli asked.

"Yeah," Berman said. "Now all the middle-aged yuppie-hippies live there. Liberals with money. A lot of gray ponytails."

"Are you willing to put this in writing?" Julius asked.

Garrett jumped in. "May I consult with my client for a moment before we continue?"

"Sure. Whatever you want," Julius said. He stood up and crooked a finger at Marvelli and Vissa, calling them over to the side of the room next to the one-way mirror. They huddled together, just inches away from Loretta. Even though she realized that they didn't know she was there, she leaned back anyway to maintain her personal space. Julius had his back to the glass. Vissa and Marvelli were facing him—and Loretta—with their backs to Berman and Garrett.

"So what do you think?" Julius asked them.

"I think he's telling the truth," Vissa said.

Marvelli nodded. "I have to agree."

Julius let out a slow breath. "Well, it looks like you two will be going out to Hippie Heaven."

Marvelli frowned. "Why do I have to go?"

Julius shrugged. "Like it or not, you're on this case now, O Marvelous One. I want you to see it through."

"But—"

"No arguments, Marvelli. Krupnick is a serious dude. He shouldn't be out and about."

"But—"

"Stop butting, Marvelli. Your die is cast. You are going to San Fran."

"But what about my daughter?" Marvelli objected. "Who's gonna watch her?"

"Her grandmother," Julius said as if it were self-evident. "Doesn't your former mother-in-law stay with Nina every time you have to go out of town?"

Marvelli didn't answer. He knew there was going to be no way out of this.

Vissa flashed a sly grin at him. "Don't worry, Marvelli. Frisco's a nice town. We may actually have some fun out there."

Loretta's eyes narrowed. *What the hell did Vissa mean by that?*

But suddenly something else caught Loretta's eye. At the conference table Garrett had bent down to get something out of his briefcase, which was sitting on the floor next to him, and while he was turned away, Berman picked up Marvelli's pint of ice cream and tossed it into a nearby wastepaper basket. It hit with a metallic clunk that made everyone take notice.

Instantly Berman put on an innocent face. "Sorry," he said to Marvelli. "I knocked it over with my elbow. It was an accident."

Loretta frowned. *What the hell was that all about?*

Three thousand miles away the real Ira Krupnick was stretched out on a cushy white-and-beige-striped couch that was positioned directly under a skylight. His eyes were closed against the rays beaming down on his face, his fingers linked behind his head as if he were sunning himself on the beach. His partner, Barry Utley, the other half of Arnie and Barry's, was pacing the carpet like a mad rhino, ranting about something or other, shouting at him and calling him "Arnie." But "Arnie" wasn't listening. "Arnie" was thinking like Ira now because in his mind he'd never stopped being Ira, and Ira was thinking about something else. He was thinking about sex. Specifically, he was thinking about having sex with Barry's wife, Dorie.

Krupnick rolled his head to the side and squinted against the sun so he could see Dorie sitting on the matching striped couch on the other side of the living room. Dorie was a cool blonde, not too smart but very sweet and very affectionate. A classic California girl, but kind of sly and cunning without really knowing it. She had brown eyes and light hair, which was a dynamite combination in his book. And freckles. He liked freckles on women.

The stripes on the couch reminded Krupnick of prison stripes, which in turn reminded him that Dorie had done some time at a women's correctional facility. The thought of her behind bars made him even hornier than he already was. Women in cages. He wished he had known Dorie back then. He would've married her for the conjugal visits alone. Sex behind bars was an awfully tasty thought— as long as he was the one getting out at the end of the day.

"Listen to me, Arnie," Barry squawked. "We have to expand our product line. That's all there is to it." Barry was waving his arms like an insane symphony conductor. "We can't depend solely on the profits from Elmer Fudge Whirl. That's just plain bad business, Arnie."

Krupnick just stared at Barry as if he were yelling at someone else. Even though he'd gotten used to answering to the name Arnie Bloomfield, Krupnick never became Arnie Bloomfield. It just wasn't him.

"Arnie, we need to work on the flavors, add some new ones. Fudge Whirl is not forever."

Yes it is, Krupnick thought. He arched his back and stretched.

"We need to develop the *next* Elmer Fudge Whirl," Barry said.

Krupnick squinted at him. The man looked like a big angry potato. His lumpy head just sat on his shoulders with no neck at all. He had tiny little eyes, and the hair that was left on his head was sort of like Larry's in the Three Stooges. As far as Krupnick was concerned, Barry was Mr. Tuber.

"I realize that creating the flavors is your thing, Arnie, but we have to do something before it's too late. Our vanilla base is blah, our coffee doesn't taste like coffee, and frankly our strawberry tastes like sweet plastic. If we don't get on this right away, we won't be here in five years."

Amen, Krupnick thought. He looked over at Dorie, who was looking out the window at the row of painted ladies across the street. Haight-Ashbury was full of these brightly painted Victorian houses, the painted ladies. Krupnick thought of them as Easter eggs because of the colors. The practice of painting them like this started with the original hippies, and now the old bourgeois hippies were keeping up the tradition. Arnie Bloomfield had been one of those old hippies. That's why Krupnick had grown the ponytail and re-painted the house beet red with orange and yellow trim.

"Hey, Dorie," he said, stretching his arms lazily. "Did you know that Grace Slick used to live in this house? With some guy, I think."

"Who?" she said, her eyes suddenly wide as if he'd just woken her up.

"Never mind," he said, slightly disappointed. He kept forget-ting how young she was. She didn't know who the Jefferson Air-plane were. Her frame of reference started with the Police.

"Do *I* know this Grace person, Arnie?" Dorie asked.

"I don't think so," Krupnick said.

"Is she still with the guy?"

"I doubt it."

Moby Potato was about to blow. *"Screw Grace Slick!"* Barry exploded. "What the hell's wrong with you two? I'm talking se-rious here."

Krupnick glared at him. "This is my house, Barry," he said quietly. "Don't yell. Only I yell in my house."

Barry glared back at him, giving him that look. Barry, of course, knew about the switch Krupnick had made with the real Arnie Bloomfield, and so he thought he had something on Krup-nick. But Barry was a putz. He liked to throw his weight around, but he was just a lot of noise. In seven years they'd never really had it out over anything, mainly because Barry was smart enough not to cross his new partner. Ira Krupnick had a way about him that Arnie Bloomfield never had. Sort of like a Komodo dragon—surprisingly big, old enough to make you think twice, and just plain dangerous.

"I like what you did with the living room," Dorie said. "White and beige with ficus trees. It's a nice improvement."

Barry turned his glare on his wife, but she was oblivious. Krupnick grinned. He knew that Dorie didn't give rat's ass about the new decor. She just brought it up to change the subject and hopefully defuse a fight. But Krupnick could see what Barry was thinking. The new decor was an improvement over what? How did she know what was here before? The Utleys had been here once since he'd bought the place three years ago, but she seemed a little more intimate with the place than she should have been. That's because she was, Krupnick thought.

"I redid the master bedroom, too," Krupnick said with an evil grin. He wanted her to say, "I know," but she just nodded, running a lazy hand through her hair as she went back to staring out the window.

The big angry potato sat down on the coffee table and leaned into Krupnick's face. "You think you control me," he hissed. "You think you've got me over a barrel. Well, you don't. You may have the formula to Fudge Whirl, but there's more to this company than just one flavor."

"Oh, yeah? What?" Krupnick's eyes were closed. He was smiling at the sun.

"I'm sick of the games, Arnie. Either we run this thing like a business, or we sell it. I'm tired of this secret-formula crap. What do you think this is? A Vincent Price movie?"

"I like Vincent Price movies. You ever see *Theatre of Blood*?"

"Sell me the formula, Arnie, and you can retire. That's what you want, isn't it? To do nothing. Just name your price."

Krupnick laughed softly as he shook his head. *It's not that simple*, he thought. *Well, actually it is. But really it isn't. Yin, yang.*

"Come on, Arnie. Don't be a pain. Sell me the Fudge Whirl formula and retire. Then I can hire someone else to create new flavors. I want to build this company into something great, something that'll last. I don't want to go down in history as a one-flavor wonder."

Krupnick shaded his eyes and stared at him. "Barry," he said, "you are one serious freakin' potato."

"What?"

"Not important," Krupnick muttered, suddenly distracted. A massive cloud had just crossed the sun, blocking it out entirely. It wasn't a storm cloud, but it wasn't a white, fluffy one either. It was sort of dingy gray and definitely sinister. He took this as a bad sign.

"Arnie, we have to do some—"

"Stop!" Krupnick thrust out his hand like a traffic cop, holding Barry off. "I have to think." He pinched the bridge of his nose and squeezed his eyes shut.

The writing's on the wall, he thought. *The signs are making themselves clear. Can't stick around here much longer. Gotta move on. A person's luck changes every seven years, and it's been just about seven years since the switch with Arnie Bloomfield. Bad luck is coming. Gotta be someone else soon.*

He opened his eyes and glanced at Dorie, her face in profile. He loved those freckles.

"What's the problem, Arnie?" Barry said without sympathy. "What? Do you have a headache?"

Krupnick clenched his jaw. "I said I'm thinking."

Barry backed off, sliding his big butt to the other end of the coffee table.

Dorie was gazing out the window, not paying any attention to either her husband or her lover. It didn't bother her one bit that they were all together in one room. It was as if she were somewhere else. La-di-da.

Krupnick was thinking hard. There was still a lot of money to be made with Elmer Fudge Whirl, but money didn't matter to him. He could always make money. Freedom, mobility, change—that's what was important. If you stop, you die—that's what he'd always believed.

Just take enough cash to get started again, he thought. *That's all. And Dorie, of course.*

He looked down at his crotch. He could feel himself growing even though he couldn't see anything through his jeans. *Easy, boy,* he thought. He was thinking about a threesome with Dorie and Sunny. Dorie had said no the first time he'd suggested it, but he could tell she was curious. He hadn't mentioned it since, but she knew the offer was still on the table.

The thought of having Dorie and Sunny together made him light-headed. He thought about their hair on the same pillow, white blond mixed with ebony black. Yin and yang. The harmony of opposites. The joy of cooking.

He shifted his hips to make some room in his pants. Women—there were so many of them . . . so many he'd missed out on when he was younger. He sighed, wishing he'd started younger, wishing he'd had more. He felt like a failure on that front, not enough names on his resume. Not nearly enough.

He looked down at his crotch again. *So what were we thinking back then?* he said to Eugene, which was what he'd always called it. *That we were being good? How stupid could we be?*

"Arnie! Talk to me!" Barry barked.

Krupnick closed one eye and stared at the big potato. "Wait!" he snapped.

This was suddenly turning into a very bad scene. Negativity from the past was creeping into his present. He had to talk to Sunny right away, have her throw the *I Ching* for him, get some direction, find out where to go next. She'd give him some ideas.

He slowly put his feet on the floor and sat up, finally ready to deal with Barry. "Hey, Dorie," he said, looking past his partner, "would you mind getting us something to drink? You know where the kitchen is, don't you? It's through that door—"

"I know where it is," she said, already off the couch and heading for the kitchen. La-di-da.

Barry's face was hot as he tracked her with his tiny little spud eyes. When she was finally out of the room, Barry curled his lip at his partner. Krupnick was grinning at him. Barry was one steamed potato.

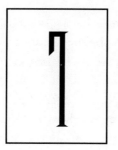

"Come on, Marvelli. Get the lead out," Vissa said, as they walked up the ramp, heading for the terminal. Their plane had just landed in San Francisco.

Marvelli was lagging behind, holding his old-fashioned gym bag over his shoulder, staring at the back of Vissa's head and her thick jet-black hair. He glanced out one of the small windows at the end of the ramp at the planes waiting in line to take off, wishing he were on one of them. He didn't like the idea of being alone in San Francisco with Vissa. After five hours of sitting shoulder-to-shoulder and thigh-to-thigh with her on the plane, he was nervous. He didn't trust her to behave. But what was worse, he didn't totally trust himself either.

Vissa was a shameless flirt, and she'd been true to form all during the flight, touching his hand, his hair, his knee, his arm, sometimes leaving her hand on him a little longer than she should have. But that was just the way Vissa was, he told himself. She was always like this. But it was *his* feelings about her behavior that bothered him. He didn't exactly dislike it when she touched him, and deep down he wanted her to keep doing it. But he *shouldn't* have felt that way, he kept telling himself. Unfortunately, he wasn't listening very well to himself. The little guy in his pants didn't have ears.

Of course, nothing had happened on the plane. Except in his mind. That was the problem, though. That's where trouble always started.

"Stop dragging your ass, Marvelli," she called back to him, wrinkling her nose and flashing that sneaky grin of hers. "We've got things to do."

What kind of things? he wondered. He was worried that they might be thinking the same thing. That's the second stage of trouble.

But it wasn't that he didn't love Loretta anymore. You don't change your mind about someone you love in just five hours. That only happens in the movies. There was just something about Vissa that was more than sexy. She was . . . comfortable. He didn't find himself having to explain things to Vissa the way he had to with Loretta. He and Vissa spoke the same language. Sometimes with Loretta, it was like dealing with a foreigner. He'd say something and she'd just stare at him as if he were from the moon because their frames of reference didn't always mesh.

With Vissa, he didn't have to explain everything. She just sort of knew the things that he knew. Like when they were on the plane, listening to music on their headsets, and she reached over to change his channel to the oldies selection. Del Shannon was singing "Runaway." She knew he'd like that.

Loretta wouldn't have done that. She liked all those depressing female singers who moaned and groaned about their dissatisfying relationships. And show tunes. She liked show tunes. And Kenny G. Marvelli had never criticized her taste in music, but it was really hard to take sometimes. Particularly when they were driving someplace together, and he had to listen to her Kenny G. tapes.

But that really didn't mean anything, he told himself. *Not in the whole scheme of things. Relationships are not based on music; they're based on trust. Right?*

"Will you come on, Marvelli?" Vissa was at the top of the ramp, waiting for him. She was wearing tight jeans, a cinnamon-colored silk disco shirt with long collar points, and black leather platforms. "Come on," she said. "Please?" She wrinkled her nose and held her hand out for him.

He wished to hell she wouldn't wrinkle her nose like that. It did something to him.

When he got to the top of the ramp, she took his hand and started pulling him along. His first urge was to pull his hand away, but he didn't. It would seem hostile, and he had to work with her. Anyway, it didn't mean anything, he told himself. Not really.

That son of a bitch! Loretta thought as soon as she spotted the two of them coming off the ramp. She didn't know what to do first—cry or scream. She'd been sitting at the gate for the past two hours, thinking how stupid she was for being here. She felt ridiculous wearing this coffee brown pageboy wig and the sunglasses with electric blue lenses, but she was too embarrassed to take them off in public. She felt like a complete ass. She'd flown cross-country in a fit of jealousy, not even knowing what she was going to do when she got here. She'd started having second thoughts before she even got off the plane. It was stupid to be jealous, she realized. Marvelli wasn't like that. She felt so stupid she couldn't bring herself to get out of her seat and arrange for a flight back home. What if the clerk asked her why she was going back to Newark just hours after she arrived? She wouldn't know what to say. But then she spotted them coming through the terminal, not wanting to believe what she was seeing. She stared at them over the tops of her shades, wanting it to be something other than what it looked like, something perfectly innocent. But it was right there in front of her. Marvelli *was* like that. They were holding hands, for God's sake. In broad daylight!

Loretta was paralyzed, digging her fingers into the arm of her leather chair. She didn't know who to blame—Marvelli for cheating on her or Vissa for seducing him. She watched them walking away, wondering what they'd do next. Without thinking, she snatched up her carry-on bag and stood up, following after them. Maybe Marvelli really was innocent, maybe this was all Vissa's doing. Maybe she came on to him and he was too polite to tell her to go to hell. It didn't look like that right now, but it was possible. Marvelli wasn't good at telling people off the way she was. But all Loretta wanted was to see some sign of resistance from him, some indication that he didn't want Vissa's affections, then she'd know that he wasn't like that.

Just let go of her hand, she urged him in her mind. *That's all. Then I'll go home, and no one will ever know I was here.*

Loretta followed them through the crowded terminal, staying a good twenty feet behind. She wanted to move in closer and eavesdrop on what they were saying, but Marvelli was pretty street savvy. He was good at spotting tails and lookouts in bad neighborhoods. If she got too close, he might sense her presence.

Loretta focused on Vissa's butt as she followed them. The woman had a sassy bubble ass that wagged like a happy little dog's tail. Loretta frowned. Why was her butt so happy?

As Loretta watched them, she noticed that Vissa seemed to be dragging him along. Marvelli seemed to be a little reluctant, and eventually he let go of her hand so that he could carry his big gym bag in his other hand. It was all Vissa, Loretta decided. It had to be. Marvelli never hung back like that whenever *she* held hands with him. At least she didn't think he did.

Loretta stayed right behind them. She remembered Freddy the

pimp's assessment of Vissa. She was a vampire, and Marvelli was vulnerable.

Vissa and Marvelli walked into the terminal and took the nearest escalator down to the baggage claim area. Loretta had already been down there. She'd called in sick from the pay phones across from the carousels, lied to Julius and told him that her doctor thought she had mono. She'd told him that she felt absolutely lousy and that she didn't know how long she'd be out. She also said she was going to be staying with an aunt until she felt better.

Well, it was partially true. She did feel lousy because she'd been up all night, worrying about Marvelli being alone with Vissa. Loretta had taken the red-eye, and she'd spent the whole night having conversations in her head with the two of them, especially Marvelli, rehearsing what she was going to say when she confronted him with the infidelity that she'd just been assuming at that point. But now she wasn't so sure which speech she'd use—the I'm Hurt speech, the Avalanche Of Righteous Indignation speech, the I Never Wanted To See You Again speech, the tearful How Could You Do This To Me? speech, or the What Have I Done Wrong? speech. (Although that last one wasn't in her nature—she rarely blamed herself for anything.)

Marvelli and Vissa waded into the baggage claim area where eight huge carousels were churning out luggage as passengers anxiously jostled for an inside position. Vissa and Marvelli found their carousel and wedged their way up to the front. Loretta knew that whenever Marvelli traveled, he never took any more than he could carry in his gym bag so she assumed it was Vissa's luggage they were waiting for. Loretta peered over her sunglasses and watched them from a distance, standing behind the waist-high gate that surrounded the carousels. She watched them as they watched the chute, which hadn't begun to spit out bags yet. As the minutes accumulated, Loretta started getting steamed just trying to imagine what kind of luggage Vissa would have. Multiple matching pieces in fuchsia alligator leather, she decided. A steamer trunk full of evening gowns to seduce Marvelli in. A round hatbox. A matching cosmetics case. A duffel bag stuffed with sexy lingerie, something for all occasions, morning, noon, and—

"Warden? Warden Kovacs? Is that you?"

The sweet languorous voice penetrated Loretta's mounting fury and set off an alarm in her head. She'd been made! Loretta looked to her right and saw a willowy blonde standing a few feet away, staring into Loretta's face and smiling as if they knew each other. The woman was wearing tight jeans and a white cotton blouse sufficiently unbuttoned to reveal the curvature of two perfectly round breasts. Loretta stared at her, trying to figure out who she was and why she was calling her *Warden* Kovacs. No one had called her that in years. She had been an assistant warden at the Pinewood Correctional Facility for Women back in Jersey, but that was a long time ago.

The blonde dropped her chin and pouted. "You don't remember me, do you, Warden?" She was shy, sly, sexy, and glum all at the same time.

Loretta narrowed her eyes and started to nod. Yes, she did remember this person. Not her name and not even her face, but the mannerisms were very familiar.

"You're—" Loretta jabbed her finger at the air to jog her memory.

"Dorie," the woman said with a wide, unabashed smile. "Dorie Utley. I used to be Dorie Jasson when you knew me. Jasson with two *S*'s."

Loretta's mouth fell open as it all came back in a rush. Dorie Jasson . . . of course. The sweetheart of Cell Block 9, the dreamiest inmate Pinewood had ever had. The guards used to call her the "eggshell bombshell," fragile but *va-va-va-voom*. Loretta could remember having to discipline more than a few of the lesbian inmates for repeatedly hitting on Dorie. As Loretta remembered it, Dorie was always vague and unhelpful about these incidents because she was a true innocent who invariably thought the best of people— even the ones who only wanted to get into her pants. She was sometimes shockingly frank, and it seemed that whatever popped into Dorie's head came out her mouth. Her attitude at Pinewood had always been so unbelievably positive, Loretta and her staff often wondered if Dorie actually realized she was serving time.

"You've changed your hair," Dorie said, still smiling.

"It's a wig," Loretta admitted.

"I know." Dorie's smile didn't waver, but Loretta wondered what she was thinking. That the wig looked terrible? That it was obviously a disguise? Loretta glanced over at the carousel where Vissa and Marvelli were standing, and suddenly she panicked. Maybe they had already made her.

"So what brings you to San Francisco?" Dorie asked. "A new prison?"

"Ah . . . no." Loretta was distracted. She didn't want to lose track of Marvelli and Vissa.

"Vacation?" Dorie asked.

"Ah . . . yeah. I'm on vacation," Loretta said without thinking, wishing Dorie would just go away.

"That's great," Dorie said, her eyes turning into slits of glee. But then suddenly she pouted again. "I wish I were going on a vacation," she sighed.

The abrupt change in her mood snagged Loretta's attention. In the blink of an eye Dorie had become terribly sad, and Loretta instantly felt for her. She recalled that Dorie had this way about her. You couldn't ignore her if you wanted to, and her mood often became your mood. If she was sad, you became sad for her.

"Is there something wrong, Dorie? Are you in trouble?"

Dorie looked down and shrugged. "No, I'm not in trouble. I'm just . . . stuck, I guess."

"What do you mean, 'stuck'?" Loretta glanced over quickly at Marvelli and Vissa again. They were still at the carousel.

Dorie sighed, and Loretta sighed with her even though she didn't know why. "I'm just stuck, that's all," Dorie said. "I married this guy about three years ago. He's got a lot of money, and I don't have to work or anything, and we have a lot of nice stuff, but . . . I don't think I love him. I don't think I've *ever* loved him."

"Have you thought about leaving him?" Loretta asked.

Dorie's eyes widened. "Why? He hasn't done anything wrong. Except be him."

"I don't understand. Is he mean to you? Does he beat on you?" Loretta was thinking of Dorie's prison relationships. Whenever she would hook up with another inmate, Dorie was always the submissive one, the femme.

"No, no, it's nothing like that," Dorie said. "He's just a bully. In his attitude, I mean. It's got to be his way or no way. He terrorizes everyone, especially the people who work for him. The only person who isn't cowed by him is Arnie, his partner. Arnie is nice."

From Dorie's wistful smile, Loretta suspected that Arnie was more than just nice to her. "Are you sleeping with Arnie?" Loretta asked.

Dorie's eyes shot open. "How'd you know?"

"Just a guess," Loretta said. *Based on past experience,* she thought.

"I like to come here to the airport and imagine that I'm going away someplace," Dorie said. "Someplace far away. Like Thailand. I think I'd like Thailand. I like Thai food. Sometimes I make believe I'm going away with Arnie. But sometimes I make believe I'm going away alone. Sometimes all I want is to be by myself. Do you ever feel that way, Warden? Do you ever feel like you don't need a man in your life? That men are just excess baggage?"

Loretta looked over at Marvelli lifting an overstuffed garment bag off the carousel, Vissa nodding and smiling as if he'd just caught a big fish. *Excess baggage,* she thought. *That wasn't Marvelli. He was an essential.* Loretta had already done the alone thing, and she didn't want to go back to it.

"You know where I'd really like to go?" Dorie said. "Someplace where they don't have ice cream. I'm so sick of ice cream. Are there any countries that don't have ice cream?"

"What?" Loretta said, turning her attention back to Dorie. "Why? What's wrong with ice cream?"

"Barry—that's my husband—he's in the ice-cream business. That's all I ever hear about. Ice cream."

Loretta stared at her as it all started to gel. "Barry is your husband? And Arnie is his partner? Are they *the* Arnie and Barry?"

Dorie nodded. "You've heard of them?"

"A little."

Marvelli and Vissa were walking away from the carousel, heading for the exit. Loretta had to get going before she lost them.

"Listen, it's been nice talking to you, Dorie, but I have to—"

Dorie grabbed her forearm. The desperate look on Dorie's face stopped Loretta cold. "I was wondering, Warden, if maybe you'd like to stay with us while you were here. Maybe just for a few days. Barry wouldn't mind. He won't even notice. We've got this huge house in Sausalito. Great views of the bay. I'd love to have you, Warden. I could show you around. It would be fun. If that's okay with you."

Dorie was clearly dying for some company, but Loretta was desperate not to lose track of Marvelli. She peered through the crowd and saw his departing back as he walked through the terminal, but Dorie's pathetic face suddenly blocked Loretta's view. Loretta was just about to make a quick excuse so she could dash off when suddenly something occurred to her. Marvelli and Vissa were here to find Arnie, right? But Dorie could get Loretta directly to Arnie through Barry, and if she found Arnie, she'd eventually rendezvous with Marvelli. Perfect.

"You know, Dorie, that would be great," Loretta said, smiling gratefully. "I'd love to stay with you and your husband."

Dorie beamed like the sun. "Fantastic," she squealed, hunching her shoulders. "I mean, it's only fair that I put you up. After all, you put me up for two and a half years at Pinewood." The woman sounded totally sincere—no irony, no sarcasm.

Loretta nodded. "You've got a point, Dorie."

Dorie led Loretta through her living room, waving her arm at the floor-to-ceiling sliding glass doors like a game-show hostess showing off the prizes. "So? Was I telling the truth or not?" she asked.

The view of the bay was truly spectacular. The Golden Gate Bridge was off to one side, San Francisco in the distance. The sun had just gone down, and the lights of the city were shimmering over the water. Loretta was very impressed.

"See that little island over there?" Dorie said, pointing with her finger.

"Yeah?"

"That's Alcatraz." Dorie was grinning with anticipation, but when Loretta didn't react, she suddenly seemed upset. "I thought you'd be interested, Warden. You being in corrections and all."

"Oh," Loretta said. "Well, actually I'm not in corrections anymore, Dorie."

"Really? What do you do?"

"I . . . I work at a private girls school. Assistant head mistress."

"Oooo! Head mistress," Dorie said, closing her eyes in mock ecstasy. "I love your title."

Loretta just let that pass. "Would you do me a favor, Dorie?"

"Sure. Anything."

"Don't call me Warden anymore."

"You'd prefer Head Mistress?"

"No. Just call me Loretta."

"Anything you say." Dorie nodded and kept nodding, staring at Loretta for way too long. "Loretta?" she finally said. "Can I ask you something?"

"Sure. What?"

"Why are you wearing that wig? Did something happen to your hair?"

"No," Loretta said abruptly. She didn't have an excuse ready.

"If you had chemo or something, and you lost all your hair, you can just tell me to shut up and mind my own business. It's okay."

"No, no, it's nothing like that," Loretta said quickly, not wanting Dorie to think she was hiding something. "It's a religious thing."

"Oh! You mean, like you're Jewish. Like the really religious ones who live in New York? All those women *have* to wear wigs, right?"

"Right, right," Loretta said.

"Gee," Dorie said, "I didn't think Kovacs was a Jewish name."

"It's not. I converted."

"Ooooohhh," Dorie said, nodding emphatically.

Loretta couldn't believe she'd just said that. Her Hungarian Catholic grandmother must be spinning in her grave.

"Arnie's Jewish," Dorie said. "You two ought to meet. But I don't think he's very religious. In fact, I know he isn't."

"I'd still like to meet him," Loretta said. *And handcuff him,* she thought.

"If you'd like, I could take you for a tour of the factory to-morrow. Arnie'll probably be there."

"Great. I'd really like that."

"Have a seat and get comfortable," Dorie said. "I'll go tell Barry we're here."

Loretta sat down on a huge L-shaped butternut leather sofa while Dorie headed up the open staircase to the second floor. She ran a pinkie along her cheek, pulling stray wig hairs out of the corner of her mouth as she wondered what Barry was like. He had to have more going on upstairs than Dorie, which made Loretta a little nervous. He might suspect that a supposedly converted Orthodox Jew with a Hungarian last name who used to be an assistant warden at a women's correctional facility in New Jersey might not be entirely kosher.

Somewhere in the house music was playing. Loretta could just about make it out. It sounded New Agey. A harp with gongs and chimes. She took in the room, which was an eclectic clutter of statues, masks, paintings, plants, and tchotchkes. No surface—wall, shelf, or table—was left uncovered. Dusting this place had to be a nightmare, she thought.

She turned around to get a better look at the paintings on the wall. The centerpiece of the room was a large oil painting of a naked mythical creature with the head of a tiger and the body of a *Playboy* centerfold. She wondered if Dorie had been the model. All the pictures seemed to have an Asian theme—rickshaws on a crowded street, pagodas, a temple in the mountains, the Great Wall of China—but one in particular grabbed her attention. It was a close-up of an unusually small foot and a pair of hands. The hands were binding the feet tight in layer after layer of cloth wrapping. It made Loretta uncomfortable just to look at it. She knew about the ancient custom of binding little girls' feet to keep them small, but seeing it was something else.

A long, glass-topped wrought-iron coffee table was littered

with all kinds of bric-a-brac—a cut-glass bowl full of chocolate Kisses, an array of glossy picture books full of sexual positions, a platoon of tiny figurines. The largest of the figurines caught her eye immediately. It was a carved ebony figure of a little man with a very big appendage. He looked like a pumpernickel version of the Pillsbury Doughboy with a super jumbo wiener sticking out of his crotch. It was so big it extended higher than his head, and he had to hold it up with both hands. The oddest thing about him was his expression—a great big sickle-moon smile and tiny, crinkled tight eyes. The little guy was totally self-satisfied and just tickled pink to be himself. Loretta thought of Marvelli and wondered if all men think of themselves that way. As long as their thing is working, the world is all right, and they're just delirious.

The sound of rapid clicking suddenly caught Loretta's attention. It was the unmistakable sound of a dog's untrimmed toenails trotting across a hardwood floor. Loretta scanned the room to locate the animal, imagining a loping Afghan hound with long, floppy, perfectly combed hair. If dogs looked like their owners, Dorie would have to have an Afghan. But what came out from behind the staircase sure as hell wasn't an Afghan. Loretta wasn't sure what it was.

It was big and mostly black with light tan markings on its huge paws and around its droopy muzzle. The dog's coat was wrinkled and rumpled, hanging in folds from its chest and flanks. Smaller folds fell from its brow, partially obscuring the eyes and giving the dog a haughty, aloof expression. It looked like a prune with an attitude.

The dog clicked over to the sofa, stopped, and stared at Loretta. After a moment it cocked its head to one side.

Loretta cocked her head to the other side. "What're *you* looking at?" she muttered.

The dog slid its front paws forward and lowered its head as if it were getting ready to lunge. The upper lip curled back, revealing a fierce row of teeth. A chill ran down Loretta's spine. Generally she wasn't afraid of dogs, but the fact that this one could bare its teeth without growling was very eerie.

"Easy, Fido," she said, deliberately keeping her hands still. "Be still, boy . . . girl . . . whatever you are."

Dorie came down the stairs. "Dragon," she said to the dog, "what are you doing here?"

The dog turned its head and a gave her a snotty look—but without the teeth.

Dorie walked right up to the beast and stared down at it. "Where's Sunny?" she asked. "Where is she, boy?"

The dog wagged his tail, but with that wrinkly immobile face he didn't seem happy.

Dorie looked at Loretta. "Did you meet Sunny?" she asked.

Loretta shook her head. "Who's Sunny?"

"Dragon's mistress. She must be around here someplace."

"I haven't seen anyone," Loretta said. "Just the dog." She noticed that Dorie wasn't reaching down to pet the beast. Maybe Dragon was a biter. "What kind of dog is that?" Loretta asked.

"Dragon is a rott-pei," Dorie said, "a cross between a rott-weiler and a shar-pei, which is why he's so wrinkly. Sunny says he's a kung-fu fighter. Aren't you, boy?" Dorie looked down at Dragon affectionately, but she still wouldn't touch him. "Shar-peis were fighting dogs in ancient China, but the fighting instinct was bred out of them a long time ago. Sunny said that crossing them with rotties brings back the old fighting spirit. Isn't that right, boy? Don't want to be a wimp, do you?"

"Does Sunny fight him?" Loretta asked. An image of cock fighting ran through her mind.

Dorie shrugged. "Gee . . . I don't know." That possibility apparently had never occurred to her.

A man came down the stairs then. He had a heavy, plodding step. As soon as Loretta saw his face, she recognized him. It was

Barry, the other guy on the ice-cream carton. He was wearing khaki shorts and a short-sleeved blue chambray shirt open to the middle of his hairy chest. He wasn't wearing anything on his feet.

"Where's Sunny?" Dorie asked him.

He pointed up to the second floor. "Meditating."

"Oh." Dorie nodded to herself. "Barry, this is Loretta Kovacs. Loretta, my husband Barry."

Loretta stood up, and they shook hands across the coffee table, but she kept an eye on Dragon. She didn't trust him.

"Nice to meet you," Barry said. He had a broad smile and a big space between his front teeth.

"You must be the most famous person I've ever met," Loretta gushed. "I love your ice cream." She figured it wouldn't hurt to suck up a little, seeing as she was going to be staying at his house.

"I'll be right back," Dorie said. "You two talk." She slide-walked on her sandals across the polished floors and disappeared behind the staircase.

"I hope you don't mind my staying with you," Loretta said. "I had planned to stay at a hotel in town, but Dorie kind of insisted."

"No problem," Barry said. "We have plenty of room here." He stepped over Dragon and took a seat on the other side of the L-shaped sofa. He linked his fingers behind his head and stretched his legs out, which lifted his shirt and exposed a triangle of hairy belly.

Dragon looked at Barry for a second, then went to the stairs and trotted up without giving Loretta a second look. *Very rude,* she thought. She usually liked dogs, but not this one.

"So, Loretta, tell me about yourself. You married?"

"No," she said. "But I'm engaged." She said that only because she didn't like the way he was looking at her. He seemed a little too interested. The man made no attempt to conceal his roving eyes, and his expression was very similar to the ebony doughboy

with the humongous cruller. With all the erotica in the room, Loretta couldn't help but think of him as some kind of kinky trip-
master. It figured that Dorie Jasson would end up marrying a guy
like this. She'd always been a magnet for users. It made Loretta
wonder who this Sunny person was and why he or she was meditating upstairs at Dorie's house?

Aren't you supposed to meditate at home? Loretta thought.
Or was meditating a private code word for something else?

Barry was staring at her hands, looking for an engagement ring
no doubt, but she wasn't going to make up an excuse for why she
didn't have one, not to Barry the ice-cream pervert. But that got
her thinking about Marvelli again. What were the chances that
he'd ever give her a ring now that Vissa the viper was on the scene?

"So were you really Dorie's warden?" Barry asked. He was
grinning as if this were amusing.

"That was a long time ago," she said. "I've been out of corrections for several years now."

Barry nodded, that weird grin plastered to his face. "You
know, you should come down to the plant while you're here. I can
arrange for you to get the private tour."

"Dorie already offered. Thanks. I'm looking forward to it."

"Great."

Why was it great? she wondered. Did he have something in
mind?

"So do you have any new flavors coming out?" she asked, to
change the subject.

All of a sudden Barry's face turned grim. He sat up straight
and put his feet flat on the floor. "I don't handle R and D. That's
Arnie's end." Clearly that had been the wrong question to ask.

"I'm back." Dorie said, sliding back into the living room. She
was carrying a teak tray with three cobalt blue bowls, three spoons,
and three pints of Arnie and Barry's ice cream. "The specialty of
the house," Dorie announced. The three flavors she'd brought were

Rainforest Rum Raisin, Nuts to You, and of course, Elmer Fudge Whirl. But as soon as she set down the tray on top of their copy of the *Kama Sutra*, Barry suddenly stood up and snatched the pint of Fudge Whirl off the tray.

"Don't eat this one," he grumbled. "Bad batch." He carried it back to the kitchen with a scowl on his face.

Loretta tracked him with her eyes until he was out of the room. "What was that all about?" she whispered to Dorie.

Dorie shrugged as she dug into the Nuts to You. "Must be a bad batch," she said, keeping her eyes on what she was doing.

Suddenly Loretta noticed a figure looming at the top of the stairs. Dragon was staring down at her, silently baring his teeth.

The next morning Loretta and Dorie were on the main floor of the Arnie and Barry's plant in Berkeley, watching empty pint containers zip along on a conveyor belt, stopping momentarily to be filled with softened Elmer Fudge Whirl, moving on, then stopping again to have a lid automatically plopped on. From here the pints raced on like lemmings to the sea, tumbling off the edge of the conveyor where a young man in a white lab coat and a hair net quickly arranged them on metal racks that were stacked on an electric trolley by second man in a lab coat and a hair net. When the trolley had a full load, it shuttled off to the freezer where the ice cream would set.

Loretta was wearing a borrowed banana-yellow parka with the Arnie and Barry's logo on the back. The main floor of the plant was kept very cool, of course, to keep the ice cream from melting. It was a huge space with a two-story ceiling to accommodate the hulking machinery. Workers in white lab coats scuttled around busily, making sure the flow of pints continued uninterrupted. On the wall above the commotion was a mural of the Arnie and

Barry's logo, their smiling faces superimposed over a rainbow-colored tie-dyed sunburst. High on the wall opposite the mural were a line of glass panels where the endless stream of people on the public tour peered down at the ice-cream works.

Loretta gazed up at them shuffling by as she tried to scratch her head through her wig. The damn thing was hot and itchy, and it was really starting to bug her. She wished she hadn't lied to Dorie and told her she was wearing it for religious reasons. Dorie had actually gone out and gotten her matzo for breakfast, which Loretta had no choice but to eat. But even with butter, eating those dry brittle sheets of unleavened bread was like eating wallboard, and Loretta knew she was going to be constipated for a month.

"You think I'll get to meet Arnie today?" Loretta asked, raising her voice over the constant clack and grind of the packaging machinery.

Dorie shrugged. "Depends," she said.

"On what?"

"How busy he is, his mood, the *I Ching* . . . lots of things."

"I should've brought my Eight Ball," Loretta muttered to herself.

"What?" Dorie said, cupping her ear.

"Nothing," Loretta shouted back.

Loretta was getting nervous about this whole thing. She still hadn't figured out what she was going to do when she met Arnie a.k.a. Ira Krupnick. If she arrested him and hauled him back to Jersey by herself just to show up Vissa, she'd be leaving Marvelli alone with her here in San Francisco, which might not be the smartest thing to do, all things considered. No telling what might happen if those two stayed together too long.

But on the other hand if Loretta let Vissa and Marvelli arrest Arnie, and Loretta just happened to be on the scene, she'd look like a jealous idiot. She chewed on her lip, trying to figure out what to do. This jealousy thing was driving her crazy. She wasn't proud of herself for feeling this way, but she couldn't help it. It was how she felt.

Please, Marvelli, she thought. *Just be the good guy I always thought you were. That's all I ask.*

"Loretta, are you all right?" Dorie asked. "You're mumbling to yourself."

"Ah . . . just saying prayers," Loretta said.

"Prayers?"

"It's a Jewish thing."

"Oh . . ." Dorie moved around to the back of a huge machine. "Look over here," she said. "You have to see this."

Loretta had to stand on her tiptoes to see what Dorie was pointing at. Inside a stainless-steel vat that was as big as a living room, metal rakes rotated through a lifetime's worth of Elmer Fudge Whirl. And it was one of three vats sitting in a row, two of them waiting in line to be hooked up to the packaging machine.

Dorie whispered into Loretta's ear. "This is where Arnie does his 'fine-tuning.' That's what he calls it. For the Fudge Whirl he always adds a little something special at this stage. His secret ingredient."

Loretta nodded, wondering if and when Arnie would pop out. With all these white-coated workers buzzing around in double time, she was beginning to feel like a refugee in the merry old land of Oz. She stared into the vat at the swirling waves of vanilla ice cream.

"They add the fudge at the very end," Dorie said, pointing to a smaller vat that loomed over the next vat in line, "so that it doesn't blend in completely."

"Right," Loretta said. The swirling ice cream was hypnotic, forcing her to stare deeper and harder. When she closed her eyes, she could see neon pinwheels. She opened her eyes and looked up, trying to focus on something else. But what she saw instantly made her see red.

Up on the walkway behind the glass, shuffling along with all the tourists, were Marvelli and Vissa. She had her arm hooked around his, grinning and hunching her shoulders as if she were a sweet little newlywed. But she was far from that. She was a flying monkey as far as Loretta was concerned. *Vissa must be short for* vicious, Loretta thought. When Vissa hugged Marvelli's arm and laid her big teased-up head on his shoulder, Loretta wanted to scream.

Loretta shaded her eyes and squinted, desperate to make out the expression on Marvelli's face. Was he enjoying this or just tolerating it? They were just pretending to be a couple while they scouted out the factory. Right? *Right, Marvelli?* she yelled in her head.

"Loretta?" Dorie was tapping Loretta on the shoulder. "There he is." Dorie nodded at the large man charging across the room. He smiled at the workers as he passed, but they all gave him a wide berth. He was carrying what looked like two pint-size metal milk cartons, one in each hand. Loretta glanced up at Arnie's painted face on the mural. Yes, this was definitely Arnie.

He marched right up to the vats and quickly dumped the contents of one of the containers into one of the vats, then did the same to the other vat. Whatever was in the containers was quickly swallowed up by the swirling ice cream because Loretta didn't even see what color it was.

"What's that?" Loretta asked Dorie.

"The secret ingredient," Dorie whispered. She waved to Arnie from across the vat to get his attention. "Arnie? I want you to meet someone."

"Not now, sweetie pie," he said. He was already halfway across the floor, heading back to the doorway he'd just come through. A small sign on the door said PRIVATE in red block letters.

Loretta glanced up at Marvelli and Vissa, who were focused

intently on Arnie. They apparently hadn't recognized her. *But why not?* she wanted to know. Shouldn't Marvelli be able to recognize her, even with the wig on? After all, they'd been practically inseparable for the past three months. And she was even wearing the white cowboy shirt with the roses embroidered on the front that she'd worn to the Jersey Devils hockey game at the Meadowlands two weeks ago. *Shouldn't he remember that?*

The door marked PRIVATE slammed shut with an abrupt bang. Loretta gritted her teeth and made a face. Arnie disappeared as quickly as he'd come, and she didn't even get to meet him.

"Friendly guy," Loretta said sarcastically.

"Oh, he is when you get to meet him," Dorie said.

"When will that be?"

"I dunno. When the planets are in harmony, and your signs are in alignment."

Loretta just stared at her, waiting for a sign that she was kidding. "You don't really believe that stuff, do you?" Loretta finally asked.

"Yes and no," Dorie said. "Put it this way. I *want* to believe."

"I can sort of understand that," Loretta said, but she was lying. She had no patience for anyone who believed in angels, crystals, pyramids, and all that other New Age crap.

"So what's the secret ingredient?" Loretta asked, changing the subject. She wanted to know more about Arnie.

Dorie shook her head as she played with her hair. "I really don't know. Arnie doesn't talk about it, and neither does Barry. I guess that's what makes it a secret."

Thanks a lot, Dorie, Loretta thought.

"So Barry takes care of the money end," Loretta said, "and Arnie creates the flavors. That sounds like a pretty good division of labor."

"I dunno about that," Dorie said, rolling her eyes toward the door marked PRIVATE. "They fight all the time."

"Really?" Loretta looked up at their smiling logo. "You'd think they were the best of friends from ads."

"Well, from what I hear they used to be. But that was long before I arrived on the scene."

"What happened? They have a falling out?"

Dorie shrugged. "Someone told me it all started when Arnie went away to a fat farm in Florida. He lost a lot of weight, but when he came back he was different. No one could exactly put their finger on it, but somehow he'd changed. And that's when things changed between him and Barry. They stopped palling around. Eventually they were at each other's throats all the time."

"So why didn't they just dissolve the partnership?"

Dorie looked down into the vat. "Because of this, the Fudge Whirl. It started to take off. The company tripled its annual earnings the year it was introduced, and it's been going strong ever since. The guys were just making too much money to split up."

"So does Arnie have a wife?" Loretta asked.

Dorie's eyes shot open. "Why? Are you interested?"

"No. Of course not. I'm just curious."

"No, Arnie's not married."

"Does he have someone special?" Loretta pried.

Dorie looked down and blushed to the roots of her hair.

"You?" Loretta whispered, trying to sound surprised. "But you're married to Barry."

"Don't worry. It's cool," Dorie said. "Barry has a girlfriend, too. Sunny. Dragon's owner?"

Loretta nodded slowly. "I thought there was more going on upstairs at your house than meditation."

"Really, Loretta. It's cool. People live that way out here." The look on Dorie's face was so ingenuous, ice cream wouldn't have melted in her mouth. She kept saying it was cool, it was cool, but privately Loretta disagreed. She wasn't a prude by any means, but some things were just plain out-of-bounds as far as she was concerned, and these people were definitely running on the warning track.

Dorie flashed a naughty grin. "Let's go get some samples," she said. "The people on the public tour only get a little tiny cup, but we can get all we want. Come on." She headed across the floor, past the steel door that led to Arnie's private laboratory.

Loretta took one last look into the vat of Elmer Fudge Whirl, and it suddenly occurred to her that maybe Arnie's secret ingredient was some kind of diabolical aphrodisiac that made people cheat on their mates and swap partners and sleep with cocker spaniels and do all kinds of kinky things, then say, "It's cool." *And Marvelli shovels that stuff in like there's no tomorrow.*

She glanced up at the tourists streaming by, but he was gone and so was Vissa.

Naw, Loretta thought. *I'm just being paranoid. Right?*

But Loretta kept staring up at all those passing faces, hoping that she'd spot Marvelli—by himself.

"Loretta?" Dorie called to her from an open doorway across the plant floor. "Is anything wrong?"

Loretta shook her head and sighed, her mouth fixed in a frown.

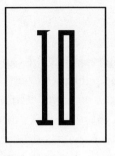

Marvelli was sitting behind the wheel of his rented white Pontiac Grand Am, Vissa in the passenger seat. They were still in the parking lot at the Arnie and Barry's plant. High clouds dotted an otherwise clear blue sky, but it was a little chilly out. The inside of the car was comfortably warm. Marvelli stared out the window, soaking in the heat like a lizard on a hot rock.

"So what do you think goes on behind that door marked 'private'?" Vissa asked. She was wearing tiny round sunglasses that just covered her eyes.

Marvelli shrugged. "Mr. Arnie seemed pretty anxious to get back inside. Did you get that impression?"

"Yeah. I did."

Marvelli turned his head to the side and squinted at her profile, focusing on her nose. She had a really cute nose. He happened to know that it was a nose job, but so what. "So what do you think?" he said. "Was that Ira Krupnick?"

She pursed her lips. "I'm not sure. We were pretty far away, plus we were looking down at him. I wouldn't put it past Krupnick to pull another switcheroo with another guy who looked like him."

"What are the chances of that?"

"With Ira Krupnick? Pretty good, I'd say."

Marvelli leaned back against the headrest. The heat melded with the quiet and covered him like a thick blanket, making him drowsy. When he glanced over at Vissa again, she was wrinkling her nose as she bit her bottom lip, which produced a sudden twinge in his groin. He wished she wouldn't do things like that.

"We could go in and try to approach him," she suggested. "But I don't know. What if it's not him, and he makes a scene? It could get into the press, and we'd have to answer to Julius."

"Worse that that," Marvelli pointed out. "The guy could press charges. False arrest, harassment, interfering with his business. He could sue us personally in civil court. He could win damages."

She turned her head and looked at him. "What's he gonna do? Garnish our wages? We don't make squat as it is."

"He could take my house."

"Oh, yeah. I forget about that. Well, I just rent." She let out a small sigh. "Of course, you could always move in with me . . . if you wanted."

Marvelli furrowed his brows at her.

"Just kidding," she said right away. "Just kidding."

He didn't say anything. He didn't want to go there.

But sitting here next to her in this warm cozy car felt sort of like lying side by side on a sunny beach, and he imagined her in a bikini, a lime green one, and suddenly the little guy in his pants moved.

Cool it, he said to the little guy. *It ain't gonna happen. Besides,* he thought, *Vissa is just a tease. None of it is serious.* He glanced at her profile again. *It doesn't mean anything.*

He felt another little tingle as if his beeper had gone off in his shorts.

"But what if it is Krupnick?" Vissa said. "Who knows what he could be into? That's one thing about Ira—he's never afraid to try something new. As long as it's illegal."

"Mmmmm . . ." Marvelli was distracted, only half-listening to her. He was thinking about that one time he'd slept with her.

He glanced at her again, studying her face, thinking that part of him would like to do it with her again, but he knew that he shouldn't even be thinking about that. It was just a physical urge that would pass. Like gas. The damage it would do, the repercussions, the complications—forget it—it wasn't worth it. One time with Vissa—even a world-class time with Vissa—wasn't worth losing Loretta over. No way.

"So," Vissa asked, "what do you want to do now?"

"Huh? What do you mean?" His heart started to thump as if he'd just been caught red-handed.

"What do you mean, 'what do you mean'? What do you want to do about Krupnick? Do we approach this guy now, or do we watch him for a while?"

"We should just watch him," Marvelli said. "Better to be safe than sorry."

"Really?"

"Yeah, really. We should go slow. Don't do anything rash."

"But I thought you were anxious to get back home to Loretta."

"We shouldn't rush this," he insisted. "If it takes a few days, so what?"

He closed his eyes and tipped his head back. The comfortable heat was starting to feel a little too warm.

Are you crazy? he asked himself. *A few days for what?* He wasn't going to do anything with her, he told himself. He wasn't the kind of person who did things like that. Other people did things like that, not him.

But he had done it . . . once.

He opened his eyes and looked down to one side. Vissa's long

tapered fingers were stretched out on her thigh. The pale pink pol-
ish shimmered in the sun. He looked at her dark hair and the
Cleopatra eyeliner.

The woman is no nun, he thought. *A person this sexy can't
possibly be. She must have had dozens of guys. Which means she
could have a sexually transmitted disease!*

His heart started slamming in his chest. *No way,* he thought.
He couldn't risk that.

"So what're we gonna *do?*" Vissa said. "Sit here all day?"

"No," he said.

"You have a plan?"

"Not yet."

"Well, you let me know when you come up with one, Marvelli." She dropped her chin and rubbed the back of her neck. He
had an urge to rub it for her, but he kept his hands in his lap.

He watched her move, shrugging her shoulders and tilting her
head. She was incredible. Everything she did was sexy. A striptease
couldn't have aroused him more than what she was doing right
now. She squirmed out of her black jeans jacket and tossed it in
the backseat. She was wearing only a tube top underneath, lime
green. Her hair brushed her bare shoulders. The geometry of her
breasts could inspire a long-term study.

*Statistically, men give women sexually transmitted diseases
more than women give them to men,* he thought. *Condoms prevent
infection. Some guys wear two.*

He sneaked a look at her flat stomach. What if he got her
pregnant? he thought in a panic. What if Vissa decided to keep the
child? He didn't want to have kids with her. How would he explain
that to Loretta? *No, forget it,* he thought. *Much, much, much too
risky.*

But then Vissa started slowly rubbing her bare arms as if she
were putting on suntan oil. She reached down for the handle on
her right side and dropped the seatback all the way so that she

was lying flat on her back right next to him. Her boobs were right there, like dessert on the table, and her tight black jeans outlined every curve and crevice. The little guy was getting jumpy.

How many times in a person's life do opportunities like this really happen? Marvelli thought. *Almost never.*

But then he wondered if what he was feeling was just a symptom of midlife crisis. He was going to be thirty-five in a month. Admittedly he was a little young for a midlife crisis, but maybe what he had was like early menopause or early Alzheimer's. Whatever it was, it was driving him nuts. He hadn't been this horny since he was fifteen.

She took off her sunglasses, but her eyes were closed. "Wake me up when you think of something, Marvelli. I'm still jet-lagged."

Marvelli clutched his seat belt. She was there for the taking.

Or is she? he thought. Maybe she didn't want any part of him. Maybe this was all in his head. Maybe he was reading in.

She opened one eye and grinned up at him. "Don't stare," she said. "I can feel it." She didn't sound displeased.

The little guy was all pumped up now. Marvelli was afraid he was going to split his pants. He had to do something. It wasn't healthy staying this way. He was totally distracted, obsessed, consumed. He needed something—a vacation, Prozac, an exorcist, something. He was definitely gonna go batty if he didn't deal with this, and then he'd be no good for anyone, Loretta included. He had to straighten himself out before he got back home. Maybe just do it once and get it over with. Then he could stop thinking about it.

He stared down at Vissa and started to sweat. *But how the hell could I do that?* he thought. *I want to, but I don't want to. I'm too chicken. I don't want to lose Loretta.* He started to knead his temples with his thumb and forefinger.

"What's wrong?" she said. Her eyes were open, a dazzling blue gray in the sun. "You okay?" she asked, laying her hand on his thigh.

Please don't do that, he thought.

"Marvelli? What is it? You don't look good." She raised her seatback.

"It's just a headache," he said. "It'll go away."

"Why don't we go back to the motel? You can lie down for a while."

"No, I'll be all right."

"It's not that far from here. Go lie down and take an aspirin."

"I don't have any," he said.

"I have some in my room. I'll bring it to you."

His breathing got shallow. A scenario unfolded in his head. *She was just bringing me some aspirin,* he could say afterward. He had a headache. One thing led to another . . .

"Come on, Marvelli. I don't want you getting sick on me. I need you to catch Krupnick." She was kneading his thigh to emphasize her point. The little bodybuilder downstairs was flexing everything he had.

"Marvelli, are you gonna be sensible about this? Let's go back to the motel."

This is wrong, Marvelli kept telling himself. *This is wrong. This is wrong.*

"Marvelli, don't be stupid."

But what if?

She reached over and felt his forehead, then his cheek. "Open your mouth," she said.

"What?"

"Just open it," she said, and suddenly she slipped her pinky between his lips and under his tongue before he could object. "I can't tell if you have a fever from your forehead. It's too hot in here. This is the only way I can tell."

"But—"

"Shush. My grandmother used to do it this way. She didn't need a thermometer."

Marvelli could feel her fingernail under his tongue. He could *taste* her. The little hard guy was going crazy.

After a few seconds, she pulled out her finger. "I can't tell for sure. Let's go back to the hotel. You should lie down for a while."

"But—"

"Marvelli, will you stop being stupid? Will you let me help you?"

He zeroed in on her nose and how it flared when she yelled at him.

"Marvelli, please," she said, suddenly quiet. Her eyes were pleading with him.

Marvelli held his breath. There was 'roid rage down below.

"Please?" she said. Her voice was somewhere between a squeak and a purr. She was pouting. "*Please?*" she whispered.

His hand was already on the ignition key.

II

Loretta was in the private bathroom in Barry Utley's office at the plant. Her wig was on top of the toilet tank, and she was desperately trying to scratch her itchy scalp through the skullcap she had to wear to hold in her own hair. She looked at herself in the mirror as she scratched and made a sour face. Why did she buy this stupid wig in the first place? A washout dye and a new hairstyle would have been a much better idea. She wished she'd thought of that first.

The bathroom was small but posh with matching polished brass fixtures on the sink and shower, and milk-glass green tiles on the walls. The tub, sink, and toilet were a darker green. It was the kind of bathroom a British barrister would have on *Masterpiece Theater*—if they ever showed bathrooms on *Masterpiece Theater*.

The framed print hanging opposite the toilet was an antique etching of a tiger in the jungle, something that might have appeared in a turn-of-the-century schoolbook. The colors were muted—the sky a peacock blue, the orange on the tiger more of a pastel Creamsicle color. The tiger's face was placid, as if it had agreed to pose for the drawing. It was a far cry from the tiger woman hanging in the living room at Barry and Dorie's house. If fact, there was nothing remotely sexual about the decor in here or anywhere in Barry's office. It was a nice cover, Loretta thought, but Barry was still a perv in her book. She was tempted to look in the cabinet under the sink for girlie magazines. Barry had to have something smutty stashed away here.

Loretta picked up the wig and smoothed out the bangs, getting ready to put it back on. Dorie was outside in the office, waiting for her. Barry was out entertaining a buyer from an East Coast supermarket chain.

"You okay in there?" Dorie called through the door.

"I'm fine," Loretta called back.

"You should have told me you didn't like Mexican food."

"No, I like it. It just doesn't like me." Loretta lied, reaching down and flushing the toilet again. She'd needed a reason for being in the bathroom so long. "Shouldn't have had those beans with my *huevos rancheros* this morning."

"I'm sorry," Dorie said. Loretta could hear from the tone of her voice that she was taking personal responsibility for Loretta's alleged gastric distress.

"You don't have to be sorry," Loretta said. "It's not your fault." She hated it when Dorie got all bent out of shape, trying to make things perfect. It seemed like Dorie was apologizing all the time. "I'll be out in a minute," Loretta said. She bent forward, positioned the wig on her head, and stood up fast, flipping it into place. She pulled out a comb and started to arrange it when she heard the door to the office open and bang shut. She frowned in the mirror, thinking Dorie was upset about something and had run out. Then she heard an unfamiliar voice.

"What the hell's going on? Answer me." It was a husky female voice. Whoever she was, she was furious, but her voice was ominously controlled.

"What do you mean?" Dorie asked innocently.

"Who's your new playmate?"

"Who? Loretta?"

"Is *that* her name?" The woman's voice oozed with contempt.

"Don't be that way, Sunny. She's a nice person."

"Really."

Loretta gazed at herself in the mirror, still fixing the wig. *So this is Dragon's mistress,* she thought. Loretta wondered why she was able to just walk into Barry's office. Probably for the same reason she could "meditate" upstairs where the bedrooms were in his house.

"So what's the deal, Dorie? And don't lie."

"Sun-ny!" Dorie whined. "Loretta is someone I knew back in New Jersey. She's an old friend."

Loretta raised her eyebrows. There weren't many ex-cons who referred to their wardens as old friends, but that was Dorie.

Sunny didn't respond, but as the silence grew, Loretta became concerned. What was going on out there? she wondered. Were they staring each other down, getting ready for a catfight? Dorie hadn't been much of a fighter in prison, and this Sunny sounded like a nasty piece of business. It was her quiet control that concerned Loretta. In her experience the shouters were almost always more talk than action. Mostly they just wanted to vent. It was the calm ones like Sunny who did the most damage because they managed to carry out their intentions.

Loretta stopped fussing with the wig and opened the bathroom door.

"If I *ever* catch you with someone else," Sunny was saying, "I'll cut your—"

"Well, that's better." Loretta said, putting on a pleasant face as if she hadn't heard a word of what had been going on. But then she got a gander of Sunny. Her first thought was *S&M Dragon Lady.*

Sunny was Asian American with pretty but hard features. Her straight jet-black hair was chopped at the neck, and she wore heavy eyeliner and dark red lipstick. She was a little on the heavy side, but obviously that was from lifting weights. The woman was buff and built with unusually broad shoulders, muscular arms, and powerful thighs. She was wearing a black leather halter, black leather shorts, and black lace-up lumberjack boots. There were big ornate rings on all her fingers, thumbs included. Her nails were moderately long and painted high-gloss violet. Both thumbnails, however, were so long they curlicued back toward her hands.

"Oh, Loretta," Dorie said. "This is Sunny Chu." If Dorie was scared or nervous, she wasn't showing it. She was one hundred percent laid-back California girl.

"Nice to meet you," Loretta said, extending her hand.

Sunny didn't say a word. She didn't shake Loretta's hand or even look at it. She just stared into Loretta's eyes, beaming hostility directly into her. Nevertheless Loretta kept smiling, determined not to let Sunny creep her out—even though she was doing a pretty good job so far.

So what's her problem? Loretta wondered.

What's her *problem?* Sunny thought as she stared this Loretta woman in the eye. *You think you're better than me—that's the problem. You think I'm dirt. I can feel what you're thinking.*

"Come on, Sunny," Dorie said. "Don't be that way." Dorie tipped her head forward and let her floppy blond hair envelop her face. She peeked through the blond tunnel and melted Sunny right down. Dorie knew how to do that. There was just something about her that Sunny couldn't resist.

Sunny turned away and stared out the window at the parking lot that went on forever. She loved Dorie, but she didn't have a clue as to what Dorie thought of her. Sure, Dorie was friendly and accommodating, but Sunny wanted more. Barry had promised her that he would get Dorie to join them in a threesome, but so far it hadn't happened, and she was getting tired of whipping that big tub of lard by herself. He was taking advantage of her now, taking more liberties with her than she'd ever allowed a client to take. But all Sunny wanted was Dorie—Dorie *alone*—and Sunny felt that she needed Barry's involvement to convince Dorie that it would be okay. Of course, nobody ever really understood what Sunny wanted. They all had expectations and assumptions about her, but they had no freaking idea what it was like to be a butch bisexual Chinese American yellow witch–dominatrix. They just didn't understand.

Her family certainly didn't understand her—not her relatives here or the ones in Hong Kong. Her sissy-boy clients didn't offer much understanding either. They were just a bunch of needy little boys who wanted spankings from Mommy, but who never dreamed that Mommy needed a little something now and then, too. Have you hugged your dominatrix today? Not likely. The people at the gym avoided her; wouldn't even use the free weights or the Stairmaster after she was through with them, as if she'd cast a spell on the equipment, which she wouldn't mind doing except she wasn't up to that yet in her witch training. The pinheads in her *wu shu* classes were just as bad, and she had no way of knowing what her conveniently inscrutable master thought of her. All the straight people she knew were afraid of her, and her lesbian friends didn't completely trust her because she was bi. Even her ancestors in the afterlife dissed her when they spoke to her. They sounded just like her Hong Kong grandparents, very disapproving. They didn't like the witchcraft she practiced and said that she was doing it all wrong, that a girl shouldn't meddle in such things. They kept telling her to stop fooling around and learn to cook so she could find a man and get married.

As if.

Out of the corner of her eye, Sunny spotted Dorie standing close to Loretta, straightening out that cheap wig she was wearing. Blind jealousy started to rise in Sunny's chest, stoked by the sight of Dorie fluffing Loretta's bangs. It burned her shoulders and scalded her abs until the heat finally reached her face. It felt as if she were standing too close to an open fire. But for Sunny this felt good. She never backed away from things that were painful. She savored her jealousy, consumed it, turned it into *chi*—inner energy—then she let it electrify her. Emotions like jealousy stoked her inner furnace and increased her power.

What's bad is good, what's good is bad, she thought. *Yin yang, yang yin, as the ancestors always say. Yadda, yadda, yadda.*

Sunny focused on Loretta's big butt. Sunny hated flab. It was evil, she thought. Unusable evil. She wished she had Dragon with her so that she could make him rip a big hunk out of Loretta's butt. Dragon would do it for her. Dragon was loyal. Dragon loved her, and Dragon was the only one who did. She wished Dorie would love her like that.

She smiled wistfully as she remembered Dragon as a pup. He was so cute and wrinkly. One of her clients—a man who was into enforced feminization—bred Dragon specially for her. He owned a small vineyard in Marin County and bred rottweilers as a hobby. He crossed one of his best bitches with a male shar-pei and gave her the pick of the litter. He'd actually brought all the puppies to her dungeon, so she could choose. There were seven of them, and they were all adorable, but she knew right away that Dragon was the one when he started to teethe on the handle of her bullwhip. She cradled him like a baby and scratched his belly, but he kept squirming and turning his head to sniff her leather bustier. Dragon still loved the scent of leather.

She closed her eyes and imagined Dragon running through an open field of wildflowers. Thorns and burrs and brambles would get caught in his coat, and she would pluck them out one by one on the deck of a big house with a view of the ocean, pricking herself repeatedly until her fingers bled. It would be heaven. Her dream was to have lots of land and a great view and a fully equipped dungeon in the country, but she wasn't so sure she'd ever have that. Agnes and Thaddeus were turning into a couple of butt-wipes. They talked big, but that's all they did, just talk. She couldn't depend on them. She was sorry she'd ever invested her hopes in those two.

But Dorie was another story. Sunny looked at her sideways through half-closed lids. Dorie was sitting on the green leather sofa next to Loretta, the two of them chatting away. Sunny would love to live in that big house in the country with Dorie. Dragon liked Dorie. (He didn't care much for Thaddeus, and he totally ignored Agnes.) And Barry would support Dorie financially, even if she left him. The man was a doormat when it came to women. Sunny knew that firsthand. She could give him an ultimatum—if he wanted to keep seeing her in the dungeon, he'd have to help pay for the house. And he'd do it, too, because he couldn't live without her approval. And even on the off chance that he could work up the gumption to find another dom, Sunny had secretly taped videos of him being trussed up like a Thanksgiving turkey. Wouldn't be too good for sales if Arnie and Barry's fans found out that Barry was a perv. Whipped cream would take on a whole new meaning for them.

Sunny allowed herself a self-satisfied smirk. She was glad that she had made extra copies of those videos. Arnie had originally commissioned her to make them, so that he could hold them over Barry, but she was no fool. In fact she had videos of *both* of them in compromising positions. Except that Arnie—well, Arnie was Arnie. Nothing bothered him, and he had nothing to be ashamed of.

His banana split could wipe out the competition in a dead heat. That man could go far in porn if he wanted to. He could go far in anything if he wanted to. Like Dragon, he was born in the year of the dragon, which made him powerful, a leader, someone to be feared and admired. People like Arnie can make magic, but they should be kept close and cherished like rubies. And they should never be messed with.

A few weeks ago she had thrown the *I Ching* for him. They were at his house, in the living room under the skylight. He'd wanted to know how he was doing in the luck department. He'd said he'd been feeling itchy lately, thought it might be time for a big change. He wanted to know if this would be wise.

She was straddling him, both of them naked, using three quarters on his bare chest, throwing them down to get the hexagrams. All heads were yin. All tails yang. A tail and two heads were yin. A head and two tails yang. She threw the coins six times—yin, yin, yang, yang, yang, yang, which according to the *I Ching* was the thirty-third hexagram, *tun*, retreating. She then picked out his primary trigram, which was heaven over mountain. The signs, she told him, were not auspicious.

"Heaven is about to confront mountain, a mounting force," she'd told him. "This force will likely increase in power, posing an undeniable threat. Be wary of people whose character and virtue remain a mystery to you. Strangers should be avoided, for they may be the agents of the mounting force."

It wasn't what he'd wanted to hear. Immediately he became sulky. He glared up at the skylight as if he were mad at heaven for wimping out to mountain. His banana split melted.

He said just one thing for the rest of the afternoon, and he'd muttered it to himself: "The time has come." Later he hummed "I Am the Walrus."

But now, looking across the room at Loretta, Sunny couldn't help but wonder if this was the stranger Arnie had to avoid.

Think about it. Loretta just arrived from the East Coast. Her character is unknown, and who knows if she has any virtues. And on top of that she's pretty big, must weigh close to two hundred pounds. Mountain. She's the mountain!

"Sunny," Dorie called over to her, "Loretta and I are going into town for lunch. You wanna come?"

Sunny stared at Dorie, ignoring her question. She slowly shifted her gaze and let her stare bore into Loretta. "Mountain is strong," she said, "but heaven has lightning. Life is uncertain. Fortune is a bucket. It can hold anything. Even snakes. Beware, Mountain. You can be crumbled."

Dorie squinted at her. "Does that mean you don't want to come?"

Loretta stared back without blinking, her face serious.

Sunny grinned and sauntered toward the door, swinging her black leather hips like weapons. "Have a nice lunch," she said.

12

"Where you going?" Vissa said.

Marvelli was already halfway out of the car. They were still in the parking lot at the Arnie and Barry's factory. He had to get away from her before he did something stupid.

Vissa put the seatback up straight and adjusted her tube top. "What's wrong? Are you gonna be sick?"

"No, no. I'm fine," he said. He was standing on the pavement, bending down and peering in through the open door.

"But what about your headache?" she asked.

"It's gone."

"So fast?"

"Yup."

He knew he was going to have a much bigger headache if he stuck around her.

She took off her sunglasses and squinted at him in puzzlement, wrinkling her nose in the process. Marvelli zeroed in on her nose and froze. He wished to God she wouldn't do that. He was tempted to get back in the car and say to hell with it, go for the gold, suffer the consequences later. Every muscle and gland in his body—particularly Mr. Man in his pants—was telling him to get in. Only his conscience was saying go away, but that was a faint voice yelling from down the end of a very long corridor, and that corridor was getting longer and the voice fainter and fainter.

"Marvelli?" she said softly. "Don't go. I'm worried about you."

He started to melt. She was asking him not to go. *She* was asking *him*. How many times does that ever happen, the woman asking the man? His foot automatically lifted off the ground and went back into the car.

"I . . . I . . ." he said, but his mind went blank. He'd thought of an excuse for getting out of the car so abruptly, but he'd already forgotten it.

"Let's go back to the motel," she said. "Come on."

Marvelli's mouth wasn't working; he couldn't get any words out. At this very moment Vissa was beyond sweet. She was . . . she was what he wanted. Badly.

But the faint voice was still struggling to be heard, shouting from down that long hallway. *Short-term goals,* the voice was yelling. *No short-term goals. Think long-term.*

Those words doused him like an ice-water shower. Short-term goals, he'd always thought, were the big problem with men and women. Guys always settle for short-term goals, which is a big mistake. Guys use tactics, but they rarely have a strategy. Basically if a guy thinks he can get what he wants, he goes for it. In Marvelli's current situation, Vissa was the short-term goal while Loretta was the long-term goal. Hands down, Loretta was the better bet for him, but if he went for the short-term goal, he would most likely screw up his chances of achieving the long-term goal, which was what he *really* wanted. And that's what the little voice down the hallway was telling him. He put his foot back on the ground.

"Marvelli," Vissa whined. She was leaning across the console, her elbow on the driver's seat, trying to get to him. "Please, Mar-velli."

But he knew what he had to do even though Mr. Man in his pants was screaming at him, telling him not to be stupid, that Loretta would never find out. Marvelli moved farther away from the car, getting way out of Vissa's reach, telling himself over and over again that he had to stay away from her even though he wasn't totally convinced why. The sperm had shot up to his head, he told himself. The fluids in his brain were too cloudy to allow him to think straight.

"Where you going?" she called to him.

"Back inside," he said, pointing at the factory.

"Why?"

"I'm gonna apply for a job."

"What?"

"If I get a job here, I'll be able to get close to Arnie, find out if he's really Krupnick."

"But you said you didn't remember him that well."

"It's all coming back to me." Marvelli reached into his pocket and pulled out the keys to the rental car. "Here," he said, tossing them through the open doorway. "I'll call you later at the motel."

"When?"

"I don't know. Depends if I get the job. Don't worry. I'll call you."

"But—"

"Don't worry. I'll be okay."

Oh, please, he thought. *Please, let me get a job and let me start today. Right this minute.*

He turned and started to walk across the parking lot. But when Vissa stopped objecting, he looked back over his shoulder, a little disappointed that she wasn't insisting more. Part of him wanted to be seduced, hoping that she had magical powers, like a siren, and when it happened, it would be totally beyond his control. But Vissa didn't say another word. She was crawling over the console, getting into the driver's seat. He felt a little disgruntled that she'd given up so easily. Maybe she didn't really want him that badly. Anyway, it was better this way.

I think, he thought.

He wedged his way past the crowd of visitors waiting to take the plant tour and wove through the crowd of shoppers waiting to get into the gift shop, which was packed with people holding up the various tie-dyed Arnie and Barry's T-shirts, trying to decide which design they wanted. The gift shop sold all kinds of junk with the Arnie and Barry's logo on it—coffee cups, ice cream bowls, ice cream scoops, pins, scarves, sweatshirts, beach balls, towels, baby bibs, decals, bumper stickers. All of it was grossly overpriced, and Marvelli couldn't believe people actually paid good money for this junk. He wasn't one for souvenirs and tchotchkes. The T-shirts and sweatshirts took up an entire wall of cubbyholes, but he noticed that one style in particular was selling much better than any of the others. As he stood there, the clerks kept having to restock those shelves. And he didn't even think the design was that attractive—a brown, red, and pale yellow tie-dye swirl pattern, sort of like a septic flush. But then he saw the words on the front—ARNIE AND BARRY'S ELMER FUDGE WHIRL. The logo was altered so that Barry was completely bald with a hunter's cap perched on top of his head, and Arnie was wearing rabbit ears and buck teeth. Marvelli gave it a second look.

Actually it's kind of clever, he thought.

He passed by the gift shop and headed for a hallway where there were several offices. At the first office he heard the rapid clicking of someone typing on a keyboard inside. He was about to go in and ask where he could apply for a job, but he stopped himself and reconsidered the idea. It was very unlikely that they'd take him on the spot—he'd have to put in an application. And all he really wanted was to get a closer look at Arnie—and put some distance between himself and Vissa. He didn't need a job to do that. He spotted a sign at the very end of the hallway that said EMPLOYEES ONLY.

Marvelli walked toward it, and without hesitating he pushed his way through as if he belonged there. But when he saw what was on the other side, he was disappointed. He had hoped this door would get him to the plant floor, but instead it was just another long hallway. He started walking down it. Maybe he'd find another way to Arnie's PRIVATE room down here.

The hallway was pretty stark, nothing but cinder-block walls painted lemon yellow and recessed fluorescents in the ceiling. There were only two doors on the entire stretch, and Marvelli discovered that they were both locked. He walked to the very end where it came to a T, hallways branching off to the right and left. Guessing that the plant floor was to his right, he turned that way.

There were more doors on this stretch and some windows, too. One room had a whole bank of windows that looked in on three rows of stainless-steel tables crammed with all kinds of electronic testing equipment. Marvelli assumed that this was where they tested the ice cream before it was packaged, but why wasn't anyone working? There was no one there. But then he spotted a clock on the wall inside the room. It was 12:25. *Everybody must be at lunch,* he thought and grinned to himself. If everyone was on lunch break, that gave him better than a half hour to find Arnie. And if he didn't find Arnie, maybe he'd find some Elmer Fudge Whirl. Now that he knew it was lunchtime, he was suddenly hungry.

Marvelli moved on down the hallway, peering through windows in doors, looking for one that was marked PRIVATE. Suddenly he saw someone coming through a doorway up ahead, a tall guy in a white lab coat and hair net. Marvelli walked toward him, keeping his eyes level, acting as if he knew exactly where he was going. As they got closer, Marvelli gave the tall guy a friendly smile, but he didn't smile back. He looked pretty sour.

"Hi," Marvelli said without slowing down, intending to walk right by.

The tall guy stopped dead right in Marvelli's path. "Don't go down there."

"Excuse me?" Marvelli didn't want any trouble. He didn't want to have to tussle with this guy.

"I said don't go down there." The man was scowling. "Friggin' Arnie's on the warpath. I was just eating my lunch at my desk, minding my own business, when suddenly he throws me out. Said I had to go outside and get some fresh air, company policy. You know how he gets when he's in one of his damn moods."

"Do I ever," Marvelli agreed.

"Just stay out of his way," the tall man warned.

"Definitely," Marvelli said. "I just need to get something and I'm outta here."

The tall man nodded and started to move on, but then he stopped abruptly and reached out toward Marvelli. "By the way, watch out. *She's* around." He rolled his eyes and smirked as if Marvelli would know exactly who he was talking about.

"Thanks for telling me," Marvelli said. *Just as long as* she *is not Vissa,* he thought.

He moved on down the hallway, passing doorways and keeping up a steady pace until the tall man was out of sight. Marvelli was about to double back to check the doors he'd missed when suddenly he noticed a doorway on the right marked PRIVATE. The sign was red, identical to the one on Arnie's door on the plant floor.

Must be the place, he thought.

He reached for the handle, then stopped himself. *Why not just knock? Arnie's probably in there.*

But before his knuckles touched wood, the door swung open, and a woman was staring at him as if he'd just climbed out from under a rock. She looked like an Asian version of Zena, Warrior Princess.

"What do you want?" she said. It was less a question than a pronouncement of his unworthiness.

"I have an appointment with Arnie Bloomfield," Marvelli said.

"Doubtful," she shot back.

"I'm with Brazilian Foods," he said, making it up on the spot. "We sell chocolate. I think you could do better with us than with your current supplier."

"Really." She was deadpan, couldn't care less.

"May I speak to Arnie?" he said, trying to look over her head. "We really do have an appointment," he lied.

"You may *not* speak to Arnie," she declared.

"Is he in?"

She stared at him as if he'd just peed on the floor.

This must be the she, he thought.

"I can demonstrate how our product will not only be cost-effective for you, it will substantially improve the flavor of your Elmer Fudge Whirl, for instance." His stomach grumbled at the mention of its name.

"Elmer Fudge Whirl is perfect the way it is," she said. Case closed.

"Maybe, maybe not," he said with a sly grin. He hoped there might be a shred of humor in her.

"Elmer Fudge Whirl is *perfect*," she repeated, her face like stone.

Not a shred, he thought.

"You said you had an appointment with Arnie?" she asked.

"Yes. I do."

She narrowed her eyes. "Do you *know* Arnie?"

"Not exactly. We've never actually met."

"I see," she said. "Then you're a stranger to him, correct?"

"Well, technically, yes."

"Interesting." She nodded to herself.

"Do you think I can get to see him today?"

She ignored the question. "Would you like some ice cream?" she asked—not exactly cordially, but not as cold as she had been earlier. "I can prove to you that Elmer Fudge Whirl needs no improving. Would you like to try some?"

Marvelli's eyes lit up, and his grin curved like a bowl. "You won't have to ask twice," he said.

"Don't worry. I won't." She stepped into the hallway and closed the door behind her. "Follow me," she said.

Marvelli forced himself to open his eyes and keep them open, but it wasn't easy. He felt extremely groggy, as if it were siesta time and he was on the equator. He kept trying to shake off the lethargy, but it wasn't going away. Twenty minutes must have passed before he could focus his eyes well enough just to see where he was.

But as he looked around, he was confused. This wasn't where he'd thought he was. He had been in the private executive dining room at the Arnie and Barry's plant, sitting at a long glossy birds'-eye maple conference table lined with plush navy-blue leather highback chairs. Sunlight streamed in from floor-to-ceiling windows, and the glare off the table was almost blinding. That woman Sunny had taken him there for some ice cream. Marvelli worked his mouth. It was bone dry, but there was still a hint of the taste of Fudge Whirl.

He blinked and squinted when he realized that he was somewhere else, a dark, windowless space. Eerie electronic mood music was oozing out of hidden speakers somewhere above him. Heavy

chains hung from the ceiling. What he thought might be a gym-
nastic horse stood in a corner, except that it was upholstered in
black leather and had straps attached it. He scanned the room with
new suspicions. Hanging on the wall was a wooden rack filled with
an assortment of whips and riding crops, including a cat-o'-nine-
tails and a braided bullwhip. A chrome coat rack was crammed
with dresses and costumes. The one on the end was a French
maid's uniform; the one right behind it looked like a little girl's
frilly party dress—but big enough to fit an adult. A makeup table
with a large lighted mirror was up against the wall. Three man-
nequin heads sat on top of the table holding wigs—blond banana
curls, a huge redheaded flip, and a black Cleopatra do. In front of
the table was a chair that looked like a top-of-the-line electric
chair—dark stained wood with black leather cushions and matching leather straps for the wrists, ankles, waist, and neck.

Marvelli glanced straight up and suddenly discovered a mirror
hanging from the ceiling right above him. A chill went through
him when he saw his own reflection. He'd been so groggy he hadn't
realized that he was naked except for his undershorts. Instantly he
was angry and humiliated.

He started to sit up, but something was holding him down.
He peered up at the mirror and saw that a black leather strap was
stretched across his ribs. His wrists and ankles were strapped
down, too. He was lying on some kind of narrow table, like an
operating table. Suddenly his heart started to pound.

"Well, hello."

Marvelli turned his head toward the voice. Sunny was coming
into the room through a door that was padded in more leather.
She was pushing a tea cart.

"What's going on?" he said, trying to control his temper, fig-
uring that he might be able to reason with her if he didn't start off
by yelling. But then he noticed what was on the tea cart: a can of
whipped cream, a plastic squeeze bottle of chocolate syrup, a bowl

full of multicolor jimmies, a jar of wet walnuts, a jar of butter-scotch sauce, and a jar of maraschino cherries. "We having a party?" he asked, trying to keep it light.

"Don't ask questions," she said sternly. "*I* will ask the questions." She pushed the cart right up to the narrow table and stood over Marvelli. She was wearing a skintight, black rubber Minnie Mouse minidress with a flared skirt and stiletto-heeled Roman gladiator sandals with straps that crisscrossed all the way up to her knees. Her fingernails were painted black, which was new. Her lips were scarlet.

"Is this like Jeopardy in reverse?" Marvelli asked. "All my questions have to be in the form of an answer?"

She sprung like a cat and dug her nails into his thigh. "I said, no questions. You will speak only when I allow you to."

"I doubt it," he said. "I have this medical condition. I can't shut up—*Ouch!*"

She dug her nails in deeper.

He looked down to see if she had drawn blood. "That wasn't very nice," he said, looking up at her. "You put something in that ice cream you gave me, didn't you."

"Of course," she said. "A touch of opium. Good for dreaming."

"I didn't dream. I just slept."

"You must have weak *chi*. That's inner energy, in case you don't know."

"I know what *chi* is. Like tai chi."

"Very good." She bowed her head to him.

"So what am I, an addict now?"

She clawed his thigh again. "You're still asking questions."

He just stared at her, refusing to let her see that the pain bothered him. "I'm waiting for an answer."

She grinned a lopsided grin. "I like your spirit. And no, you are not an addict."

"How do you know? I'm an addictive personality."

"You are a meddlesome personality."

"Oh, I'm not *that* bad," he said. "Untie me and I'll show you what a nice guy I can be." He was smiling at her, but his heart was hammering. Sunny could definitely be a genuine wackarino. With all the S&M stuff she had in here, there was no telling what she might try to do to him. His eye went to the extra-large Shirley Temple dress, and his stomach bottomed out.

She let go of his thigh and ran the side of her index fingernail down his sternum as if she were making an incision. "Why are you here?" she breathed in his face.

"Because you brought me here. By the way, where are we?"

She pressed the point of her nail into his nipple. "No questions." She sounded sultry all of a sudden. "There is one thing I want to know from you. Are you here to harm Arnie?"

Marvelli laughed nervously. "No, of course not." *If you don't count bringing him in to serve twenty-five to life as harm,* he thought.

"You're lying," she said in a whisper, pressing on his nipple as if it were a faulty doorbell.

"Why would I want to harm Arnie? I want to sell him chocolate."

"Please don't insult me. I didn't buy that story when you first told me, and I don't buy it now."

"Well, it's true."

She reached over to the cart and picked up a ballpoint pen and a small pad. She dropped the pad on his chest, then picked up something else. "To get a truthful answer, I must ask the *I Ching.*"

She shook her fist as if she were throwing dice, then dropped something on his chest. He looked down and saw three quarters nested in his chest hairs. She clicked the ballpoint and marked down on the pad two short lines side by side. She picked up the quarters and threw them again. This time she drew one longer line above the first two. She kept doing this, marking down new lines each time she threw quarters. Marvelli tried to figure out what combination of heads and tails produced a long single line as opposed to two short lines, but lying flat on his back, he couldn't always see what she was writing down. Finally he just asked.

"What're you doing?"

"I told you."

"Consulting the *I Ching*."

"Exactly."

"Of course," he said wryly.

"Of course *not*," she replied.

They stared at each other for a moment.

"I get it," he said. "I say 'of course,' and you say 'of course not.' Yin, yang."

She scowled at him. "Don't get cute. You don't understand a thing about this."

"You're right. What the hell do I know?" he said with a shrug. "I'm Italian."

She kept throwing down the quarters on his chest until she had two sets of lines, six in each set. She picked up the pad and studied it for a while, her expression growing tighter and grimmer. Suddenly she tossed the pad across the room and glowered at him. "Mountain over earth, earth over earth," she seethed.

"Is that bad?" Marvelli asked.

"You tell me."

He stuck out his bottom lip and shrugged.

"The foundation is uncertain," she said. "Movement in any direction can cause disaster. Treachery is possible everywhere. And *you* are the cause."

"Come on now. You can't lay everything on me."

"So you're saying you're *not* the source of all treachery?" Her glossy scarlet lips loomed over him, gleaming moistly in the dim light.

"You've got me all wrong. I'm not who you think I am."

"Who do you think I think you are?"

"I don't know who you think I am . . . not exactly."

"Then how can you say that you're not who I think you are?"

"Can we start from the beginning? I'm getting confused."

"Confusion is the child of deception."

He squeezed his eyes shut. This woman wouldn't know a straight answer if it bit her on the ass. "Are you going to untie me?"

"I don't think so," she said.

"Why not?"

"I must have the truth first."

Marvelli rolled his eyes. "Can I at least have a towel or something? It's cold in here."

"I was planning on covering you."

"Good. With what?"

She flashed her lopsided high-gloss grin. He followed her eyes to the tray full of sundae toppings. He sighed inwardly. "You're not serious, are you?"

"I'm nothing but serious."

"I don't want that stuff all over me."

"I don't intend to put it *all* over you."

Marvelli furrowed his brow. He didn't like the sound of this.

She laid her hand on his crotch. "I'm sending my *chi*," she declared.

"Please don't do that," he said. Her hand was very warm. She curled her fingers, and her nails moved lightly over his skin. Her breasts were hovering right above him, flesh encased in black rubber. The little guy couldn't help but respond. "Stop. Please," he said.

She just grinned. "I can't. You need a banana to make a banana split."

"Then let's go to Dairy Queen."

"A mighty big banana," she purred with satisfaction.

He swallowed hard. *Of all times to go for the gold,* he thought in annoyance. She kept curling her fingers, brushing his skin. His whole body was throbbing.

"Enough. Please," he begged.

"Yes, I guess that's big enough," she said matter-of-factly, as she reached for the can of whipped cream. "Brace yourself."

She pressed the spout, and whipped cream spurted out in a rush. It was icy cold, and it made him shiver. She concentrated the whipped cream on his crotch, covering it completely in high fluffy peaks. When she was through, he looked like he was wearing a lemon meringue pie.

She took a hand towel and used it to pick up the plastic squeeze bottle of chocolate sauce. "I microwaved this before I came in. I wanted *hot* fudge." Sunny inverted the bottle and dripped squiggles of steaming chocolate sauce over the whipped cream.

"Hey! Watch it!" he blurted, as her swirling movements became freer and more artistic, straying from her target and leaving lines of hot chocolate on his bare thighs.

"There," she said, squeezing out the last drops of chocolate with a farty whoosh. "How about a little hot butterscotch now?" she asked.

"I don't think so," Marvelli said, squirming under the leather straps. "Either hot fudge or butterscotch, but not both. That's what I always say."

"Who said it's for you?" she said with an evil giggle as she dripped butterscotch sauce all over Marvelli's crotch until the jar was empty.

She moved on to the wet nuts, carefully spooning out the walnuts in maple syrup, making sure there was an even distribution.

Then came the multicolored jimmies, which she sprinkled by hand, like precious seeds. "I've never thought these added much to the taste," she said as she worked, "but they do add some color to all that brownness."

"Whatever you say." Marvelli's voice constricted as he felt the hot toppings seeping through the whipped cream. *No pictures,* he thought. *Please, don't take pictures.* If Loretta ever saw him like this . . .

Finally Sunny unscrewed the jar of maraschino cherries and speared one on the nail of her index finger. She leaned down close to his face, twirling the cherry in front of his nose. "These are supposed to be very bad for you. The red dye causes cancer. What do you think?"

"Yeah, I think I read that somewhere."

"Are you worried about what this cherry will do to you?"

"Yeah. I am." He pressed his head back into the padding of the table, but the cherry was so close he saw two of them.

She reared back and started to laugh, a full-throated belly laugh. Then she abruptly stopped laughing and plunged the cherry into the mess of toppings, sinking her finger deep into the whipped cream until it was up to her knuckles. He could feel the cherry pressed against him, fruit to nuts.

I swear to God I am not enjoying this, he thought. *The little guy might be having a ball down there, but I am definitely not.*

She wiggled her finger and scraped it against him until the cherry was dislodged from her fingernail. She extracted her finger and left the cherry under the pile.

Sunny licked whipped cream from her finger. "Mmmmm," she said.

"Now what?" he asked. His forehead was beaded with sweat.

"Now I'm going to bring someone in. Someone who has a great big sweet tooth."

The beads turned into little streams, like droplets coursing down a windshield. "Who is this person?"

"You'll see," she said as she went out through the padded leather door. A moment later she returned with a strange-looking dog on a black leather leash. It had an odd face, no expression whatsoever, and it was staring right at Marvelli.

"This is Dragon. Say hello, Dragon." The dog bared its teeth but didn't make a sound. It held that expression like some kind of tribal devil mask. A chill ran down Marvelli's arms from his shoulders to his fingertips.

"Now I'm going to ask you one more time," Sunny said evenly. "And if you don't give me a truthful answer, I will let Dragon go."

"He doesn't look very active," Marvelli said.

Sunny scooped up a finger full of whipped cream and chocolate sauce and quickly smeared it on Dragon's muzzle. The dog inhaled it with an ungodly snort, then started to whine urgently. The sound was supernatural, unlike anything Marvelli had ever heard coming out of a dog. Dragon raised his head and started sniffing madly. He got up on his back legs, straining at the leash. Sunny had to lean back like a water skier to keep Dragon off. Marvelli was afraid that if she tottered on her stiletto heels and lost her balance, Dragon would lunge and make it to the "banana split," and Marvelli had a sinking feeling that Dragon wouldn't stop with the toppings.

"Okay," Sunny said, as she struggled with the dog. "Your last chance. Yes or no. Are you here to harm Arnie?"

The hellhound pawed at the air frantically. Spit was dripping from his teeth.

14

Loretta was in the passenger seat of Dorie's vanilla-white Lexus coupe, waiting for a break in the conversation. "You know, Dorie," she quickly said, "I was thinking. Maybe I should check into a hotel after all. I don't want to impose on you and Barry any more than I already have."

"Don't be silly, Loretta. You're not imposing." Dorie was sitting behind the wheel. She'd just pulled into the short driveway of a big Victorian in the Haight-Asbury district, stopping inches from the garage door. She yanked the parking brake and looked over at Loretta. "Come on. I want to introduce you to Arnie." She went to open her door, but Loretta grabbed her wrist.

"Hold on," Loretta said. She was biting her bottom lip as she gazed up through the windshield at the garishly painted house.

"What's wrong, Loretta? I thought you wanted to meet Arnie." Dorie was distressed. She was all set to blame herself if Loretta wasn't happy.

"I *do* want to meet Arnie. It's just that"—*Think fast*, she told herself—"it's just that I'm . . . shy."

Dorie's eyes doubled in size. "Shy? You?"

"Yes, me. I don't want him to think I'm a groupie or anything. Do you know what I mean? Anyway, Arnie must be a busy guy. He's got more important things to do than meet me."

But in truth, that wasn't the reason she'd changed her mind. She was afraid that if she made contact with Krupnick, she might run into Marvelli, and she didn't want to face him now. What if he had decided to dump her for Vissa? If that was the case, Loretta didn't want to hear any bullshit excuses from him, and she didn't want any scenes. If it was over between them, then it was over. She didn't want to break down and cry in front of him, and she didn't want to hear his side of it. Forgiveness and understanding weren't in her repertoire. Going off by herself and sulking with a half-gallon of ice cream while she plotted a couple of murders was more her style.

But that really wasn't her style either. She could deal with being angry better than she could deal with being hurt. She could make a good show out of being furious, but being hurt meant that she was vulnerable, and Loretta Kovacs never wanted anyone to know that she could be vulnerable.

Fat girls aren't allowed to cry, she thought. *The little skinny minnies can cry and get away with it because they look cute crying. We just look pathetic. Fat girls have to be strong. Always.*

"Loretta? Are you all right?" Dorie touched Loretta's arm, and suddenly Loretta snapped out of it. She was so upset she'd fuzzed out for a minute.

Loretta cleared her throat. "I'm fine," she said, but her throat was so tight it ached as if she had been crying her eyes out. She blinked back the mere possibility of tears and tipped her head back to catch her breath. "Dorie, I really don't think we should be bothering Arnie—"

Dorie pointed at the front porch. "But he's already here."

The man Loretta had briefly seen at the plant was standing at the front door. He was wearing a mocha-colored collarless shirt, blue jeans, white socks, and no shoes. Loretta stared at his face— the smarmy smile, the broad nose, the peaked eyebrows—and compared it to the mug shots she'd seen of Ira Krupnick. It was definitely him, she decided, but she didn't care. He wasn't her case. *Let Vissa and Marvelli worry about it,* she thought.

He waved and curled his finger, signaling for them to come in.

"Come on," Dorie said enthusiastically. "You're gonna love this house. You won't believe what he's done with it."

Loretta sighed. She didn't see any way out of this. "Okay, but let's not stay too long."

But Dorie was already out of the car. She ran up onto the porch and gave Krupnick a big hug. But even as he embraced her, his eyes were on Loretta, which made her a little uneasy. Why was he staring at her like that? she wondered.

As she mounted the steps, Krupnick's smile broadened, show- ing his teeth. "Hello," he said over Dorie's shoulder. "Nice of you to come."

Not really, Loretta thought glumly.

"Come in, come in," Krupnick said. "It's Loretta, right?" He extended his hand to her even though Dorie was still hanging on to his neck. He had to get to know her before she came into the house. Sunny had told him that she shouldn't enter as a stranger.

Loretta took his hand—not exactly warmly—but her touch startled him. *Soft electricity,* he thought. She had a lot of *chi,* pow- erful *chi.* Suddenly he changed his mind about her. There was a lot more to this Loretta than he'd thought. She was interesting as well as dangerous.

"I told Dorie I really didn't want to impose on you," Loretta said.

Krupnick smiled. "What would life be without impositions? Boring, right?"

"Are you sure we're not bothering you?"

"Not at all," he said. *The lady doth protest too much*, he thought. *What's she hiding?* "Come on in," he said.

Dorie led the way in, heading upstairs to the living room. Loretta followed her, and Krupnick brought up the rear. He kept his eye on her, watching her face when she wasn't looking. When they reached the top of the stairs, Loretta scanned the room and zoomed in on the large oil painting, a bold full-frontal nude. Loretta stared at it, studying it frankly. Krupnick looked for signs of disapproval, shock, or apprehension, but her expression remained neutral—neutral but curious. Most people looked away from that picture and pretended it wasn't there, but Loretta acknowledged it. She was an interesting woman, this Loretta.

"Sit down, sit down." He motioned toward one of the beige-and-white-striped couches. He took his usual position on the couch under the skylight, lounging on his hip with his elbow propped on the arm.

"So," he said when they were all settled, "what do you do for fun?" He was looking right at Loretta.

"Excuse me?" There was a little attitude in her voice. He liked women with attitude. Like Sunny.

"I mean, what have you been doing for fun? On your visit."

"Not a whole lot," Loretta said. "I really just got here."

"I took her to the plant," Dorie volunteered.

"Really?" He wondered why Loretta hadn't mentioned that. Was she hiding something? Like her true intentions?

He watched Loretta's eyes as she scanned the erotic books on the coffee table. She grinned despite herself. Arnie grinned, too. *She was a go-er*, he thought.

Loretta had set down her pocketbook on top of his copy of *The Joy of Sex*. He wished she'd go to the bathroom so that he could go through it, find her driver's license, a credit card, something that would tell him who she really was. Maybe she wasn't that dangerous after all. Maybe she was harmless—well, not harmless, just not a threat. He was thinking hard about seducing her. He'd never done it with a woman that big. Actually he'd never given much thought to large women before, but Loretta was exceptional. There was a lot going on behind those emerald eyes, and there was a lot of Loretta to play with.

"Can I give Loretta the house tour?" Dorie asked. "This is really a fantastic house," she said to Loretta.

"Sure," he said. "By all means. But can I get you anything to drink first."

"Not for me, thanks," Loretta said.

"Me neither," Dorie said.

"Then go ahead, show Loretta around. I'll wait here, though. I've already seen the place." They all laughed; Loretta was being polite.

"Come on. I'll show you the top floor first," Dorie said, and the two of them headed for the stairs.

He watched them going up, comparing Dorie's skinny derriere to Loretta's ample butt. He couldn't believe how much she was turning him on. He'd never felt this way about a big woman. The feeling itself turned him on even more.

After they'd disappeared up the stairs, he glanced at the coffee table, but Loretta's purse wasn't there anymore. She'd taken it with her. *Why?* he wondered. Was she paranoid? Didn't she trust him? Or was she hiding something in there? He had a bad feeling about this. But still, she was really making him horny.

But horny isn't always good, he thought. Horny had gotten him into trouble before. *Most women are not what they seem,* he told himself. *Forget about this one. Just get her out of here. She's a stranger.*

But then he looked up at the naked woman in the painting,

and his opinion started to change, like a jewel turning to face the light. Loretta in a threesome with him and Dorie. Loretta in a *foursome* with him, Dorie, and Sunny. Loretta with Sunny—that would be interesting.

He looked at *The Joy of Sex. Horny isn't bad,* he thought. *For the most part horny is good. Sex is a positive. It creates good* chi, *spreads it all around.* He shifted his position on the couch because his shorts were getting tight. *Sex is definitely a positive,* he kept thinking. He had to shift his position again.

After a while the two women returned to the top of the stairs. He could see their ankles from where he was sitting. Loretta didn't have bad legs, he thought. Not bad at all. They were big but very shapely. He watched her legs descending the stairs, taking in her body one slice at a time until he could see her face. Her purse was hanging from her shoulder on a strap. All he wanted was a little peek. Just two minutes to go through her wallet. He wanted Sunny to be wrong. He wanted Loretta to be all right.

"You have a beautiful house," Loretta said, as she went back to the couch.

"Thank you."

"Loretta really likes the skylights in your bedroom," Dorie said.

"Do you really?" *They're great to wake up to,* he thought. He shifted his position again, trying to get comfortable.

Loretta raised a devilish eyebrow. Her expression made him raise his eyebrows. They were like dueling Jack Nicholsons.

"Would anybody like some ice cream?" he asked. "I have some private stock Elmer Fudge Whirl."

"I could be tempted," Loretta said.

I'll bet you could, he thought. In his head he sounded just like Jack Nicholson.

Marvelli's eyes were bugging out of his head. Dragon's upper lip was curled back over his teeth. He looked like he should be growling or barking, but he didn't make a sound. It was like watching a scary silent movie starring Dragon as a ghost dog.

But what frightened Marvelli even more than Dragon was the fact that his shorts were tighter than ever, and for the life of him he couldn't figure out why. The little guy down below had gone berserk; he was responding to all the wrong stimuli. Marvelli glanced down at the sloppy sundae dribbling over his thighs. He looked at Dragon's slobbering yellow-fanged jaws. He looked at Sunny in her rubber Minnie Mouse skirt, her cleavage in bondage. She was tottering precariously on her stiletto heels, barely keeping her dog at bay.

This is no time to be aroused! he shouted in his head at the not-so-little guy.

But the little guy wasn't listening. Underneath the whipped cream and hot fudge, the butterscotch, the wet nuts, and the jimmies lurked a very dumb banana. Dragon had a sweet tooth—a lot of them in fact—and they were all sharp. If the beast got to the toppings, dollars to doughnuts, he'd scarf up the little guy, too.

The little guy could die! Marvelli thought. *Like Pinocchio inside the whale, but without a happy ending.*

Marvelli winced at the thought of a bleeding crotch wound. It occurred to him that he could bleed out and die right here.

But if I lose the little guy, I may as well be dead, he thought. *Life wouldn't be worth living.*

"What's wrong?" Sunny said with a strange giggle. "You look a little nervous."

The giggle was totally unexpected coming out of her. It suddenly made her sound girlish and playful, and of course that just turned the little guy on more.

Stop it! Marvelli ordered the little guy. *Cease! Desist! Reduce!*

"What's wrong?" Sunny asked. "You seem to be a little hot under the . . . collar." She was staring at his crotch, leaning closer to get a better look. But the closer she came, the closer Dragon came. The dog was inches away, so close Marvelli could feel hot dog breath on his thighs.

"Why don't you put the dog away?" he asked, trying not to sound as scared as he was. "Please?"

"But why?" Sunny said with mock innocence. "All he wants to do is lick the sweet stuff off. Don't you *want* him to lick it off?"

"No. I'd rather he didn't."

"Then who would you like to lick it off?" She was running her tongue slowly across her upper lip.

Not you, he thought, but he didn't dare say it. He didn't want to piss her off.

Dragon was still straining at the leash. The whites of his tiny eyes were showing under the fuzzy folds that covered his brow. That dog didn't just want the toppings, Marvelli thought. That dog was a meat eater.

A dark cloud of loss, regret, and resignation passed over Marvelli. The little guy was doomed. Sadly Marvelli recalled the fun the two of them had had over the years, the tender moments, the rollicking times. He thought back to the women they had been with—Loretta, his late wife, high-school flames, relationships that never really got off the ground but that he still remembered fondly. He even felt sad about the women he liked who never got to meet the little guy. Then out of the blue he remembered that one time with Vissa, and suddenly the little guy was a pole vault trying to set a record without a vaulter.

Stop! Marvelli screamed in his head, but he couldn't stop thinking about her. It had happened years ago, but Marvelli still remembered every detail. It had been intoxicating, mesmerizing, overwhelming. He couldn't really put it into words, but there was just something out-of-this-world about Vissa. But as good as it had been, he knew he should never have done it with her. It wasn't right—he was married, his wife was sick. He'd regretted it while he was doing it practically. He should have kept the little guy locked up in his Levi's because if he had never done it with Vissa, then he wouldn't have anything to remember now, and he wouldn't be bursting at the seams. The little guy would be that much smaller, that much less for Dragon to find in the whipped cream. But thanks to that one time with Vissa, the little guy was standing up straight, saluting the flag. No way Dragon could miss him now.

"Hey! Hey!" Sunny said, raising her voice. "Come back. You're a million miles away. I hate when people do that."

"Don't take it personal," he said with a pained groan.

"I do take it personal. I'm standing right here. Don't go feasting on your fantasies without me."

"Sorry. I won't do it again."

"So don't keep it to yourself. Share it with me."

Marvelli's face flushed. "I can't do that." It wasn't that he was embarrassed because he was thinking about Vissa. He was ashamed that he wasn't thinking about Loretta.

"Why are you groaning like that?" she demanded. "Are you hurt? Dragon hasn't touched you yet."

Marvelli could only groan again.

Her lopsided grin suddenly returned. "Is there yeast in that whipped cream?" she asked. "Or are you just glad to see me?" She reeled in Dragon and picked up the wooden spoon she had used to spread the wet nuts. Stretching her arm out as far as it would go, so that she could hold Dragon back, she scraped away some of the toppings.

"Oh, me, oh, my," she said deadpan, when she found fabric. "Your assets certainly have been growing, haven't they?" She scraped off most of the whipped cream and examined the bulge in Marvelli's shorts with clinical detachment. "I wouldn't have expected anything like this from someone like you. You seem like such a . . . white guy."

"Well, I am Italian," he muttered.

"Be quiet," she snapped. She was back to being the commandant. "Most men disgust me," she said. "But I do appreciate outstanding anatomical achievements." She pushed Dragon's head down and let him lick up the toppings that had spattered to the floor. His slurping and snuffling were the loudest sounds Dragon had made so far. As soon as he'd licked the floor clean, he sniffed around frantically for more, and when he realized there was none, he jumped up and tried to clean Marvelli's sticky shorts, standing on his hind legs straining against the leash, clawing at the air with his front paws.

"Sorry, Dragon," Sunny said, as she pulled him away. She dragged him to the other side of the room and tied his leash to one of the manacles bolted to the wall. "Stay" was all she had to say. Dragon lowered his rump and sat erect, staring hard at Marvelli and silently showing his teeth, but not moving a muscle.

Sunny snatched up a riding crop from the wall rack as she walked back to Marvelli. "Now," she said. "As for you." She tapped the formerly little man with the end of the crop, testing it for firmness. "Impressive," she said. "*Very* impressive."

She turned away from him and reached behind her for the zipper that ran down her back.

Marvelli panicked. "What're you doing?"

She turned her head and looked at him over her bare shoulder. "Are you that stupid?" she said.

"No. Maybe. Come on, you can't do what I think you're gonna do."

"I can't? Why not?"

"Because."

"Because why?"

"Because I don't want to."

"You have no say in the matter," she said. "And from the looks of things, I'd say at least part of you has another opinion."

"He's not serious," Marvelli said. "He's just kidding."

Sunny exhaled a flat laugh. "I've never met a penis that had a sense of humor. Penises are incapable of kidding. Trust me on that." She started to pull down her zipper, and soon Marvelli could see where her spine became her tailbone. It was much more than he wanted to see. She peeled the rubber dress down to her knees— it took some doing to pull it off completely and kick it aside. She was wearing a black spandex bra and black thong panties. With her black-leather stiletto centurion sandals, she looked like a super-vixen, a comic-book she-villain.

Sunny turned around and beamed an evil grin at him. "Don't worry," she said. "You won't have to do a thing. Just sit back and enjoy it."

"No way," Marvelli muttered. He was thinking about Loretta, worrying about what she'd think if she ever found out about this. It wouldn't be his fault, but he'd still feel as if it were.

Sunny walked around his head to a lacquered black Chinese cabinet that was pushed into a corner. It was as high as Sunny's shoulders and had dozens of small drawers, each one marked with a Chinese character painted in red. She opened a few drawers until she found what she was looking for. When she came back, she was holding a big pair of scissors that almost could have doubled for hedge clippers.

Marvelli felt sick to his stomach when he saw them. He struggled against the straps. "What're you gonna do with those?"

"Relax." She threw her leg over him with the agility of a ballerina and hopped up on his thighs. "You're very pale," she said. "Do you know that?" She was snipping the air with the scissors.

"What're you gonna do?" he demanded. His throat was tight. He kept thinking about Lorena Bobbit, the woman who got ticked off at her husband a couple of years back and cut his little guy off, then threw it in a field. The cops eventually found it, and a team of surgeons sewed it back on. Supposedly they did a pretty good job, and they basically got it to work again. Still, Marvelli felt like throwing up. It was as if someone had just kicked him in the crotch. Who knew what this nutcase had in mind? She just might do something like that to his little guy. *Oh, God!*

No, no, he thought, *that's not gonna happen. Sunny's bad, but she's not that bad. Right?*

But what if she did? He could just imagine what the crime scene photos would look like. *God, no!* he thought. The whole world would see him trussed up like a parfait in bondage . . . but without the little guy. *No, God, no!*

Sunny was humming to herself as she stuck a finger into the elastic waistband of his shorts and stretched it away from his belly. Marvelli's heart was pounding like crazy as he struggled for breath.

"No," he gasped. "Don't. Please. Whatever you want. Just tell me."

She grinned at him. "But this is what I want." She lowered the scissors and snipped through his underwear in three big bites. Mr. Happy was liberated. He didn't have a clue, the *stunade*.

"Please, no," he pleaded. "Money. I'll give you money."

"I don't want money," Sunny said.

"Then what do you want? What can I give you?"

She stopped smiling. "You can't give me anything. I take what I want for myself."

Marvelli's eyebrows were up in his hairline. His fingers and toes were ice cold.

She arched one eyebrow and snipped the air between them with the scissors. Then she started to hum again. Marvelli suddenly recognized the tune. It was from *Mary Poppins*. Julie Andrews sang it. "Just a Spoon Full of Sugar."

Marvelli glanced down at the little guy standing at attention. "Can we just talk about this first?" he asked.

She shook her head no.

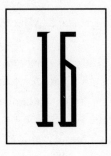

16

"I think someone's down there," Dorie said.

"You think so?" Krupnick said. They were standing at the top of the narrow stairway that led down to the basement.

Loretta was standing right behind them, still carrying the bowl of Elmer Fudge Whirl that Krupnick had given her. She hadn't touched it, and it was starting to melt. She didn't have any appetite. She just wanted to get the hell out of there and leave San Francisco because she had a new life to start now that Marvelli had abandoned her. But for some strange reason Krupnick had insisted that she get the rest of the house tour, and it was just easier to go along with what he wanted than to argue about it. They'd done all three floors, and all that was left was the basement. Well, as soon as she saw his rec room, she was out of there. She didn't care if he was Ira Krupnick. He wasn't her problem.

Dorie didn't seem upset that someone might be in the basement. She led the way down the steps, followed by Loretta, then Krupnick. But when Dorie opened the door at the bottom of the stairway, she stopped short and put her hand to her face. "Uh-oh," she said.

"What's wrong?" Krupnick demanded. He was crowding Loretta from behind.

Loretta moved forward to get away from him, but Dorie was in the way. Loretta looked over Dorie's shoulder to see what the "uh-oh" was all about, expecting a burst pipe or something like that, but what she saw made her jaw hit the floor. Krupnick's basement was an S&M dungeon, and his old chum Sunny was straddling some nearly naked pervert strapped to a massage table and smeared with chocolate sauce and jimmies. She couldn't see the perv's face because Sunny was blocking the view.

Krupnick was crawling up Loretta's back, desperate to get into the room, but Loretta didn't want any part of this, and she intended to go right back upstairs and leave as soon as she could free herself from this logjam. But Krupnick kept pushing from behind, forcing Dorie and Loretta to enter the room. When Loretta stepped over the threshold, she finally got a look at the pervert's face, and instantly she stopped breathing.

"Marvelli?" She was barely able to voice his name.

At the sound of her voice, he whipped his head around and strained his neck to see where she was. "Loretta? Is that you?"

She didn't answer. The words just wouldn't come.

"Loretta, this isn't what it seems," Marvelli said. "Don't jump to conclusions."

But she was only half-listening to him. She was suddenly so exhausted all she wanted to do was sit down—on the floor if necessary. After expending so much energy being furious with him for running off with Vissa, now she had to start all over and be furious at him for being with Sunny. A lot more furious.

"I didn't know you were here, Sunny," Krupnick said. He sounded angry, but he was keeping a lid on it. "So who's your friend?"

"He's *your* friend," Sunny replied indignantly, tossing her head to get the hair out of her face.

Krupnick stepped closer to get a better look at Marvelli. "I don't know him," he said.

Marvelli was desperately trying to get Loretta's attention. "Loretta?" he kept saying over and over, straining his neck to get her to look at him. "Loretta? You came just in time. Nothing happened."

But she didn't want to talk to him ever again. There was no explaining this away. It was what it was, and it was more than she could ever forgive.

Krupnick's gaze bounced back and forth from Loretta to Marvelli. "You two know each other?"

Loretta ignored him. She had enough to contend with.

Krupnick turned to Sunny. "Where'd you find this guy?"

"He was snooping around the plant. He said he had an appointment with you." Sunny scraped some butterscotch off Marvelli's thigh and licked her finger.

"I didn't have any appointments with anyone today," Krupnick said. The color was draining from his face.

"He's a stranger, Arnie," Sunny purred malevolently. "And so is she." Sunny nodded at Loretta. "Remember what the *I Ching* told you: Beware of strangers. They mean you harm."

A look of rage passed over Krupnick's face. It was such a sudden and dramatic transformation, everyone in the room stopped and stared at him. It wasn't anything like the smiling face on the Arnie and Barry's logo. If Loretta had ever had any doubts that this was really Ira Krupnick, she was certain now. This was without question the face of a violent felon.

"What the hell do we do now?" he yelled to Sunny. "Kill them both?" As he said this, he was gazing around the room at the whips and chains and torture devices. He was looking for something he could use.

Instinctively Loretta felt the bottom of her purse, wanting to feel the reassuring heft of her gun. She squeezed the leather purse, but she wasn't getting that old familiar feeling. There was nothing there. Then she remembered that she'd left her weapon back home in New Jersey. Since she wasn't coming here on official business, she hadn't bothered to make arrangements to bring her gun with her on the plane.

"Easy boy," Sunny said to Krupnick, unfazed by his temper. "Remember what I told you about letting the mud settle so you can see the waters clearly? Don't do something you'll regret later."

But Krupnick didn't seem to be listening. He was glaring down at Marvelli, flexing his hands, warming up to do something.

Loretta slid her purse strap off her shoulder. She was ready to use it like a bolo around Krupnick's neck if he made a move toward Marvelli.

Marvelli may be a worthless piece of crap, she thought, *but he's my defenseless worthless piece of crap.*

The room was absolutely still, everyone waiting for Krupnick to go crazy. Loretta's focus was so intent on Krupnick she didn't hear the scratching noises right away. When she finally noticed them, she scanned the room and saw Dragon pawing at the back door. A normal dog would have been whining or barking to go out, but Dragon wasn't normal. No one around here was.

Krupnick suddenly erupted, wheeling around and screaming at the dog. "What? What do you want?"

"He wants to go out," Sunny said in a bored voice. She was still straddling Marvelli, scraping toppings off his skin and licking her fingers.

"Why?" Krupnick snapped. "Does he have to go pee?"

"No," she said. "There must be someone on the other side."

Krupnick's scowl grew deeper. He went to the door, nudged Dragon aside with his leg, threw the dead bolt, and whipped the door open. Dragon raced outside.

A short surprised scream came in through the doorway. "Let go, you stupid fleabag. Ooowwww! Let go of me."

The sound of struggling footsteps on a gravel path preceded Dragon's reentry. He was tugging on something, digging his heels in and inching backward. It was an arm, a human arm in a jeans-jacket sleeve. The hand was holding something, but Dragon had the wrist in his mouth, and he was thrashing his head so violently Loretta couldn't tell what the hand was holding. Dragon shook it loose, and it banged against the door and bounced into the room. A long-barrel revolver lay on the carpeting like a dead fish.

"Let go, dammit!" the person on the other end of the arm shouted as Dragon dragged her all the way into the dungeon. It was Vissa.

Marvelli and Krupnick called out simultaneously: "Vissa! What're you doing here?"

Vissa was bent over sideways and wincing, trying to free herself from Dragon. "Call off the beast!" she demanded. "Call him off!"

Krupnick picked up her gun from the floor and shut the back door. He threw the bolt with a loud click, then looked at Sunny. "Call him off."

"Dragon," Sunny said, and immediately the dog let go. He trotted over to his mistress and flopped down on his rump next to her leg. She scooped up a finger full of butterscotch and jimmies and gave him a reward. Dragon noisily licked her finger clean. "Good dog," she said. There was more feeling in her voice for the dog than she'd shown for any of the humans in the room.

"Vissa," Marvelli said. "Are you okay?"

"Yeah, I'm okay," she said, rubbing her wrist and looking daggers at the dog.

Loretta wondered if Vissa could recognize her with the wig on, but Vissa wasn't paying attention to anyone but Krupnick. They were glaring hotly at one another.

"It's been a long time, Vissa," he said. All of a sudden he was calm. He seemed resigned. In an odd way it seemed as if he was sort of glad to see her. "How ya been?"

"Just shut up," she snapped at him.

He grinned at her, shaking his head. "That's what I always liked about you, Vissa. Pure, unadulterated, one hundred percent USDA-approved Jersey girl."

"I said, shut up." She was massaging her wrist with a vengeance, giving Krupnick a look that could kill. Loretta wondered if there was more to their history than she knew about.

"How's tricks?" he asked.

"Don't start with me," she said, brandishing her index finger and its killer fingernail at him.

"I had no intention of starting with you . . . unless you want to." He flashed a naughty grin.

She showed him another finger.

"Well, come on, Vissa. With all these beautiful women all in one place, it does sort of give a man ideas. How could it not?" He was looking at Loretta, Dorie, and Sunny.

Vissa made a face at him. "In your dreams, pal."

He grinned at her. "In my dreams," he repeated. "Yes, indeed." He inspected her revolver admiringly, running his finger along the length of the barrel. "This is quite a gun you've got here, Vissa. Of course, you always were a pistol."

"Are we interrupting something here?" Loretta blurted out. "I can leave if you'd like."

Vissa shot her a dirty look, but Krupnick just smiled at her. "How can you interrupt when you're an integral part of it all?" he said.

Marvelli struggled against his straps. "What's that supposed to mean?" he snapped.

Krupnick ignored him.

"A foursome," Dorie said, speculating out loud. "You've never done *that*, have you, Arnie?"

Sunny rolled her eyes. "Been there, done that."

"Listen to me, Krupnick," Marvelli said.

Krupnick's contented expression changed as soon as he heard Marvelli using his real name, like instant Jekyll and Hyde. "Why the hell should I listen to you?" he snarled. "Why should I listen to *anyone*?"

"Because I'm talking to you, that's why," Marvelli shot back. "Leave right now while you still have a chance. Leave the women here, and I'll give you a head start. I promise."

Krupnick started howling with laughter. He couldn't stop. "You're an original. . . . What's your name?"

"Marvelli."

"You are something else, man." Krupnick was wiping tears from his eyes. But when his laughter trailed off, Mr. Hyde came back. "Six shots," he said, shaking the pistol like a sun-crazed bandito. "One, two, three." He pointed the barrel at Marvelli, Visa, and Loretta in turn. "Two shots each. Head start my butt, pal. Why not just eliminate the problem entirely? Huh?"

No one dared answer him back. His eyes were wild, and they all knew he was capable of all kinds of weirdness. He stroked his beard in a rough rhythm, thinking hard.

Loretta stood absolutely still, wishing to hell she had her gun with her.

"Okay, okay," Krupnick finally said. "Here it is." He was talking to Sunny. "We leave Vissa and Loretta here, and we take Jell-O Marvello or whatever his name is with us."

"Why?" Marvelli demanded. "What do you need me for?"

Krupnick spun on his heel and leaned into Marvelli's face. "Because, stupid, you're the one most likely to lead the charge against me. I *can't* leave you here. You're the male, the threat. They're not." He pointed with the gun at Loretta and Vissa.

"And what exactly do we *do* with them?" Sunny nodded at the two female parole officers.

"Just leave them here," Krupnick said.

"And you expect them to sit nicely with their hands in their laps?" Sunny said sarcastically.

Krupnick grinned under his bushy beard. "We leave Dragon."

"No," Sunny said flatly.

"Come on, Sunny," Krupnick cajoled her. "He'll be all right."

"No."

"Come on," he said. "The *I Ching* said it was time for a change."

Sunny didn't respond.

"He's right, Sunny," Dorie said, trying to mediate. "Dragon will be fine."

"How about us?" Loretta cut in. "Will we be fine?"

"Finer than if I stick around," Krupnick said ominously. He was twisting the revolver in his hand as if he wanted to twirl it like a gunslinger.

"Why do you have to take Marvelli?" she asked defiantly. "Why don't you just go?"

"God," Krupnick said in frustration, "is everybody stupid here? I just told you. Marvelli's a guy. He'll come after me like nobody's business. It's a male alpha thing." He turned to Dorie. "Find him something to wear." He nodded toward the rack of S&M dress-up clothes.

Marvelli tried to do a sit-up. "Hey, I'm not wearing a dress. You can kill me—I don't care—but I'm not wearing a dress."

Dorie sorted through the rack and picked out a black leather jumpsuit with a matching leather ski mask that had a zipper over the mouth.

"I'm not wearing that," Marvelli said.

"Okay, fine," Krupnick said, and in one smooth move he went right over to Vissa and stuck the gun barrel deep into her neck. "I'm gonna have to go with Plan B then. Shoot everybody."

Vissa winced and tried to pull away from him, but he had a fistful of her denim jacket.

"Okay, okay," Marvelli said. "Whatever you want."

Loretta wanted to be furious with him for rolling over as soon as Vissa was in the slightest bit of danger, but it was clear that Krupnick was desperate and liable to do anything.

"You won't have to worry," Dorie said cheerfully to Marvelli as she took the leather jumpsuit off the rack. "You wear this, no one will even notice. This is San Francisco." She wasn't trying to be funny.

"Unbuckle him," Krupnick said, letting go of Vissa but taking a step back so he could train the gun on both her and Loretta.

Sunny went to work undoing the straps. When Marvelli sat up, he had wide red marks all over his body. The whipped cream clung to his privates.

"You look like a zebra," Vissa said.

"I was thinking barber pole," Loretta said.

"Get dressed," Krupnick ordered. "Hurry up."

Reluctantly Marvelli took the jumpsuit from Dorie and made a face. "I'm all sticky. Can't I take a shower first?"

"No," Sunny said.

Dorie shrugged. "Sorry."

"Dorie," Loretta said, "you're not gonna go with them, are you?"

Dorie sighed. "I have to, Loretta."

"But, Dorie, you can be charged with kidnapping if you go with them. You don't want to go back to prison, do you?"

"Well, no," she said, but it wasn't a very convincing no. "I did meet some nice girls in prison. It wasn't all bad."

Loretta shook her head. Dorie was a hopeless slave to her

hormones. Loretta glanced at Vissa and Krupnick and wondered about their hormones.

Marvelli was zipping up the jumpsuit, careful not to get his pubic hair caught. He didn't look happy. "This feels terrible," he said with a disgusted frown.

"Quiet," Sunny ordered, as she handed him a pair of black satin ninja booties. "Put these on."

"Why?" he said defiantly.

Krupnick grabbed Loretta by the front of her blouse and hauled her across the room, jamming the gun barrel square in the middle of her forehead. "Why?" he yelled at the top of his lungs. "You really want to know why? Because I'll do your friend here and not even think about it if you don't put those friggin' booties on. That's why!"

Loretta's heart was in her throat.

"Okay, okay, I'm putting them on," Marvelli said quickly. "Take it easy."

Krupnick shoved Loretta away and indicated with the gun barrel that she should go back to where she'd been standing next to Vissa. Loretta's heart was a frantic little bird, but there was a hint of a satisfied grin on her lips. Marvelli had conceded to Krupnick just as quickly for her as he had for Vissa.

Sunny was pulling the leather ski mask down over Marvelli's head, zipping the mouth hole shut. It matched the jumpsuit perfectly. Krupnick poked him in the back with the gun barrel, prodding him to stand up. When he did, his movements were stiff and unnatural. He looked like a gingerbread man who'd been left in the oven way too long. "Okay, move," Krupnick said, shoving Marvelli toward the door. "Come on, let's go," he said to Sunny and Dorie.

Dorie hopped to, but Sunny stooped down to say good-bye to Dragon. "I'll see you later, okay? I'll make you something nice."

She fondled the dog's jowls and kissed his wrinkled forehead. She seemed genuinely concerned about the animal. But if Dragon felt anything for Sunny, his wrinkly face didn't show it.

Sunny locked the padded door that led upstairs before she went out the back door, which she also locked but from the outside. Loretta could see that there were no handles to turn the dead bolts on either door, which she supposed made sense since this was a dungeon, after all.

She glanced sideways at Vissa, who was already glaring at her. Loretta glared back.

Vissa was just about to say something when a sound came out of Dragon that made them both stare at him in amazement. The dog did have a voice. He was growling as he bared his teeth, but it was a hissy, high-pitched sound that reminded Loretta of a chain-smoker on his deathbed.

When neither of the women responded to him, he growled a little louder and half an octave higher.

Loretta curled her upper lip at him. "Don't start with me," she warned. Then she looked Vissa in the eye. "You either."

Vissa moved away from Loretta, going around to the other side of the table where Marvelli had been strapped, Loretta holding her ground near the door that led upstairs. They stared at each other like professional wrestlers getting psyched for a bout. The only difference was, this was for real.

"What the hell're you doing here?" Vissa said with an Elvis sneer.

"What the hell're *you* doing with Marvelli?" Loretta shot back.

Vissa pushed the hair out of her eyes. "Is *that* why you're here? Because you're jealous?" She looked up at the ceiling and shook her head in amazement. "Take me, Lord. I've heard everything now."

Dragon emitted another high-pitched growl and showed a few more teeth than he had before. He was anxious and upset, turning his head back and forth from Loretta to Vissa. He didn't like them positioned this way. He wanted them standing together so he could watch them both.

Loretta was about to throw what she had in her hand, hoping that he'd go fetch it, when she realized that she was still holding that bowl of Elmer Fudge Whirl Arnie had given her upstairs. It was almost completely melted now. "Here," she said, stooping down and sliding the bowl across the floor. It tottered to a stop in front of the dog's paws.

Dragon tilted his head and stared at it, then he bent down and sniffed it. A split second later he was scarfing it down and cleaning the bowl, his pink tongue darting in and out of his wrinkled jowls like lightning from a rain cloud.

Loretta turned her attention back to Vissa. "So why shouldn't I be jealous? You don't think I have a right to be?"

"No one has a *right* to be jealous," Vissa said, tossing her head. "Jealousy is stupid."

"Only when you're the cause of it," Loretta said. Her face was hot. She had an overpowering urge to grab Vissa by her Annette Funicello flip and drag her around the room a few hundred times.

"Oh, get real," Vissa said dismissively. "I'm not interested in Marvelli."

"Oh, really? Then how come I saw you two strolling through the airport holding hands?"

Vissa crossed her arms and tucked in her chin. "Last time I checked, hands weren't sex organs."

"No, but they know where to find them."

"Yeah, well, mine didn't. Not Marvelli's."

"Yeah, right," Loretta grumbled. Vissa was looking her dead in the eye, as forthright as a judge, which started to give Loretta second thoughts. The woman's denials sounded genuine.

"So what is it with you?" Loretta asked. "What are you, a guy magnet? They just flock to you?"

"You know, I'm getting sick and tired of hearing people say that about me. You make it sound like I'm some kind of sideshow freak, like I can put guys under a spell and do whatever I want with them. Sure, I'm sexy, and I'm proud of that. I use it to my advantage. But I've had my problems, too—more than you'd think."

Vissa was frowning defiantly, but Loretta could see that she was upset. For the first time since Loretta had met her, Vissa seemed vulnerable. "What kind of problems?" Loretta asked.

Vissa didn't answer immediately. She looked away and heaved a big sigh. "I'm thirty-nine, and I've never had a halfway decent relationship in my life. Not even close to one because guys don't get serious about girls like me. I did not touch Marvelli, and he didn't touch me because he wouldn't want me, not the way I'd want him. Besides, I couldn't have done anything with him if I'd wanted to because he's stuck on you. He talks about you all the time." Vissa brushed away a tear with the flat of her hand, trying not to ruin her mascara. "And if you don't believe me," she blurted, "well, too damn bad."

Loretta didn't know what to say. If what Vissa had said was true, then Loretta should be ashamed of herself. But she wasn't exactly ready to buy the whole package yet. Still, she was beginning to feel foolish for jumping to conclusions and coming all the way out to San Francisco to spy on them.

"I . . ." she started. "I . . ." In her heart she wanted to believe Vissa, but her stubborn head just didn't want to be wrong. "Vissa, I—"

Ka-thump!

Loretta looked down and saw Dragon lying flat on his side with his long pink tongue hanging out. He'd just keeled over. The bowl was absolutely clean, and Dragon seemed to be having a hard time keeping his eyes open. If he were a cartoon dog, he'd have had little imaginary birds circling his head.

Loretta furrowed her brow. "What the hell's in that stuff?"

"What? The ice cream?" Vissa moved closer to the dog.

Loretta got down on one knee and stroked Dragon's flank. His breathing seemed to be a little slow for a dog, and she thought she could see a doggie smile under the folds around his muzzle. "This is weird," she said. "There must be something in this stuff, something that's not kosher."

"Like what?"

"I don't know, but I did see Arnie putting his secret ingredient into a vat of Fudge Whirl at the plant."

"What did it look like?"

"I didn't get to see it. He threw it in too fast."

"Poor dog," Vissa said, kneeling down next to Loretta. "You think he'll be all right?"

Loretta shrugged. "I don't know anything about dogs." She kept stroking his wrinkly coat. He felt like a fuzzy prune. She pulled off her brunette wig and skullcap and tossed them aside, shaking out her long, dirty blond hair. "Poor Dragon," she moaned. "I wish we could get him to a vet."

"We'd better find Marvelli first," Vissa said.

Loretta narrowed her eyes and gave Vissa a look.

"Not because I'm lusting for his bod," Vissa clarified, "though I must admit it isn't a bad bod. It's because of Krupnick. He's a very dangerous person. I'm afraid of what he might do."

"What do you mean?"

Vissa suddenly became very serious. "Krupnick will do anything to get his way, and he doesn't care who he hurts. He's also got a nasty temper. I've seen it in action. If he starts to feel squeezed, he'll take it out on Marvelli. I know it."

"*How* will he take it out on Marvelli?"

Vissa smacked her forehead with the heel of her hand. "God, do I have to draw you a picture?"

"Yes."

Vissa sighed in frustration. "Now I don't know this for a fact, but I was told that there was a guy who owed Krupnick money once. It was something like twenty thousand dollars. When the guy didn't pay on the day he'd promised, Krupnick kidnapped his wife, and every day that Krupnick didn't get paid, he did something to the wife. The first day he shaved her head and sent the hair to her husband FedEx. The second day he sent one of the woman's front teeth. Do I have to go on?"

"How long did it take for the guy to come up with the money?"

"A week."

Loretta shuddered. "I don't want to know."

Dragon let out a dreamy moan. Loretta pushed back the fold of his brow and checked his eyes. They were out of focus. The dog was out of it.

"We have to get out of here," Loretta said. "We're gonna drop this animal off at a vet and then find Marvelli." She was saying this more to herself than to Vissa, thinking out loud and putting together a battle plan as she went along. "Is there anything in here we can use to break the door down?"

Vissa got up and started checking out Sunny's equipment. "We could whip it open," Vissa said sarcastically. "She's got plenty of those."

Loretta scanned the room, searching for an idea. There were chains hanging from the ceiling and all kinds of restraints but nothing heavy enough to batter down a door. But then she noticed something on the legs of the table that Marvelli had been strapped to. It was on wheels.

"Give me a hand," she said to Vissa. She unlocked the wheels and swiveled the table around so that it was aimed at the back door.

Vissa came over to help. "It looks like it's made out of solid wood," she said hopefully. "It might work."

"On three, push as hard as you can," Loretta said. "Ready? One . . . two . . . three!"

They ran with the heavy table, like bobsled racers at the start of a race, crashing it into the back door with a loud *thud*. But instead of splintering the door, it did absolutely nothing. Both the door and the table were unaffected. They'd only managed to put a two-inch scar in the door.

"Again," Loretta shouted and pulled the table back. "One, two, three."

They ran with the table, and it boomed like a shotgun when it hit the door this time, but nothing broke. The door remained intact.

"Again," Loretta yelled. "Come on."

They tried it again, shoving the table as hard as they could, but the collision only stung their hands and rattled their eardrums. The door stood solid—sturdy and arrogant about it.

Tears welled in Loretta's eyes. She ran her fingers through her hair and leaned over the table, ready to try it again. She didn't want Marvelli back in pieces.

Vissa laid her hand on Loretta's shoulder. She was crying, too. "I want you to know something. I didn't do anything with him while we were here. We did do it once, but that was a long time ago. Before he met you. And it was only one time. I guess I wasn't the girl he wanted to bring home to Mom. Anyway, the point is, I'm not after him. I swear. I may be a flirt, but I'm not a slut. I want you to believe that."

Loretta looked into Vissa's eyes. Mascara was running down the woman's cheeks in vertical lines. Loretta sniffed back her own tears and laid a hand on top of Vissa's. "I believe you," she said softly, her voice breaking.

"Let's try it again," Vissa said. "Come on. We can do it."

Loretta sighed. She knew Vissa was just trying to be encouraging because a stick of dynamite wouldn't knock that door down. But Loretta also knew that she had to do something because she refused to give up hope. "All right," she said. "One more try."

They took their positions on either side of the table. "On three," Vissa said, and they both counted together. "One . . . two . . . three!"

They pushed as hard as they could and ran with the table, Loretta putting all of her determination into it.

For Marvelli, she thought.

The table crashed into the door, but this time they heard something different, not a *thud* or a *boom.* The women looked at each other, unwilling to believe it until the other confirmed it, but they knew something had happened. Something had cracked.

"Again," Loretta said.

They pulled the table back into the room, adjusted the angle, and charged again, smashing directly into their target.

They searched each other's faces for affirmation. *Yes!* Wood had cracked again, louder and more pronounced this time.

Neither of them had to say a word. They knew what to do, pulling the table back, getting into position, and ramming it into the door once more.

CRACK!

This time the door screeched in agony, drowning out the boom of the initial impact. Loretta looked at the door and could see the damage clearly now, a fissure running along the grain from the bottom to just above the point of impact.

"Keep going," she yelled, and that's just what they did, slamming the heavy table into the door again and again, smashing it until it cried out for mercy, then smashing it some more until there wasn't much of a sound at all. The formerly rock-solid door was a ragged fresco of shreds and strips. Spears of daylight filtered into the gloomy basement from outside through a wide crack. The table had started to split as well, and the leather padding had taken a beating, but it didn't look half as bad as the door. Loretta shoved the table aside with her hip as she went over to the door and gave it a good boot. She kicked it a few more times until the crack opened up clear to the top; then using her hands she pulled the unhinged side down, letting it crash to the floor. The hinged side swung open meekly on squeaky hinges. Fresh air wafted into the dank room and cooled the sweat on Loretta's face.

She fanned her blouse against her chest. "Do you have a car?" she asked Vissa.

Vissa nodded. "On the street."

"The dog," Loretta said, nodding toward Dragon, who was still in a stupor. "I'll take the front. You take the back."

Together they stooped down to pick up Dragon, Loretta cradling his head as she got a hand under his shoulder, Vissa linking her fingers around his midriff. But when they went to pick him up, they were both startled by how heavy he was.

"Jeez!" Vissa said. "He weighs a ton."

Loretta struggled with her end, trying to get a better grip on the floppy animal. "He'd better lay off the Arnie and Barry's," she grunted.

Dragon dozed blissfully as they carried him out the door and into the sunshine. A tiny flower garden clung to the side of the house. Rose bushes in big terra cotta pots climbed a long trellis that ran along the property line.

"This way," Vissa said, pointing with her head to a walkway that led to a cement staircase. "The steps go down to the street."

They went as fast as they could with the cumbersome dog, but it was hard keeping a hold on him. His skin was loose, and his coat was slippery. Getting him down the stairs was like trying to carry a leaking sack of sand.

"I want you to know one thing," Vissa said, as she strained to hold up her end.

"What's that?" Loretta was trying to keep Dragon's head from flopping around too much without dropping him.

"I want you to know that I wasn't trying to steal Marvelli away from you. That was never my intention. Ira Krupnick's the one I really want."

Loretta's eyes shot open. She almost dropped Dragon. "What did you say?"

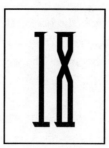

"I don't believe this." **Loretta was still reeling from Vissa's reve-**
lation. She was sitting in the passenger seat of the rented Pontiac,
Vissa, behind the wheel, racing down a steep San Francisco hill.
As she sped through an intersection, the muffler hit bottom and
scraped the pavement. "Hey, take it easy," Loretta said.

"Sorry." Vissa had both hands on the wheel, every knuckle
white. She was biting her bottom lip.

Loretta watched Vissa's face. Originally Loretta had thought
that Vissa was a straight arrow when it came to parole work, but
her confession had come as a complete shock. Vissa just didn't
seem like the type who'd get involved with a jumper.

"Stop staring at me like that," Vissa complained. "You know
what it's like to be in love. You do stupid things."

"Not that stupid," Loretta said. "You told me yourself that
Krupnick was dangerous. Why would you ever get involved with
him?"

Vissa cringed. "Smart women, stupid choices?"

Loretta frowned. "Too easy. Try again."

A loud groan came from the backseat. Loretta peered over the headrest and saw Dragon trying to untangle his legs and sit up. His eyes were open, and his nose was wet.

"I think he's coming to," Loretta said. "He looks a lot better than he did before."

"You think he still needs a vet?" Vissa asked. "Maybe if we hold on to him, he'll lead us to his mistress."

"That's not a bad idea. Forget the vet. Go straight to the ice-cream plant," Loretta said. "Now getting back to Krupnick."

"Come on, don't beat me up with this."

"I'm just trying to understand," Loretta said. "You fell in love with him, then you set it up so that he could escape?"

Vissa was nodding guiltily. "That's why I left him with Marvelli and didn't tell him who Ira was. I knew Marvelli would just assume he was all right and let him walk away."

"But why did you arrest him in the first place if you were in love with him?"

"I was mad at him. But by the time we got to the office, I had changed my mind."

Loretta noticed that Vissa referred to Krupnick as Ira. She also recognized the distressed note in Vissa's voice. Loretta had heard it in her own more than a few times. The girl had it bad for that man, and in this case that definitely wasn't good.

"You know how it is," Vissa said. "You try to be intelligent about men. You try to stay away from the jerks, the ones you know are gonna be nothing but trouble. You look for the nice guys, the ones like Marvelli. But then someone like Ira Krupnick comes along, and you know he's all wrong for you, but you can't help yourself. There's just something about him."

"And you thought you could change him," Loretta said half-sarcastically. She'd once tried to do the same thing herself with a computer nerd she'd dated once upon a time.

"Yeah, I suppose I did think that," Vissa grumbled. Her cheeks were flushed from embarrassment.

They fell silent for a moment, but Loretta just had to ask. "He was great in bed, right?"

The color of Vissa's cheeks went a few shades toward scarlet. "Yeah," she admitted, "something like that." She jerked the steering wheel and took a hard left onto a three-lane major artery, making the tires screech. "I feel like a real idiot."

Loretta sighed. "You're not the only one."

Sometimes she wondered if men were just a bad idea in general. They weren't like ice cream—they weren't guaranteed to make you happy. Although, like ice cream, sometimes they made you regret that you'd had too much of them. At one time Loretta had thought about giving up men entirely—or at least until they came out with a new and improved model. But then good things started to happen with Marvelli, and her feelings changed. She glanced at Vissa's forlorn expression and wondered if perhaps there wasn't a little bit of Ira Krupnick in every man.

"How far are we from the plant?" Loretta asked. The tone of her own voice startled her. She sounded like someone in distress, but someone else. She was anxious to find Marvelli before something happened to him. *If it hasn't happened already,* she fretted.

"Arnie and Barry's is just across the bridge, except I can't find a damn entrance for the freeway."

They were on a major thoroughfare full of stores and businesses, and Loretta could see the elevated freeway on their left, but there were no signs that showed where they could get on. They drove along this avenue for more than a mile, Vissa cursing all the way. Loretta clawed the upholstery at every interminable red light they had to endure. Finally Loretta spotted a red, white, and blue sign for Interstate 80.

"There! There!" Loretta pointed frantically. "Turn! Left!"

"I see it, I see it," Vissa said.

As soon as Vissa made the turn, a big green sign with white letters hanging over the road pointed the way to SAN FRANCISCO BAY BRIDGE and OAKLAND.

"Take this right," Loretta shouted. "Right here!"

"I'm not blind, Loretta." Vissa was getting annoyed with her, but Loretta didn't care. Marvelli's life was at stake.

Vissa steered the car onto the entrance ramp, and soon they were sailing down the freeway with sparkling expanses of deep blue water on either side of them. Oakland was in the distance at the end of the long bridge. The women fell into a tense silence. The sounds of the road and the cars around them became white noise, buffering their separate anxieties. Only the roar of an occasional trailer truck invaded their private thoughts.

"Can I ask you something?" Loretta said after they had been on the bridge for a few minutes

"What's that?" Vissa kept her eyes on the road.

"What did you intend to do when you found Krupnick? Before all this happened."

"What do you mean?"

"Were you going to arrest him or run away with him?"

Vissa gave her a dirty look.

But Loretta wanted to know. "You can tell me the truth. I don't care."

Vissa made a sour face. "I don't know what I was going to do. I just wanted to find him."

Loretta nodded, her brows slanted back in sympathy. "I know just what you mean."

From the backseat Dragon made a sound that seemed like a yawn, a groan, and a sigh all in one. It was exactly how Loretta felt.

•   •   •

By the time they reached the Arnie and Barry's plant, it was quitting time, and workers were walking through the parking lot in small groups, heading for their cars. Some of the women were brushing their hair as they walked, fluffing it out after having it imprisoned in hair nets all day. A tall bald man had kept his light blue lab coat on, the tails flying behind him as he hurried across the lot. Most of the employees were too busy smoking and gabbing to notice Loretta and Vissa moving against the tide back toward the plant. And if any of them noticed the grimace on Loretta's face or the fact that she was carrying something heavy under a black jeans jacket, they didn't show it. All they wanted was to get home.

"God, this dog is heavy," Loretta grunted through clenched teeth. Dragon was curled in her arms like a puppy, his muzzle snuggled up against her breast. She shifted her shoulders to get his nose off her nipple. "Don't get any ideas, junior," she warned.

"I think he likes you," Vissa said.

"Lucky me."

"Go that way," Vissa said as they came up to the building. All the workers were coming out of one doorway. Unfortunately it locked whenever it slammed shut, and now Loretta and Vissa had to wait for someone to come out.

"Come on, come on," Loretta said. "My back is breaking."

Dragon groaned contentedly.

Finally the door opened, and two men in light blue lab coats came out. One was too busy lighting a cigarette to pay any attention to them, and the other just didn't care.

"Good night," Vissa said to them with a smile.

"Good night," Loretta echoed, forcing a smile.

" 'Night," the man with the cigarette said, not even looking at them.

The other man was in his own world, heading off by himself.

Vissa held the door open, and Loretta rushed into a long corridor with cinder-block walls painted marigold yellow. A few more workers were coming down the hall, the stragglers, but like the others they were tired from a day's work and didn't pay much attention to the two women.

"Maybe they think we're the cleaning ladies," Vissa whispered.

"I don't care what they think," Loretta whispered back. "I have to put this damn dog down."

"Not here," Vissa said.

"I know that," Loretta said, beginning to get testy.

"Let me find an empty room," Vissa said. As soon as the last of the workers had passed them by, she started trying doors at random, hoping to find one that was unlocked. The first few she tried were locked tight.

"Come on, come on," Loretta urged. "I'm dying here."

Dragon moved his nose back onto Loretta's nipple.

"Stop it!" she snapped, and shrugged him off.

The dog emitted a weak cry from under the jacket.

"Oh, break my heart," Loretta said sarcastically. She didn't want to admit that she was beginning to like him.

"In here," Vissa hissed from farther down the hall. She'd found an open door.

Loretta speed-walked over to the door and slipped in, setting Dragon down on the concrete floor as soon as she was inside. "Oy, my back!" she muttered. As she bent backward to stretch, she realized where she was: the factory floor where the big vats of ice cream stood. The lighting was dim now, only a few fluorescent lights casting long shadows across the floor. The mural of smiling Arnie and Barry under a rainbow took on a sinister aspect in this light. Loretta studied their faces. They were both schmucks, she thought angrily.

Vissa found a huge spindle of plastic baling cord that was used to tie the stacked trays of pints together after they were shrink-wrapped. She helped herself to a twelve-foot length, cutting it off with the sharp metal nib that was attached to the spindle.

"I'm making a leash for Dragon," she said as she doubled the cord and tied one end to the dog's collar. "Okay, boy, let's go find Marvelli." She ruffled the dog's ears, trying to encourage him. "Come on, let's find Sunny."

"Hang on," Loretta said, her voice echoing through the cavernous space. She focused on the gray metal door with the red PRIVATE sign. That was Krupnick's room, the place where he kept the secret ingredient for Elmer Fudge Whirl. Loretta remembered the stealthy way Krupnick had added his secret ingredient to the vats the first time she'd been here. She also remembered how the real Arnie Bloomfield had surreptitiously dumped a pint of Fudge Whirl into the trash back at the Jump Squad in Newark. And how Barry had kept Dorie from serving it at his house. And how Krupnick had insisted she have some back at his place. She glanced at Dragon who was still woozy after having devoured a whole bowl, which was the same bowl that Krupnick had given to her. Dragon had eaten the ice cream the same way Marvelli always ate it, like there was no tomorrow. She gazed across the factory floor, and her eye caught the little golf-cart contraption that shuttled the stacks of pints out to the freezer. Loretta tapped her upper lip with her index finger. She had to find out what the hell was in that ice cream.

"Loretta, let's go," Vissa called to her in a stage whisper.

"One minute," Loretta said, as she walked toward the golf cart.

"What're you doing?" Vissa said. "We have to find Marvelli."

"This won't take long," Loretta said with determination. She had a sneaky suspicion that she knew what was behind that door, but she had to make sure.

"Loretta, what're you doing?"

But Loretta was already in the driver's seat of the cart. She turned the key in the ignition and stomped on the only pedal on the floor. The golf cart jerked forward, the empty trailer jolting into its rear end. The cart was heading straight for one of the vats. Loretta spun the wheel and changed course. The golf cart stopped bucking and the ride evened out, but by now Loretta had her sights set on that gray metal door. The PRIVATE sign was in her crosshairs.

"Loretta!" Vissa hissed.

Dragon sensed the excitement and lifted his sleepy head to track the golf cart whizzing across the factory floor.

"Loretta!"

SMASH! The cart plowed into the metal door, a head-on collision.

Loretta was jolted out of her seat, hit the steering wheel with her belly, then plopped back into place. She blinked, wondering for a second if she was hurt, but she didn't feel any pain, so she decided she was okay. The door, however, had a huge dent in it. Loretta tried to find the gear shift so she could put the cart into reverse, but there didn't seem to be one. She got out and pushed the cart away from the door until there was enough clearance for her to make a U-turn.

"I feel like I've been here before," Vissa said, coming over with Dragon to survey the damage.

"Yup," Loretta said tersely, as she got back into the cart. "It worked the last time. No reason why it won't now."

She turned the cart around and drove all the way back to the far end of the room. "Look out," she called to Vissa, as she came barreling across the floor, heading for the door again.

"Be careful!" Vissa shouted.

But Loretta was a golf-cart kamikaze with just one objective in mind.

"Be careful!" Vissa yelled.

SMASH!

The cart knocked the door off its hinges, breaking the deadbolt. It kept on going and got through the doorway, but the caboose cart was too wide, and it brought the train to an abrupt halt. Loretta was jolted out of her seat again, and this time the steering wheel knocked the wind out of her.

"Loretta! Loretta! Are you all right?" Vissa called to her, unable to get into the room through the pileup.

Dragon managed to crawl under the wreckage and make it into Krupnick's room, barking his high-pitched bark as he jumped into the golf cart and put his paws on Loretta's chest. He was barking in her face, showing doggy concern.

Loretta scratched his head to settle him down. "I'm okay, boy. Don't worry," she said. She was going to be bruised and sore from this, but she didn't think anything was broken.

She sat there for a few moments to catch her breath, and gradually she began to focus on what was in the room. She blinked several times to clear her vision, expecting a small room with a desk and file cabinets and a bin full of sugary granules, the secret ingredient, but that wasn't what she saw at all. The room was much bigger than she'd expected, and the only things in it were barrels, heavy brown cardboard barrels with metal lids. There must've been almost a hundred of them stacked three high straight up to the ceiling. Each one had POWERED SUGAR stenciled on it.

Loretta got out of the cart, Dragon trailing behind her. The lid on the closest barrel had been pried open and was just resting on top. Loretta lifted it and peered inside. Two metal measuring cups were half-buried in white powder.

"What is it?" Vissa said as she climbed over the carts to get inside.

"I'm not sure," Loretta said. She licked her pinkie and touched the powder, then brought her finger to her lips and tasted it. It wasn't sweet. She remembered the taste from her days as an assistant warden. Prisoners were always smuggling in contraband. No wonder Elmer Fudge Whirl was so addictive: The secret ingredient was heroin.

"All right, put your hands up," someone shouted.

Loretta looked up to see Barry Utley moving out of the shadows behind the stacks of barrels. He must have come in another way. He was holding a gun, a Luger.

"I said, put your hands up. Both of you." His face was gray, and his eyes were bugging out of his head. The gun was shaking in his hand.

Loretta looked back at Vissa, who had just made it over the pileup. Vissa shrugged. Barry had the drop on them, so they had no choice but to do what he said.

Dragon flopped onto his haunches, looked up at Loretta, and whined for attention.

"Shut up!" Barry snapped. "Stupid flea bag."

Dragon started to whimper.

Loretta's nostrils flared. "Take that back," she said.

Barry stared at her. "What did you say?"

"I said take it back."

Barry's eyes became wild, and his gun hand was shaking more than before. A twisted grin grew across his fleshy face like a root. "What did you say?" he repeated.

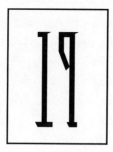

19

Marvelli was in the dark, his hands cuffed behind him, his knees tucked up toward his chest. His face was drenched in sweat beneath the leather mask, and he wasn't getting enough air because the nose holes weren't exactly generous. He was lying on his side in the trunk of some big sedan. He didn't get a real good look at it, but he was pretty sure it was an American-made car, the color sort of a taupe brown. Krupnick had shoved him in as soon as Sunny unlocked the trunk. That must have been at least a half hour ago. Maybe more. It was hard to tell.

The rumble of the engine vibrated the trunk floor, and every time the transmission shifted gears, he felt it. He could also hear the whir of the tires on the pavement. He imagined them spinning right under him. Every so often the car stopped.

Must be traffic lights, he thought. *If we were on the highway, we wouldn't be stopping so much. We must still be in town then.*

He twitched his nose as sweat accumulated around his face. The mouth-hole zipper was right up against his lips.

Bastards, he thought, as he tried to shift his position, wishing he could roll over on his other side, but there was a lot of other junk in here taking up all the room. He knew that in a lot of the newer cars there was a latch somewhere inside the trunk that released the lid, but he had no idea where it was. If they hadn't crammed all their junk back here, he would have been able to feel around for it. He might have been able to pull out the bulbs in the taillights, too. Then a cop might have pulled them over. He could've kicked and hollered to get cop's attention.

Of course, if the cop got suspicious and demanded to see what was in the trunk, Krupnick might just shoot the guy dead. He was that crazy. Marvelli couldn't risk letting that happen. He kicked the sidewall in frustration, anger swelling inside of him.

"Son of a bitch!" he yelled. "You're a freakin' son of a bitch, Krupnick. I hope you can hear me."

Suddenly Marvelli could see, although the only thing he could see were his own knees. He arched his head back and blinked as he saw a rectangle of light right in front of his face. The hatch behind the armrest in the backseat was open. He could see the frontseat headrests and blue sky through the windshield. The head behind the wheel had straight jet-black hair—Sunny.

"Hi," someone said, and a hand was waving in front of the hatch. A big face appeared, not twelve inches from his. It startled him at first, but he guessed from the fluffy, white blond hair that it was Dorie.

"Dorie?" he said. "Dorie?" But his words were muffled by the mask.

The curly, graying blond head in the front passenger seat turned around. "Unzip his mouth," Krupnick said. "I can't understand him."

Dorie peered into the hole. "Bring your face closer," she shouted.

Marvelli winced. "I'm not deaf."

"What?" she said louder.

"Never mind," he shouted.

"What did you say?"

I said, never mind! he thought loudly.

He used his legs to work his way closer to the hole. Dorie reached in and felt around for his face until her fingers found the zipper. He pressed his lips together as she worked the stubborn zipper, not wanting to get his flesh caught. When she finally got it unzipped, the air from outside suddenly felt cold compared to the clammy heat inside the mask.

"What did you say?" Dorie repeated.

"You don't have to yell," Marvelli said. "I can hear you."

"Oh . . . sorry," she said. "By the way, I don't think we've been properly introduced. I'm Dorie." She stuck her hand into the hole, blocking out the light.

"He can't shake your hand, Dorie," Krupnick said, his sarcasm barely disguised as patience. "He's handcuffed. Remember?"

"Oh, you're right," she said, pulling her hand out. "Sorry," she said into the hole.

"No problem," Marvelli replied.

"So who are you?" Dorie asked, her big blue eyes wide and innocent. He felt like a bug looking up at a human.

"Yeah, who are you?" Krupnick echoed. He turned around completely and knelt on the front seat.

Even Sunny glanced over her shoulder to look even though she was driving.

"Take the mask off, and I'll tell you," Marvelli said.

"Close the hatch," Krupnick ordered. "He just wants to be cute."

"No!" Marvelli said quickly. The terror of claustrophobia suddenly grabbed him by the gut. In the dark he'd been all right, but now that he could see light, the thought of being closed in again made him panic. He clung to that rectangle of light like a drowning man trying to keep his head above water.

"So what's your name, chief?" Krupnick said. "Last chance."

"Frank Marvelli."

"Frank Marvelli . . ." Krupnick nodded, scratching his beard in thought. "That sounds familiar. You're not the guy Vissa left me with all those years ago back in Jersey? The guy who just let me walk away?"

"You remember me?" Marvelli asked.

"I remember the name."

"Really?"

So who would have told him my name? Mavelli wondered, but he kept his mouth shut. He didn't want to get Krupnick riled.

"I'm pretty good with names," Krupnick said. "Better with names than with faces sometimes."

"Not me," Marvelli said. "Faces, I can remember. Names? Forget about it."

"That's fascinating," Krupnick said, his voice dripping with sarcasm. "Close the hatch, Dorie. He's boring."

"Okay," she said.

"No, wait!" Marvelli blurted, his heart beating like a tom-tom. He was worried about Loretta, worried that he'd never see her again. "Where's Loretta? Is she gonna be all right?"

Krupnick looked annoyed. "You mean the fat broad? Is that who you're talking about?"

"I thought you were good with names," Sunny said snidely.

Krupnick sneered at her. "Just pay attention to the road." But Sunny just laughed at him.

"What're you gonna do with Loretta?" Marvelli asked. "That's all I want to know. Just tell me she's gonna be all right."

"She'll be fine. You happy now?" Krupnick said. "Now close the hatch, Dorie."

"No!" Marvelli shouted. He was sweating so much under the leather jumpsuit he could hear himself *squoosh.* "Just tell me the truth. Is she gonna be all right? *Tell me!"*

No one said anything. Sunny kept her eyes on the road. Krup-nick stroked his beard in silence.

Dorie put her face in front of the hole. "You love her, don't you?"

"Of course, I love her."

"That is so sweet," Dorie said. "Men never say that kind of stuff out loud and really mean it. But you mean it, I can tell. Lor-etta is so lucky she found someone like you. She really is."

"What're you talking about?" Krupnick barked. "I tell you I love you all the time."

"Yeah, but Frank means it," Dorie said. "I can tell the differ-ence." All of a sudden she didn't sound like an airhead anymore.

An awkward silence filled all the space in the car. It seeped through the hole and into the trunk. Marvelli's heart wasn't pounding, but he felt worse than before. He felt hopeless. "What're you gonna do with me?" he asked quietly. "Am I ever gonna see Loretta again?"

Krupnick snickered. "Sure, you are."

"In heaven?"

Krupnick laughed out loud. "You're a funny guy, you know that?"

"You're gonna kill me, aren't you?"

"Don't worry about it," Krupnick said. "Live in the moment."

"Don't worry about it? If you're planning on doing me, I'll start saying some 'Hail Marys.' Just let me know. Okay?"

Sunny sighed out loud to let Marvelli know how bored she was with this conversation. "Why don't we just tell you every-thing? We'll write a script for you. Don't you believe in being spontaneous?"

"Not in this situation, no."

Sunny turned around in her seat and raised her voice to a near shriek. "You want to know everything? Well, how about this?" she said. "We're going to kill you and eat you. With carrots!"

"You're a vegan, Sunny," Dorie pointed out. "You would never eat him."

"I'd force myself," Sunny huffed.

"No, you wouldn't," Dorie said. "You're very particular about what you put into your body. You won't even eat Fudge Whirl."

"That's different," Sunny said.

Marvelli noticed Krupnick giving Sunny a dirty look.

"Can we change the subject?" Sunny said, trying to be bored again.

"Okay," Krupnick said. He peered into the hole. "You, Marvelli. Say something."

Marvelli ignored him. "Dorie?" he called out.

"I'm here, honey." She waved her hand in front of the hole.

"Dorie, if I tell you something, will you listen to me?"

"Sure, I will."

"Dump this loser," Marvelli said.

"Which loser?" Dorie said with total innocence.

"I wouldn't exactly say Sunny is a loser," Marvelli said, "even though she is weird." He tilted his head so he could see the back of Sunny's head. "No offense, Sunny. You may be a nice person down deep, but from what I've seen so far, you're pretty freakin' strange."

"You don't know the half of it," Sunny purred.

"Dorie," Marvelli said, "I'm not talking about Sunny. The loser I'm talking about is your boyfriend Krupnick."

"Who? Arnie?"

"Yeah, Arnie, whatever you call him."

Krupnick stared at him through the hatch. "Why should she dump me? I've been very good to her."

"Because she's gonna end up back in prison if she sticks with you. Is that what you want, Dorie?"

"No. Of course not."

"You, too, Sunny," Marvelli said, getting all worked up despite himself. "He'll drag you down, too. If you kill me, you and Dorie will take the fall. Not him. He'll slip out of it somehow. I guarantee you that's how it'll happen."

"Shut the hell up," Krupnick said lazily.

But Sunny was staring hard at her partner in crime.

"What're you staring at?" Krupnick snapped. "Watch the road."

Dorie said, "You're not really gonna kill him, are you? He's a nice guy. Loretta would be devastated."

"Like I give a crap about her." Krupnick was getting nasty, losing his cool.

"Let me give you some advice, Krupnick," Marvelli said, gulping air and gasping for breath. "Just leave us. Go on your own. You'll be faster that way. You'll get away."

"I don't want your advice," Krupnick growled. "So just shut the hell up."

"Leave us here," Marvelli insisted. "We're baggage. All of us. We'll drag you down. You'll get caught."

"I said, *shut up!*" Krupnick shouted.

"You know I'm right," Marvelli persisted. "You've done time. If you go back, it'll be hard time. You don't want that. I know you don't."

"Shut the hatch!" Krupnick ordered, but Dorie didn't listen, so he screamed at her. "Shut the friggin' hatch, Dorie!"

"I want to hear what he has to say," she said.

Sunny didn't say a word, but her head was cocked, taking it all in.

"What're you slowing down for?" Krupnick yelled at her. "Pay attention to the road!"

"Listen to me," Marvelli pleaded. "Leave us here. Take the car and go on your own."

"Don't try to play mind games with me, Marvelli—"

"I'm not playing mind games," Marvelli shouted. "I don't give a shit about you. All I care about is living. You want your freedom, right? Listen to me and we both get what we want." But what Marvelli really wanted was Loretta. He wanted to know that she was all right.

"Stop looking out for my welfare, okay? I can handle my own life. I've been doing it pretty well so far."

"You know, Arnie," Sunny said, "the *I Ching* says—"

"I don't give a damn about the *I Ching*."

"I think you should listen to him, Arnie," Dorie said. "I think he's making sense."

"Okay, that's it!" Krupnick exploded. His eyes were on fire. "Pull over!"

"Pull over?" Sunny said.

"Pull over! Right here!" Krupnick was a mad dog.

"Whatever you want," Sunny mumbled.

Marvelli could feel her braking the car. He strained to look through the windshield, but it didn't give him any clue as to where they were. All he could see was sky. They could be out in the middle of nowhere as far as he knew. Maybe down by the docks. Or on one of the big bridges.

All good places for a murder, he thought.

Barry Utley's gun hand was trembling as he nervously shifted his aim back and forth from Loretta to Vissa. They were standing in Ira Krupnick's crowded storeroom, crammed in with a hundred barrels full of heroin. Barry's pistol was a dull metallic gray Luger, the kind of gun the Nazis always use in the movies. The tapered barrel looked like a deadly little viper.

"Put that stupid thing down," Loretta said, annoyed that a yuppie slimeball like Barry would have the money and the nerve to buy a Nazi relic.

Barry gritted his teeth. "Don't talk to me that way. I'll shoot you."

"Yeah, sure. You couldn't shoot yourself with that thing."

"Loretta," Vissa said, her hands up over her big hair, "what in the hell is wrong with you? He's got a gun, for God's sake."

"A Luger? Who's he supposed to be, Colonel Klink? Who uses a Luger? C'mon, Barry. Get real. What is it? A cigarette lighter? A toy gun you had when you were a little boy?" Loretta was totally fed up. She was going to tell off anybody who got in her face.

"Oh, don't worry, it works," Barry said with quiet conviction. "It's old, but it works."

"Bull!" Loretta said.

"Oh, yeah?"

Crack! The gun went off, and a puff of white powder jumped out of a bullet hole in the side of the barrel closest to Loretta's leg. A thin wisp of smoke snaked out of the Luger's muzzle.

"Son of a bitch," Loretta cursed under her breath. The gun did work. She hated being wrong.

"Nice call," Vissa said sarcastically.

Loretta gave her a dirty look.

"I'm going to have to do something about you two," Barry said, but it sounded as if he was talking to himself, trying to put together a plan.

But the shot hadn't changed Loretta's attitude. She was still fed up. "Why don't you just grind us up and put us in the ice cream? You can make a new flavor. Call it 'Jersey Girl Supreme.' "

Barry narrowed his eyes. "Don't joke around."

"Loretta," Vissa said through her teeth, "don't get him riled up."

"Don't get *me* riled. You listen to me, Barry. Have you thought this through yet? I hope you don't think you can just kill us in a room full of heroin and get away with it. Wake up, Barry. It's *your* factory. The police will think it's a little strange, and with Krupnick gone, you're gonna be the one who'll have to face the music. Am I getting through to you? You are in deep doo-doo, pal. You're drowning in it."

"The heroin isn't mine. It's his." Barry's face was dripping with sweat.

Loretta rolled her eyes. "Tell it to the judge. I'm sure he'll be very understanding."

"I'm serious," Barry protested. "The dope is Arnie's. It was all his idea."

Vissa's eyes narrowed. "What do you mean, it was his idea? Explain."

Barry was breathing hard. "Arnie stole it from a drug dealer in Chicago. A guy named Batman."

"Batman Jessup?" Loretta asked, taking a guess.

"Yeah. You know him?"

"I've heard of him. Twenty years ago the Bat controlled all upper Midwest distribution—Chicago, Cleveland, Detroit, Milwaukee."

Vissa seemed skeptical. "Ira Krupnick stole this much dope and he's still breathing?"

Barry shrugged, palms up, as if he didn't know a thing about it. "All he told me was that he got some inside information that Batman was getting a trailer-truckload of smack, coming in by ship through Newark. He hijacked the trailer and took off with it."

"When did this happen?" Vissa asked.

"Nineteen ninety-one."

Vissa turned to Loretta. "Right after he was let out on parole in Jersey."

"Typical repeater," Loretta said.

"So how did it get here?" Vissa asked. Her fists were propped on her hips now. The woman wanted answers.

"Arnie was afraid to put the stuff out on the street," Barry said. "He figured Batman would find him if he tried, so he went to my partner, the real Arnie, who sold Krupnick his identity. I was totally against it at the time, but Ira Krupnick is hard to say no to—in case you don't know."

"Yeah, I know," Vissa said with a sigh.

Loretta looked at her. Vissa's expression was odd, more hurt than angry. Her interest in this story seemed more than just professional.

"I figured Krupnick was gonna keep a low profile and just let me run the company," Barry continued, "but as soon as he gets here he starts doing Arnie's job, dreaming up new flavors. I didn't know that he was looking for a way to use up the dope. I only found out later on. His first batch of flavors was awful. Peppermint Twist, Halloween Scare—that was orange sherbet with black licorice swirls—Raspberry Ho, Java Jingle. Nothing would hide the taste of the heroin. Then he came up with Elmer Fudge Whirl. He's got some secret formula for the chocolate fudge swirls combined with white chocolate in the base and who knows what else—he won't tell me. He was test-marketing it in Portland before I even knew it existed. I found out from the regional distributor who called me up one day, screaming for as much as we could make. In no time Fudge Whirl was flying out of the stores. That's when Krupnick told me he was spiking the ice cream. I should have tried to shut him down right then and there, but the profits were . . . well, how do you shut down a gold mine? Especially when you've got a psycho like Krupnick running the operation."

"Am I supposed to feel sorry for you?" Loretta said. "You made a mint getting people addicted to your stupid ice cream." She was thinking of Marvelli.

"There's not supposed to be enough in it to cause a serious addiction," Barry quickly pointed out. "Krupnick swore he was very careful about that. 'Just enough for a little buzz,' he always said. 'Not enough to bug the fuzz.' He puts extra heroin only in his own private stock."

"You mean, he's an addict?" Vissa asked.

Barry shrugged. "I suppose."

Vissa's brow was creased. She seemed very upset.

Loretta put her hand on Vissa's shoulder. This guy was still in her head in a major way. "Hey, look," Loretta said, "scummy people do scummy things. What do you expect?"

Vissa wouldn't look at her.

But Loretta was less concerned about Vissa still carrying the torch for Krupnick than she was about Marvelli. He was definitely addicted to Elmer Fudge Whirl, she was convinced. He'd have to go into ice-cream detox. What would the doctors give him for that? Methadone Fudgesicles?

"So what do we do now?" Barry suddenly shouted. "Huh?" He was more jittery than ever, tottering between belligerence and self-pity.

"You're holding the damn gun," Loretta pointed out. "*You* tell *me* what happens." She was really fed up now.

"Don't yell at me," Barry yelled. "You don't understand. Nobody understands."

"Well, why don't you tell us about it?" Vissa said soothingly. "We might understand."

Loretta muttered out of the side of her mouth. "What is this, the *Oprah* show?"

"You want him to go *Jerry Springer* on us?" Vissa muttered back.

Loretta frowned. She had to admit Vissa had a point.

"I won't go nuts on you if that's what you're worried about," Barry said glumly. "Guys like me never go nuts. We're not allowed."

"What're you talking about?" Loretta said.

"Guys like Krupnick, they go nuts and everybody thinks they're really something. They're dashing and romantic. Women love them. *My* women love him."

"You mean Dorie?" Loretta asked.

"And Sunny," Barry said. His lower lip trembled for a second, and Loretta's heart melted.

Poor guy, she thought. *First his wife, then his dominatrix.*

"He's taken over my whole life," Barry complained. "He's like Attila the Hun."

"Hang on, I'm confused," Vissa said. "Are you saying Sunny was your girlfriend? I thought she was just—you know—the person who beat you up."

"Doms have personal lives, too," Barry said defensively.

Vissa was skeptical. "But you . . . you . . ." She was waving at his body.

"What?" Barry snapped. "I'm not her type? I'm the schlumpy one, the accountant, the vanilla-bean counter? Is that what you think?"

"I didn't say that," Vissa said.

"You don't have to. I know what people think of me."

Loretta held up her hand in order to be heard. "So you're saying Krupnick stole your wife *and* your girlfriend? What is he, Secretariat?"

Vissa sighed longingly.

Loretta rolled her eyes. "Oh, please."

"Don't make fun," Barry shouted. "It's not funny."

"Nobody's laughing," Loretta shouted back. She reached out to him. "Why don't you give me the gun before we have an accident?"

"No!" He pulled it away abruptly. "I'm thinking about killing myself now."

"Don't talk stupid," Loretta said.

Vissa scowled at her. "You don't badger someone who's suicidal."

Loretta scowled back. "You don't coddle him, either." She turned back to Barry. "Just put the gun away. It'll make it easier for us to talk."

"There's nothing to talk about," he said. "I'm screwed. May as well kill myself and get it over with."

"Stop talking that way," Loretta insisted. "Nothing is hopeless until you're dead."

"Well, just stick around a minute." He lifted the gun and stuck the barrel under his chin.

Loretta reached out to him again. "Barry, don't," she said softly. "Please."

"You gonna tell me it'll be all right? That everything can be fixed? My life *can't* be fixed. I loved Dorie and I loved Sunny. We had a solid relationship, the three of us, until Krupnick stuck his big you-know-what into our business. Feelings are feelings. Mine are gone now, and you can't bring them back. Just like you can't make a ton of heroin disappear. You were right about that. The stuff is here in my factory. If I stick around, I'm screwed. I'll go to jail for the rest of my life." His bottom lip was trembling, and his eyes were squeezed shut as if he were praying. Or building up the nerve to pull the trigger.

"Don't do it," Vissa said.

"Wait!" Loretta said at the same time.

"Be quiet," he shouted in anguish. "This is my factory. Let me die in peace."

"Listen, listen, listen," Loretta said frantically, "we can make you a deal." She caught Vissa's eye and raised her eyebrows, wordlessly pleading with her to just go along with this. "If you help us, Barry, we'll help you."

"That's right," Vissa said. "We'll talk to the police for you, explain that there are extenuating circumstances."

"For a ton of heroin?" Barry wailed. "What're you going to tell them? That I kept it for medicinal purposes?"

"I'm serious," Loretta said. "A man's life is at stake. His name is Frank Marvelli. If you give us information that will help us locate Krupnick before he can harm Marvelli, that will weigh heavily in your favor."

"She's right," Vissa added, nodding emphatically. "That's the way it works. You help us, we help you."

"What's to help? My life isn't worth a pint of store-brand vanilla. I've got only one option left." He squeezed his eyes shut again and pressed the barrel of the Luger into the flesh under his chin.

"Wait!" Loretta yelped. "What about Dorie?"

He opened one eye. "What about her?"

"You still love her, don't you? I mean, that's pretty obvious, isn't it?"

"Sure, I love her. But she doesn't love me."

"Not necessarily. Yes, she may be infatuated with Krupnick, but that doesn't mean she's stopped loving you."

"Gimme a break. You sound like a country-and-western song."

"No," Loretta insisted. "That's the way it is with women sometimes. We're not like men. We're not always shooting for a bull's-eye the way guys do. We can have two different kinds of feelings for two different people."

"That's right," Vissa chimed in. "I mean, look at yourself. Were your feelings for Dorie and Sunny exactly the same?"

"That's different," he mumbled.

"Yeah, probably," Vissa said, "but that's only because you're a man. To you, they were possessions, things to be acquired. But women don't want to own, they want to—"

"Lease," he finished for her. "Yeah, yeah, I know all that. Men are from Mars. Blah-blah-blah."

"Well, it's true," Loretta said, talking over him. "Men are aliens. It's a proven fact."

Except for Marvelli, she thought sadly. *He doesn't even leave the toilet seat up.*

Barry's eyes were squeezed shut again, his finger poised on the trigger. Tears were streaming from the corners of his eyes. His voice was choked. "If I'm an alien, then I'm beaming myself up. So long, world. Take it easy."

"Stop!" Loretta shouted angrily. "This isn't about you, dammit. It's about Dorie. And Sunny."

He opened his eyes and frowned at her. "Are you saying this is all *my* fault?"

"Well, it is," Loretta said. "Well, not yet, but it will be if they end up going to prison."

He shook his head in confusion. "What're you talking about?"

"If Krupnick kills Marvelli, Dorie and Sunny will be charged as accessories. Think about it. Accessories to murder. And Dorie's already got a record. She could face the death penalty."

Barry slowly lowered the gun. Loretta could tell from his expression that her words were sinking in.

"If you love them," she said, "help us find Krupnick before it's too late."

He was gesturing helplessly. "If I knew where they were, I'd tell you. I swear."

"Think," Vissa urged. "Does Krupnick have another house, an apartment, a good friend, another girlfriend maybe?"

Barry shook his head, his face contorted in frustration. "We didn't pal around at all. I don't know who he hangs out with. Except for Dorie and Sunny."

"How about them?" Loretta asked. "Do *they* have any friends, anybody they'd run to if they were in trouble, anyone they might contact?"

"Well, Sunny has a lover."

Loretta's eyes shot open. "Another one?"

"Her *lesbian* lover," he said with disdain. "Agnes. I used to think *she* was my competition until I found out about Arnie."

"What's Agnes's last name?" Vissa said. "Do you know?"

"Where does this Agnes work?" Loretta said. "Where does she live?"

Barry wrinkled his nose and scratched his head with the barrel of the Luger. "Hmmm . . . I'll have to give that some thought."

"Pull over! Right here, dammit!" Krupnick was pointing through the windshield at the 7-Eleven convenience store on the side of the road.

"Easy, ace," Sunny said out of the side of her mouth as she pulled into the parking lot. "You're gonna have an aneurysm the way you're going."

"Yeah," Dorie agreed from the backseat. "You are."

"Where we going?" Marvelli said through the hatch.

Krupnick turned around and glared at Marvelli's masked face. He could see Marvelli's eyes glimmering through eye holes. This guy was really annoying him. He looked like an S&M Señor Wencas, a wiseass head in a box. A stranger who meant trouble.

"Shut the hatch," Krupnick ordered.

Dorie started to object again, but Krupnick overrode her before she could get a word in. "I said, shut the friggin' hatch," he shouted. "What part of that don't you understand? Huh?"

Dorie's chin crumpled, and her brows were bunched. "Goodbye, Frank," she said softly. "Sorry, but I have to."

"I understand," Marvelli said, as she shut the hatch and pushed the armrest into the seat.

Sunny had brought the car to a stop and left it running. Krupnick threw his door open and got out. "Stay here. I'll be right back."

"Aren't you gonna ask us if we want anything?" Sunny purred.

"No," he said, slamming his door closed. He pointed back through the window at Dorie. "And don't talk to him. You hear me?"

Dorie just looked at him, giving him her sad puppy-dog eyes. That was the problem with her, he thought. She knew him too well. She knew how to get to him. Sunny, too. But in a different way.

He stomped off into the store, pushing the door so hard it crashed into a wire rack of tabloid newspapers on the other side. One of the headlines caught his eye: ELVIS'S GHOST HAUNTS WHITE HOUSE.

Thankyouverymuch, Krupnick thought, curling his lip. The thought of Elvis with the president made him smile despite his foul mood.

A very petite Asian woman stood behind the cash register. She had fabulous long ebony hair, but she also had a pale, doughy face. Krupnick headed directly for the freezer case at the back of the store.

He quickly scanned the glass case, looking for the Arnie and Barry's pints. He found their section right away, zeroing in on his own face on one of the cartons.

Arnie Ira, Ira Arnie, he thought. *Screw 'em both. Call me Elvis from now on. The King. Thankyouverymuch.*

He sorted through the pints, looking for an Elmer Fudge Whirl. He found Macadamia Smash, Rococo Cocoa, and Impossible Orange Sherbet, but no Elmer Fudge Whirl.

Damn! he thought. *Why is this stuff so damn popular? Is everyone a freakin' junkie these days?*

He kept digging through the pints, pawing like a bear in a garbage can, sweeping pints of Arnie and Barry onto the other brands so that he could dig deeper. His fingers were red and chapped, but he didn't care. He needed some Fudge Whirl. Now!

Finally, at the very bottom, he found one last pint of Fudge Whirl. It was slightly crushed and the clear cellophane window on the lid was ripped, but so what? It was Fudge Whirl, and he needed it so he could think.

He stomped back to the cashier, grabbed a white plastic spoon from an open paper coffee cup next to the cash register, slapped a five-dollar bill on the counter, and left without waiting for his change. As soon as he was out the door, he pried off the lid and tossed it away like a Frisbee. He tried to stick the spoon in to get a bite, but the ice cream was rock hard from being at the bottom of the freezer for so long. He scraped a bit off the top and licked it off the spoon, but that wasn't enough. He wanted more. Right now!

Tiny ice crystals on the surface of the Fudge Whirl shimmered in the sun. He tried to plunge the spoon into the ice cream again, but it splintered. He cursed and threw the broken spoon on the ground as he thought about going back inside for another one. *But all those goddamn spoons are cheap and flimsy,* he thought, and he sure as hell wasn't going to wait for the ice cream to melt. Instead he improvised and brought the pint to his mouth, licking off the top. He intended to eat it out of the carton as if it were an ice-cream cone. A *big* ice-cream cone.

He went back to the car and sat on the fender as he bit into the frozen Fudge Whirl. His teeth ached from the cold, but that didn't matter. He had an urgent need for some "secret ingredient."

The motor vibrated his butt. Sunny hadn't shut it off. Eventually the heat from his hand started to melt the edges of the ice cream, so he could run his tongue around the rim and finally get a decent mouthful. Gradually a warm swell began to course through his veins. After a few minutes he felt as if he were radiating heat.

Like the sun, he thought. *Sun Records. Elvis's first label. Radiating like the Sun. The Sun King. It's good to be king.*

He smiled to himself as he looked through the windshield, shading his eyes against the glare. It was too bright to see their faces, but he could see the shapes of Dorie's and Sunny's heads and shoulders. Maybe he should be like Elvis, he thought. Go away and come back. Come back as somebody else.

I'd still be the king, he thought. *I'd be a better king.*

But to do that, he'd have to leave it all behind. He'd have to get rid of a few things, too. No loose ends. Marvelli in the trunk would have to go for sure, he thought. Sunny and Dorie should go, too, unfortunately. They knew too much about him. *Dorie's a dim bulb—she'll blab to anyone who's nice to her,* he thought. *And Sunny's got a lot of yang in her yin. She'd try to screw him—blackmail, extortion, something like that. Maybe even assassination. She'd get into it, do it just because she's never done it before. That's the trouble with people like her, they'll do anything. Sex is one thing, but then there's the rest of life. You need limits. Dominatrices don't have any. That's why Sunny is dangerous.*

He licked the Fudge Whirl, feeling downright toasty, staring at the dark shapes of the two women through the glare of the windshield, thinking about what he had to do to them. Putting together a plan was making him feel good. It was giving him energy, giving him a good shot of positive *chi.* He had to reinvent himself—that was a definite. Shed this skin and grow another one. Same way he had the last time.

The ice cream was getting soft. He squeezed the carton to make it rise to the top so he could get more. He studied the logo on the carton and thought about the money. He had accumulated a lot of money as Arnie Bloomfield. And he had the house in Haight-Ashbury. And the condo in Costa Rica. He had a lot of goodies as Arnie Bloomfield.

But what's money? he thought. *Screw it. I can always make more. That's no problem. There's always something to steal.*

But what about the smack? That was major.

He'd started out with a ton of it, and he'd hardly made a dent. He had enough "secret ingredient" to keep making Elmer Fudge Whirl for the next thirty years.

He thought about it for a minute, then started shaking his head. "Bad reasoning," he mumbled to himself, swiping ice cream from the corner of his mouth with the back of his hand. "Nothing is forever. Nobody's lucky *chi* holds out of that long."

Sunny poked her head out the window. "You say something?"

"I'm chanting," he said.

"Bull."

"Dharma bull." He flashed a silly grin at her.

"You're *so* Grateful Dead," she said with a sneer.

"So? That's good."

"It's old," she said.

"Do you think I'm old?"

"Definitely."

"So why do you hang around with me?"

"You have money. You can afford me."

"Oh." Krupnick nodded to himself. It was all coming clear to him. Sunny didn't give a crap about him. The only one she cared about was that dishrag Agnes—and that stupid dog. Sunny only wanted him for his money. Somehow he always knew that, but now that she'd come right out and said it, he had to do something. Things had to change.

"Hey, Dorie," he called out.

Dorie stuck her pretty head out the window.

"Do you love me for my money, too?" he asked.

"Of course not."

"You love Barry for his money?"

She shrugged her shoulder and tilted her head forward, trying to figure out what answer he wanted to hear. "What I feel for Barry is different," she said. "You know that."

"I'm not sure I do."

"I'm married to Barry."

"But you hang out with me."

"Right." She brightened up as if he'd solved the puzzle for her.

"So Barry's your husband, and I'm, like, what? You're bimbo?"

"No," she said with a deep frown.

"Bimbu, bimbino, bimbop—what's the male version of a bimbo?"

"*Him*bo" Sunny said. "But in this case *chump* will do." She was doing her dominatrix thing, trying to hurt him, but she didn't realize that she was the one who was going to get hurt. Big time. Her ticket was about to expire.

And remember, Sunny. No tickie, no shirty.

He tipped the carton to his mouth and drank the last dribs of the ice cream. It was almost milk shake consistency. He felt better now, confident again. In fact, he felt great.

"Okay," he said, dropping the empty carton on the pavement, "let's get his show on the road." He got back into the car and slammed the door closed. "Drive!"

"Drive where?" Sunny said, looking as bored as could be.

"Where I tell you."

"Oh, really?"

"Yes, really."

Dorie stuck her face between the bucket seats. "Where do you want to go, Arnie?" she asked, trying to mediate before he and Sunny really got into it.

He hesitated for a moment, thinking it might be bad karma to answer to his old name. He should be rejecting the old stuff. He had to look forward. "I've got someplace in mind," he said, grinning with his eyebrows.

"Someplace fun?" she asked.

"*I* think so."

"Where's that?" Sunny said, not at all amused.

He grinned at both of them in turn. "Let me surprise you. You'll have a ball. Trust me."

"I never trust anyone," Sunny declared.

"You can trust Arnie," Dorie said.

Krupnick just sat there grinning and shining like ole Mr. Sun. *Yeah, you can trust Arnie,* he thought. *You just can't trust Ira.*

"I don't think anybody's here," Vissa said. "I think this building's been condemned." She was at the top of a rickety, dimly lit staircase in a dilapidated tenement in a neighborhood that looked more like Newark than San Francisco. The plaster walls were so water-damaged, there was more lathing showing than plaster.

"Knock on the door anyway," Loretta said from the bottom of the staircase. "Barry said Agnes lives here and works here, too." Loretta was holding Dragon by the rope that was serving as his leash. The dog was still a little groggy, but he was coming around. He'd taken a liking to Loretta and would lean against her leg whenever she would let him. At the moment he was on his haunches, sitting on her foot.

"Do you mind?" she said, pulling her foot out.

"What?" Vissa said.

"Nothing. I was talking to the dog."

"Why don't you bring him up here? I've got a bad feeling about this place."

Loretta looked down at Dragon's wrinkly face. "She expects *you* to protect us? I don't think so."

He wagged his tail a few times, then heaved a deep sigh as if he were about to fall asleep again.

She tugged on the rope and got him to his feet. "No offense, Dragon, but I wish I had my gun with me. Too many weirdos out here. Even if you were clean and sober, I don't think you'd be much help."

"Will you stop talking to that dog and get up here?" Vissa said, getting testy. She had her fists propped on her hips, doing her Jersey-girl routine.

"Chill out, will ya?" Loretta said, as she made her way up the steps. It was slow going with Dragon because he kept trying to sit down. She could feel Vissa's impatience raining down on her, but she didn't say anything. Loretta still couldn't make up her mind about Vissa. They'd been through a lot in the last few hours, but Loretta wasn't about to call her "girlfriend" yet. Even though it had all happened years ago—seducing Marvelli, falling in love with Krupnick, and then helping the bum escape—they weren't the kind of things Loretta could just overlook. Vissa seemed okay, but she also seemed to have her own agenda, and little things like morality, scruples, and right and wrong didn't get in her way.

Loretta made it to the top of the stairs, but Dragon was still four steps behind. "Go ahead, knock," she said to Vissa. "He'll make it."

Reluctantly Vissa knocked on the door, which was very loose on its hinges. From the sound of it, Loretta figured she could easily crash through it with a good hip check. All of a sudden her heart started to thump in anticipation. Maybe Marvelli was in there, she thought. Maybe he was okay. Maybe Krupnick just left him here.

But then the blood drained out of Loretta's face as she considered the possibility that maybe Krupnick had left Marvelli's body here.

"Look out," Loretta said, shoving her way past Vissa in a panic. She had to get in there. She had to find Marvelli.

But just as she was about to crash through the door, it squeaked open.

"What do you want?" A woman was standing in the doorway. She had some kind of Scandinavian accent, Loretta guessed. She seemed to be in her mid to late twenties and was very thin and bony. Her elbows, knees, and cheekbones were like knobs under her skin. She was wearing brown corduroy shorts, a gauzy white top with crisscross lacing in front, and no shoes. Her hair was thin and almost colorless, hanging dead-straight to her shoulders. Her complexion was translucent, and Loretta doubted that makeup had ever touched it. She was an anti-California girl.

"What do you want?" the woman repeated in the same monotone.

"Are you Agnes?" Loretta asked.

The woman looked at Loretta blankly. "Do you want a rub?"

Loretta exchanged glances with Vissa. "Excuse me?"

"A rub, a rubdown. That's what I do. Massage."

Loretta checked out her skinny arms. This girl didn't look like she had the strength to squeeze a marshmallow.

The woman's tiny gray eyes narrowed suspiciously. "Who sent you here?"

"Barry Utley," Vissa said. "Are you Agnes?"

But now the woman noticed Dragon, who had finally dragged himself up to the top step. "Dragon!" she said, squatting down to get on the dog's level. "What's wrong, Dragon? Your energy is so depleted." Her gaze followed the leash back to Loretta. "His aura is purple black," she said accusingly.

Loretta looked down at the dog. "He looks black and brown to me."

"What are you doing with him? Where's Sunny?" The woman

stood up suddenly and switched gears from sleepwalker to guided missile.

"We're baby-sitting him," Vissa said. "And actually we're looking for Sunny ourselves. So are you Agnes or not?"

"Yes, I'm Agnes. But I want to know how you got Dragon. Sunny doesn't leave him with just anyone." She stooped down again and stroked Dragon's head, but the dog was too out of it to respond.

"We're watching him for Sunny," Vissa said. "Do you know where she is?"

Agnes glared at her. "Are you sleeping with my Sunny? Are you *both* sleeping with her?"

Loretta almost laughed out loud. "Are you crazy? I've been struggling since college to stay heterosexual. I just couldn't find a guy who wanted to be hetero with me."

"I know how my Sunny is. She likes to experiment with people. Have you experimented with her?" Agnes's outrage had dissipated. She sounded prim and matter-of-fact now.

"You have my solemn vow," Loretta said. "I have not experimented with her."

"Me neither," Vissa said. "So do you know where Sunny is?"

Agnes ignored the question. "Dragon looks thirsty. Have you given him water?"

"No," Loretta said quickly before Vissa could answer. In fact they had give Dragon plenty of water. "Do you think you could give him some?"

"Of course," Agnes said. "Stay right here. I have a client."

Agnes went off to get some water, and as soon as she was out of sight, Loretta went right in.

"What're you doing?" Vissa whispered.

"Ssshhh." Loretta gave her the leash. She was determined to find Marvelli.

Agnes's apartment was a very raw loft space with spots of

exquisite renovation. One section of the battered, wide-plank, solid wood floor had been sanded and painted with a floor mural depicting a starry night sky. The mortar on the bare brick walls was disintegrating, leaving little piles of concrete dust all along the baseboards, but part of that wall was decorated with a series of four medieval tapestries depicting the hunt, capture, and escape of a white unicorn. All the furniture looked like it came from a thrift shop except for a Danish modern, brown leather reading chair and a brass floor lamp that arched over it like a big question mark. A freestanding fabric screen blocked off a space over by the front windows. It was white with black reeds painted on it. Loretta could see the end of a massage table sticking out from behind the screen. A pair of big bare feet hung over the side, pointing down.

Her heart tried to jump out of her throat. *Marvelli!* she thought. *Marvelli on a slab!*

She raced toward the table as Agnes was coming out of the kitchen area with a glazed blue bowl full of water.

"Hey!" Agnes shouted. "What are you doing?"

But Loretta ignored her. Tears were in her eyes, blurring her vision. She had to get to Marvelli. His name was a lump in her throat as she came around the screen. "Mar—"

But then she saw the body that was attached to the feet. It was not pretty, and it was definitely not Marvelli. Not unless they'd force-fed him a vat of ice cream. She walked softly as she moved around the motionless body, taking it in cautiously, incredulously, like a beachcomber finding a beached whale. The body was lying facedown, and it would have been difficult to pinpoint the gender without the completely bald head. Rolls of fat bulged out from under the armpits. The butt was a huge double round mound that threatened to roll off the table and crash through the floor. Loretta moved in a little closer, then moved right back as soon as she got a whiff of him. It was pungent and vinegary. Filthy clothes were heaped on the floor like elephant droppings.

"What are you doing?" Agnes hissed at her. "He's sleeping."

"I can see that," Loretta said. "He also stinks."

"Yes, of course, he stinks," Agnes said indignantly. "He's homeless. Poor people deserve massages, too, you know."

Loretta eyed the sleeping mountain of flesh and tried to imagine touching him. She glanced at Agnes. *Better you than me,* she thought.

"Come. Come," Agnes whispered sternly, fluttering her bony hands as if she were shooing geese. "You are going to wake him."

"Not likely," Loretta muttered, as she moved around to the other side of the screen. She noticed that Vissa had stepped inside the doorway with Dragon. He was making a mess slurping up water from Agnes's blue bowl.

"I want you and your friend to leave this minute, and I want you to leave Dragon with me," Agnes demanded.

"And *I* want a house in Maui," Loretta said. "Doesn't mean I'm gonna get it."

Just the barest hint of color rose in Agnes's colorless cheeks. "Get out right now or I'm calling the police."

"No, you're not," Loretta said. "You're a squatter. The police will throw you out."

"Nonsense."

Loretta nodded at the octopus of extension cords plugged into a single power strip on the floor. Orange and blue cords snaked all through the loft. The source wire ran under the front door and out into the hallway. Agnes was clearly stealing her electricity from somewhere else. "Nonsense, huh?" Loretta said.

Agnes grumbled something in a foreign language.

"Where are you from?" Loretta asked. "Norway?"

"Finland," Agnes declared angrily.

"Are you legal? I can get INS on your tail if you don't watch it."

"Go on, call them," Agnes shot back. "I have my green card."

"Loretta, let's go," Vissa called from across the room. "We're not gonna get anything out of her. Believe me."

"And what is it that you want to get out of me? Huh?" Agnes said. "You've already stolen my Sunny *and* her dog."

"We haven't 'stolen' anyone," Loretta said. "Sunny left Dragon with us."

"I seriously doubt that."

"He's a loaner dog," Loretta said. "Ours is in the shop."

"Stop joking." Agnes narrowed her eyes suspiciously. "You *must* be sleeping with my Sunny. Both of you. And now she has sent you here to rub my nose in it."

"We are not sleeping with Sunny," Vissa said, moving as close as the leash would allow since Dragon was still working on the water. "We don't go that way."

"Sunny goes *all* ways," Agnes said. "That's the whole problem."

"That's what problem?" Loretta asked. "I thought you were her lover."

"*One* of her lovers." Agnes crossed her ankles and sank to the floor, falling naturally into a half-lotus position. Loretta was impressed. She took the easy chair.

"Are you saying that Sunny has other women?" Loretta asked.

"Women, men, animals maybe, I don't know. Her love for me is not like my love for her." Agnes looked like a sad little doll, her hair falling limply over her face. "I am not going to let you find her. She has too many people in her life already."

"I told you," Loretta said, "we don't go that way. Sunny's on the run with a man who kidnapped my boyfriend."

"You mean, the ice-cream man?" Agnes asked. "I warned Sunny about him. I told her he was no good."

"Listen to me," Loretta said. "If the police catch her, she could get into a lot of trouble. She could go to prison. All I want is my boyfriend back in one piece. Help me find them before it's too late."

Agnes became very quiet. Loretta could hear the fat man breathing behind the screen. Dragon finished the rest of the water and was pushing the bowl across the wood floor with his nose.

Agnes might have been crying, but it was hard to tell. She spoke softly. "I can only think of one person who would get involved in such craziness."

"Who?"

"The geek, who else?"

"Who's the geek?"

"Thaddeus." Agnes spat the name out as if it were a bitter taste in her mouth.

"And who's Thaddeus?"

"Sunny's other serious lover—supposedly. She wants us all to live together like Hansel and Gretel and the Gingerbread Man. I say *no* to that."

Loretta really didn't want to hear Agnes's problems right now. "Do you think this Thaddeus would get involved with a kidnapping?"

"Yes, of course!" Agnes suddenly shrieked. "He is a geek! Isn't it obvious?" Her outburst reverberated off the brick walls.

The fat man snuffled and pointed his toes as he stretched his legs. He was awake. "Agnes, honey," he called out. "Did'ja just leave me?"

"No, Hank, I am right here." She stood up to go to him. "Please leave," she said to Loretta and Vissa. "You have told me bad things. Please go."

"Wait," Loretta said. "Just tell me one thing."

"What?" Agnes was holding on to the edge of the screen, eager to get back to Hank the whale.

"What's Thaddeus's last name?"

"He has no last name. He is just Thaddeus." She started to turn away.

"Wait!" Loretta said. "Where can we find him?"

"Where else do you find a geek? The circus, of course." She disappeared behind the screen.

The circus? Loretta thought.

Dragon was at her feet, looking up at her expectantly.

It took Loretta and Vissa more than an hour to find the "circus." When she finally saw it, Loretta doubted that it was the kind of circus she remembered from when she was a child. This circus was all by itself on a pier underneath the San Francisco Bay Bridge, and it wasn't the kind of place you'd want to take the kids. A colorful sailcloth banner stretched between two poles gave the establishment's full name: PHRANK'S TENT PHUL OF PHREAKS—AN ALTERNATIVE CIRCUS. Other banners with imitation old-time drawings advertised the main attractions: Kanisha the World's Phattest Phreak, who wasn't fat at all—just very hip-hop. Paul the Platypus Boy. Bim, Bam, and Boom the Siamese Terrier Triplets. Henrietta the Human Cell Phone. Yvette the Cigar-Smoking Deer. And Thaddeus, the World's Leakiest Man.

Vissa had parked the car at the end of the pier, and they had walked out to the tent with Dragon on the leash intently sniffing the weathered timbers. He was still under the influence of Elmer Fudge Whirl, doing everything a dog should but doing it very slowly and deliberately. He hadn't gone to the bathroom in a while, and every time he sniffed and circled, Loretta and Vissa watched him closely, but he always seemed to forget what he was doing and would have to start sniffing all over again, trying to remember his original intention. He was doing that right now, holding up their progress.

"This is gonna take forever," Loretta said, holding the leash and heaving an annoyed sigh.

"I don't think he should go in there anyway," Vissa said. She'd gone ahead and was peering through the flaps of the big top. It was pretty dark inside. "One of us should stay out here with the dog," she said, walking back toward Loretta and Dragon. "I'll duke you for who goes in. Odds or evens?" Vissa held her fist up by her collarbone, ready to throw down one or two fingers to determine who'd go talk to Thaddeus.

"I'll go," Loretta volunteered. She was still worried that Krupnick had dumped Marvelli somewhere, and she felt that she should be the one to find him if he was here. Her hands were trembling a bit as she eyed the banners, assuming that this place would be filled with all kinds of weirdness, *dangerous* weirdness. She imagined finding Marvelli in a magician's box, sawed in half—but for real, no tricks.

"You sure you want to go?" Vissa asked. "You look a little shaky."

"I'm okay," Loretta said, as she handed the leash to Vissa and walked toward the big top.

Yeah, I'm just dandy, she thought to herself.

The box office at the entrance to the tent was empty, so she just walked right in. Her eyes didn't adjust to the dark right away, so she walked slowly, feeling the sawdust under her feet. Remembering the Siamese triplet dogs and the cigar-smoking deer, she hoped she didn't feel anything else under her feet.

Gradually she was able to make out shapes and shadows. Several small stages were set up around the tent. There were no bleachers or chairs, so Phrank's Tent Phul of Phreaks was apparently more of a glorified sideshow than a circus. At the far end of the tent, Loretta spotted a slit of light. Another flap, she assumed. Walking carefully, she glided through the sawdust toward the light. When she flipped it open, bright sunlight blinded her. She shaded her eyes and squinted at the shimmering water on the bay.

"I'm losing you. I'm losing you. Are you there?"

Loretta turned toward the voice off to her side. She had to stare to make sure she was seeing what she was seeing. A young woman in a silver lamé cocktail dress and silver platforms was talking to herself. Her long dark hair was piled on top of her head and decorated with dozens of small aluminum-foil bowties. Her fingernails were silver, and scores of thin copper bracelets jiggled from her wrists. Extra-long earrings made out of soda-can pop-tops dangled to her armpits.

"Hello? Hello?" she said to herself, raising her voice. "Are you there? *Are you there? I can't hear you. Hello!* Damn!"

Loretta stared at her. The woman had to be an escapee from a mental hospital.

"Oh, hi," the woman said with a broad smile as soon as she noticed Loretta.

"Hi," Loretta said from where she stood, not wanting to get too close.

"The reception is terrible today," the woman said, pointing at the sky. "Must be sunspots."

Loretta nodded. *No sudden moves,* she thought.

"Ruins the act," the woman continued as she positioned her arms at different angles. Loretta looked across the bay. She thought the woman might be doing semaphore. "Can't pick up any calls on days like this," the woman said.

"Oh . . ." Loretta said, as it started to make sense. "You're the Human Cell Phone, aren't you."

"That's me," the woman said, beaming proudly. "Henrietta." She extended her hand to Loretta.

Reluctantly Loretta stepped forward and shook hands, but when she tried to disengage, Henrietta hung on tight.

"Wait!" Henrietta said, cocking her head to one side. "I think I'm getting something. You're a good ground."

Loretta tried to pull her hand back, but Henrietta wasn't letting go. She tilted her head one way, then the other. "Crap, I lost it," she said. "Oh, well. Thanks, anyway." She dropped Loretta's hand. "So have you seen my act?"

Loretta shook her head.

"Well, see, I have people in the audience call home or call a friend or whatever, then I tell them to tell those people to call me at my number with a personal message. I get the message—without a phone, mind you—and relay it. It's always best when the message is something intimate or kind of personal, something that only the person calling would know. It's sort of like when magicians used to read minds. One night I got this guy in the audience who called his wife on his cell and told her to call me. The wife thought it was some kind of sick joke he was playing on her with his girlfriend. She called me and told me to tell him that she was leaving him, and that she was gonna kill all his tropical fish before he got home. Turns out the guy actually did have a girlfriend, a longtime one. I don't know what happened to the fish, but I think he got what he deserved."

"I'm looking for Thaddeus," Loretta said. "Is he here?"

Henrietta was holding her earrings up like rabbit ears. "If he's here, he'll be in his tent." She pointed with her nose to a group of small tents over by the edge of the pier.

"Which one is his?" Loretta asked.

"The wet one," Henrietta said.

"What?"

"The ground is always wet around his tent. He's always working on new leaks."

Loretta felt sick to her stomach just imagining what the
World's Leakiest Man could be doing. Forcing a smile, she said
thanks as she headed for the tents. She could hear Henrietta still
at it behind her. "Hello! Hello! Say something. You're breaking
up. *I'm losing you!*"

When Loretta came up to the canvas tents, she looked at the
ground, and sure enough, it was wet around one of them. It wasn't
just water that had caused all this wetness. Some of it seemed to
be milk. Loretta's stomach clenched. She didn't want to see this.

She went up to the flap of the tent and mentally prepared
herself. *This could be too disgusting for words,* she thought. But
then she thought of Marvelli. *Don't be a weenie,* she thought. *Just
do it.*

"Hello?" she called out, parting the flap a few inches.

"Come on in," a man's voice called back.

Loretta braced herself and threw the flap open. But instead of
finding a huge, jiggly water bag of a man shot through with pin-
holes, sprouting more leaks than a lawn sprinkler, she found a
startlingly handsome young man with floppy blond hair and riv-
eting blue eyes. He looked sort of like Brad Pitt, but actually better-
looking. He wasn't wearing a shirt, and he was built like a Greek
god—just the right amount of muscle and definition. The only
clothes he had on were a pair of cutoff jeans and black canvas
hightop sneakers. He was sitting on a wooden stool with a plastic
gallon of milk on the ground next to him. Other than a cot, a
steamer trunk, and a plastic ice chest, there was nothing else in the
tent, not even a ground cover.

"Hi," he said with a disarming smile.

Loretta couldn't stop staring at his eyes. "Hi," she said. "Are
you Thaddeus?"

"Yup." He nodded.

"Do you—?" She couldn't put a sentence together, mainly because she was wishing he'd stand up so she could see his butt. "Have you—? What I mean is . . . are you really the world's leakiest man?"

He grinned bashfully and ran a hand through his floppy hair. "I dunno," he said. "I'm the only one I know of."

"Oh," she said. "You mean, like, there aren't any others in the *Guinness Book of Records?*"

He shrugged. "I dunno. I've never checked."

"So what exactly"—she gestured awkwardly with her hands—"do you leak?"

"Liquids. Water, milk, coffee, Kool-Aid. Not soda, unless it's gone flat. The bubbles do a real job on my sinuses."

"So you drink this stuff . . . and then what?"

"I make it come out somewhere else." He grinned sheepishly. "Somewhere, like, different."

Loretta almost didn't want to ask. "Like where?"

"Well, like, I can drink milk and make it come out my eyes. Wanna see?" He reached down for the gallon.

"That's okay," Loretta said quickly.

"I can make it come out my ears, too, but that doesn't work all the time. I'm practicing, though, so I can put it in the act."

"That's really . . . great."

"I can sweat coffee, too, but that takes a while."

"I'll bet it does."

"I'm studying tantric yoga so I can eventually suck a bowl of pea soup up my—"

"Let me ask you something," she interrupted. "Do you know a woman named Sunny?"

"Sunny Chu? Sure, I know her."

"Have you seen her lately?"

"I saw her last weekend."

"She's your . . ." Loretta waited for him to fill in the blank.

"My lover, I guess. One of them."

"You have others?"

"Sure. We both do. You looking for her?"

"Yes, I am." Thaddeus seemed to be totally guileless, but she wasn't sure how much she should tell him. "She's with a guy named Arnie," she said, assuming that Thaddeus wouldn't know Krupnick by his real name. "The ice cream Arnie?"

"Oh, sure," he said. "Sunny hangs out with him a lot. They sleep together."

Loretta was stunned by his attitude. It was beyond cool. "And you're okay with her sleeping with him?"

"Sure. As long as she makes sure it's always safe sex, I don't care."

Loretta knew she shouldn't pry, but she couldn't help herself. "How about Agnes?" she asked. "How do you feel about Sunny being with her?"

"You know Agnes?"

Loretta shrugged. "I only met her once."

"A real sourpuss. I don't know what Sunny sees in her."

"You mean, you don't like Sunny being with women."

"Nah. It's not that. I switch-hit myself sometimes."

"I see." She nodded. "Look, I'm gonna level with you, Thaddeus," she said. "Arnie kidnapped my boyfriend, and Sunny is with them. I'm worried. Arnie's crazy and I think Sunny eggs him on. I need to find them before something bad happens. Can you help me?"

Thaddeus nodded thoughtfully. "Yeah, you're right. Sunny does egg people on. And not always for the best."

"Do you have any idea where they might be?"

"Did you check her dungeon at Arnie's?"

Loretta nodded.

He raised his eyebrows and shrugged. "This is a tough one. I wish I could help you, but they could be anywhere. Sunny doesn't like to stay put."

"You don't have any ideas?" Loretta could feel her throat constricting.

"I'd help you if I could. I really would."

He was so sweet she hated Sunny for being with him. He was too good for her. But as sweet as he was, Thaddeus wasn't going to be much help, and Loretta started to panic as the hard reality of the situation finally struck home: Marvelli might actually die, and she'd have to face a world without him. Her mouth contorted into a clown frown, and tears dribbled from her eyes.

"They're gonna kill him," she sobbed. "And the police are gonna find him in that leather suit. The papers will run photos. They'll say Marvelli was into S&M, and he isn't. He isn't like that. He's gentle and loving and . . . he's gonna be gone."

"Is he wearing a leather jumpsuit?" Thaddeus asked. "Black? With a mask?"

Loretta swiped the tears from her eyes and nodded.

"Well, it's a long shot, but I can think of one place where they might take him if he's dressed like that."

"Where?"

"There's this sex club in town that Sunny likes to go to called Deep. They do all kinds of stuff there. Snuff included, from what I hear."

"You mean, as in snuff films where they actually kill people?"

"Yup. I hear they even get rid of bodies right on the premises. A real full-service establishment."

"Please don't smile," she said.

"Sorry." He looked down at the ground.

"Where is this place?" she asked. "I'll call the police and have them check it out." Maybe Henrietta could make the call for her, she thought.

"Don't bother with the police. From what I've been told, the people who own Deep pay them off very well. How else could they get away with the stuff they do?"

"Well, where is this place? I'll go there myself."

Thaddeus looked her up and down. He squinted dubiously. "There's no sign on the door, and you have to pass muster with the doorman to get in. But frankly, I don't think you'll make the cut."

"Why not?" Loretta said defensively.

"You're too straight. You'll never get in looking like that."

"What do you mean?"

"No offense, but the Suzie Creamcheese look just doesn't cut it there."

She glared at him and held her tongue until her temper boiled down to a simmer. "Just give me the address, please. I'll get in."

"I really don't think so."

She got in his face, moving in so close her breasts threatened to poke out his eyeballs. She brandished a no-nonsense finger at him. "Tell me where Deep is," she growled through gritted teeth.

"But—"

She jabbed her finger closer to his face, which crossed his eyes and shut him up immediately. "Do you want me to make some new leaks for you?" she asked. "Huh?"

Still in the trunk, Marvelli felt the car pulling to a stop, but he rolled slightly toward the back of the car rather than toward the front, which meant that Sunny had been backing up. He was drenched with sweat underneath the leather mask and jumpsuit, and groggy from being cooped up in the cramped, stuffy space. He may have fallen asleep or passed out, he wasn't sure, but he'd lost track of time and couldn't figure out how long he'd been in there. He was hungry, but that was no indication of anything because he was always hungry.

He heard the car doors slamming shut, three in a row—*bam, bam, bam.* He wondered why they were all getting out—Sunny, Dorie, and Krupnick. He imagined them abandoning the car somewhere remote, like at a junkyard or in a field, and his heart started to pound, wrenching him out of his stupor. They were abandoning him. He could smother in here, he thought in a panic. He could die from hypothermia. He could starve to death!

But just as he was starting to hyperventilate, the trunk popped open, and a rush of cool air pulled him out of it. The harsh light of naked lightbulbs blinded him. He closed his eyes and tried to turn away, but with his arms handcuffed behind him, there wasn't much he could do.

"Take the mask off," he pleaded. "Please! I can't breathe." But the mouth hole was zipped shut, and his words were hopelessly muffled.

A large dark figure loomed into view, partially blocking the glare of the lightbulbs. "I don't know what the hell you're talking about, Marvelli." It was Krupnick, and there was a wiseass smirk in his voice. He reached in, grabbed Marvelli's arm, and pulled him into a sitting position.

Marvelli winced. He was cramped and stiff and sore all over.

"Give me a hand," Krupnick said, and two more silhouettes appeared, blocking out the rest of the light. "Sunny, you take his feet," he said. "Help me with this end, Dorie."

Hands were all over Marvelli, pulling him out of the trunk and setting him down on his feet. He felt light-headed and weak. He figured he had to be terribly dehydrated from all the sweating he'd done.

He blinked and shook his head, forcing himself to stay conscious. Even though the three faces were in shadow, he knew which one was Dorie from the blond halo that the lightbulbs put around her head. "Where's Loretta?" he asked her in a raspy voice. "Is she all right?"

"Don't waste your breath, my friend," Krupnick said. "We can't hear you."

"Why don't you unzip his mask?" Dorie suggested.

"Because I don't want to hear whatever it is he has to say," Krupnick replied.

But Dorie persisted. "Don't you think you're being a little cruel to him? I mean, enough is enough."

"Not yet," Sunny said, her voice clipped and cold.

"You heard the lady," Krupnick said with a wry snort. "She's the boss."

"But Marvelli seems like such a nice guy," Dorie said. "And Loretta really loves him. She told me so."

Marvelli's pulse jumped. He needed to know about Loretta.

"I don't want to see him getting hurt," Dorie said.

"Then don't look," Sunny said.

Dorie thought about that for a moment. "Okay," she said.

Marvelli winced. Dorie wasn't going to be any help.

Krupnick burst out laughing as if he'd just remembered a very good joke, one that he wasn't going to share. "Come on, let's get him inside," he said.

Sunny took Marvelli by one arm, Krupnick grabbed the other, and they forced him to walk up a short flight of concrete steps to the landing of a loading dock. The building attached to the loading dock was made of red brick and appeared to be an old factory. A big, gray green Dumpster was parked next to the car. It reminded Marvelli of a sleeping triceratops. A pale full moon was pinned to the sky, illuminating the alleyway.

"This way," Sunny said, and they turned him around. Shoe leather scraped on concrete as they led him to a rusted metal door. Sunny unlocked it with a key and shouldered it open. They hustled Marvelli down a harshly lit hallway with glossy, black-painted walls to another door. Sunny unlocked that one as well, and Marvelli was pushed inside.

Between the glaring lights and the restricting mask, Marvelli couldn't tell where he was. Sunny and Krupnick kept pushing and shoving him until he crashed into something hard. It knocked the wind out of him, and his knees buckled, but Sunny and Krupnick held him up and kept pushing him again, wanting him to go somewhere else. He couldn't have cooperated even if he'd wanted to. He was on the verge of blacking out.

"Wait! Wait!" Dorie shouted. "Take the mask off. He can't breathe. Can't you see?"

"Oh, all right," Krupnick said in annoyance. "Take it off."

Marvelli was spun around, and Sunny undid the strap around his neck and pulled the mask off. His eyes shot open, and he sucked in air as if he'd just come up from a deep dive. He scanned the room and saw that it was another dungeon, like Sunny's back at Krupnick's house, but this one was bigger and much better equipped with elaborate instruments of torture. The ceiling was at least two stories high. An iron maiden stood in one corner next to a full set of armor as if she were his lady. A narrow torture table like the one Sunny had used earlier that day was in an adjacent corner, but this one had a rack. An old-fashioned barber's chair fitted with restraints was set up in front of a makeup table. Marvelli turned his head and saw what he'd crashed into before. It was the centerpiece of the room, a large tiger's cage attached to cables that led up to a block and tackle on the ceiling. He followed the cables back down with his eyes. They were attached to a power winch that was bolted to the floor.

"In," Sunny said, shoving him roughly toward the open door of the cage.

"Hold on," Dorie protested, and she pushed her way past Sunny to unzip Marvelli's jumpsuit all the way to his navel.

"Thanks," he gasped. "It's hot in this thing."

"We know," Sunny hissed, and she shoved his chest with both hands. He stumbled backward, landing on his butt inside the cage and wrenching his wrists, which were still handcuffed behind him. The door slammed closed with a deafening clang that reverberated throughout the room and rattled the armor and his lady.

Sunny marched over to a neat rack of iron cattle brands and what looked like a big black iron wok. "Hey, this is what I need for *my* dungeon, Arnie," she said with envy and delight. "A scarification set. What do think? Should we scar him? Arnie? Did you hear what I said?"

But Krupnick was busy rummaging through the walk-in closet. "All right!" he declared as he came out holding up a pair of black leather pants. "I didn't think they made these in size forty-two." A black leather biker's jacket was slung over his shoulder. In his other hand he was holding a pair of greasy black jackboots.

"Here," Sunny said sarcastically, flinging the mask that Marvelli had been wearing. "Accessorize."

With his hands full, Krupnick caught the mask awkwardly against his chest. "Thanks," he said, unfazed by her sarcasm. "Don't mind if I do." He stripped down to his underpants and put on the complete leather outfit except for the mask, wearing the jacket zipped to the middle of his hairy chest. He fiddled with his crotch, getting himself adjusted. The pants had a codpiece where the fly should have been. "Hey, what do you think?" he asked, stuffing the mask into the jacket pocket. "Is this the new me or what?"

Sunny shook her head like a stern mommy.

"It looks nice," Dorie said. "But what's wrong with the old you?"

Krupnick ignored her and strutted over to the cage. "What do *you* think?" he said to Marvelli.

Marvelli looked up at him. "Black is very slimming. You look good."

"Thank you." Krupnick did a few turns, then sashayed over to the door. "I'll be back in a little while."

"What're we supposed to do until you get back?" Dorie asked.

Krupnick nodded at Marvelli. "Play with the Boy Toy. Sunny will show you how."

Sunny grinned malevolently, but Dorie just looked confused.

"But don't kill him," Krupnick said to Sunny. "Wait for me."

He sounded dead serious. He walked out the door, stomping hard in his new jackboots. The door slammed shut behind him, rattling the armor again.

Sunny stared at the armor.

This is nuts, Marvelli thought as he rolled over onto his knees, then climbed to his feet. *These people are nuts.*

"Come on," he said to the women. "Let's get serious here. Just let me out, and I won't press charges."

Sunny burst out laughing, but she was clearly forcing it.

"I don't think we can do that," Dorie said in a timid little voice. "Can we, Sunny?"

Sunny ignored her.

"Hey!" Marvelli shouted. "What the hell's your problem, Sunny?" He'd had just about enough of her crappy attitude. "Dorie asked you a simple question. You can't answer her?"

Sunny turned on her heel and stared at him, her bowl cut shushing over her cheek in the wake of her abrupt movement. She crossed her arms and let her glare burn into him like a laser beam. "What's *your* problem?"

"Spare me the attitude," he said. "I'm not impressed."

Sunny kept glaring at him. She started to circle his cage slowly.

"You know, you're the one with the problem," he said, turning in place so he could stay in her face. "I'm usually not this rude, but you deserve it."

Sunny's chest was rising and falling with her breathing.

"What the hell's wrong with you?" he said. "I've been trying to reason with you all day, but you're like some kind of sado-maso windup doll. All you know is one thing, how to hurt people, and I don't think you even enjoy it. You have to be just a little bit human to get off on that kind of stuff because if you can't relate to what other people are feeling, then it means nothing to you. It's just aerobics or . . . machinery."

Sunny was kneading her own biceps like a cat sharpening her claws.

"Marvelli?" Dorie said. "I wouldn't get her mad if I were you."

"Quiet," Sunny snapped.

"See, there you go again," Marvelli said. "What'd Dorie ever do to you that you have to treat her like this? Does Krupnick like her better? Is that it? You're jealous?"

"Marvelli, don't," Dorie pleaded in a pained whisper.

"No, I'm sorry, Dorie, but I'm not gonna shut up. Krupnick wants me dead and Sunny's just itching to do it for him. Well, let me tell you something, Sunny. I want to live, and I'm *gonna* live. You know why? 'Cause I can't die. I've got a daughter back home, and I've got Loretta, and I won't do that to them. Loretta wouldn't go dying on me, not if she could help it. That's 'cause we have something special together, something real. But that's something I don't think you'd understand, Sunny. You have to be a human being with human feelings to understand that kind of thing. Dorie, I think you'd better explain it to her 'cause she doesn't know what the hell love is—not real love." Marvelli's face was flushed, and his biceps were bulging. He looked like he was going to Hulk out and rip through the bars.

"I don't know what you're talking about," Sunny said. Her words were like droplets of water falling into a sizzling hot wok.

Dorie's brows were slanted back, and she was biting her bottom lip. "Marvelli," she squeaked, "I think you said the wrong thing."

Sunny could feel the tears welling in her eyes, but she kept her gaze locked on that bastard in the cage, refusing to let him or Dorie or anyone see her cry. No one would *ever* see her cry.

"Sunny?" Dorie said. "Say something, Sunny. You're scaring me."

And you're *annoying the hell out of me, Dorie,* Sunny thought.

But in fact she wished she could be like Dorie, a dizzy blonde who slid through life without a thought or a care or a qualm— *que sera sera.* Dorie didn't know what it was like to have a brain and heart and soul that all worked together. She didn't know about second thoughts and hard choices and fitting in. And she didn't know a thing about how hard it is to make love work. It just sort of happened for her. *Like, whatever.*

Well, it wasn't that way for Sunny. It was a full-time job for her. No, it was more like a vocation, like being a nun who had to pray to God every waking minute of the day, never knowing if she was getting through to Him. She didn't even know if she was getting a dial tone.

Sunny stopped circling and stood in front of the door to the cage, her feet apart, her stiletto heels nailed to the floor as she stared at Marvelli and fought back the tears.

These two didn't understand what it was like, she thought. They had no idea. They were straights. They were breeders, for chrissake. Sure, Dorie fooled around with women, but only if there was a man in bed, too. She never really got *involved* with women. She just floated through the experience and let things happen to her until she got her turn with the man. Then she was happy.

And Marvelli, what the hell did he know? He was vibrating on a *Brady Bunch* level, except that he took it all seriously. *Mr. Lovey-Dovey longing for his lovely large Loretta,* Sunny thought. *Oh, please! The man cannot be for real. No one loves anyone like that anymore. No one that I know of. Marvelli's living in a dream world. Love is negotiation, arrangement, and extortion. It's strategy and compromise. It's warfare. His lovely Loretta doesn't think about him the way he thinks about her. She couldn't. She's a woman. Marvelli is a dinosaur. People like him just don't exist anymore.*

But as she stared at him, she considered for a moment the impossible possibility that he *was* for real, that a few nice guys like this really did exist in the world.

Well, if they do exist, she thought, *then why haven't I found one? What's wrong with me? Why do I always have to be the freak? I'm tired of being the freak. I want to live in a big house in the Sonoma Valley with Agnes and Thaddeus. I want to open a mail-order business—lingerie, dom accessories, fantasy footwear. I want Dragon to run in open fields every day. I want to be freakin' normal for a change!*

She stared at Marvelli with venom in her eyes. *I hate you,* she thought. *I really, really, really hate you.*

She went to the door of the cage and unlocked it.

"What're you doing, Sunny?" Dorie asked.

"I'm going to put your friend here to the test."

Marvelli frowned. "What're you talking about?"

Sunny took off her jacket and threw it aside. "You're the poster boy for up-straight, monogamous, together-forever relation-ships, right? Well, I want to see how goody-two-shoes you are when opportunity comes knocking you over the head." She kicked off her boots and started to undo her jeans.

Marvelli's mouth dropped. "Don't come in here," he said.

"Tough," she said, as she pulled down her fly. "I am going to seduce you, Marvelli. I am going to *make* you cheat."

"No, you're not."

"Yes, I am," she said. "Your little wang-dang-doodle will stand up and salute the flag, and I'll just do the rest."

"Forget about it. It's not gonna happen."

She stared at his crotch and grinned. "Are you standing at attention right now, Marvelli? Are you thinking about it? Who are you thinking about? Me or your lovely Loretta?" Sunny pulled off her top and let it drop to the floor. "How about I unzip you and we find out what you're thinking?"

"No!" Marvelli said, backing up into the bars. "Stay out."

"It's gonna be good, Marvelli. I can promise you that. Why don't you just relax and go with it? Come on, face facts. You don't really love her the way you think you do."

"Stay out." Marvelli was up against the bars, squirming uncomfortably.

"Must be getting pretty tight down below," Sunny said. She opened the door and stepped in. The cage was just big enough for them to stand up in—or lie down.

"Get out, Sunny. This isn't funny."

"Who said anything about funny?" She was grinning from ear to ear, still staring at his crotch. "Let me just relieve some of that pressure for you."

"Dorie!" Marvelli called out. "Help me out here. Do something."

But Dorie was pulling her sweater over her head, her jeans already a puddle on the floor. "Hang on, Sunny," she said. "Wait for me."

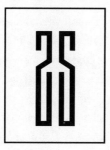

"I don't like this," Vissa said.

"Just play along," Loretta said out the side of her mouth. "Please?"

A full moon cast long shadows on the sidewalk as they stood outside an old brick building on the outskirts of San Francisco's Mission District. Most of the buildings on this block looked like they were abandoned, and so did this one, except that there was a long line of people waiting at the reinforced metal door, and a bouncer the size of Rhode Island standing guard, deciding who got in and who didn't. The man's head, face, and bulging arms were completely hairless, and Loretta wondered if he dipped himself in Nair every night.

"We are not going to pass," Vissa whispered into Loretta's ear. "This guy will never believe that we're lovers. And even if he does buy it, he's still not gonna let us in. We look too normal."

In fact the people waiting to get in didn't exactly look like the suburban Kmart crowd. There were three other couples in line before Loretta and Vissa. The pair of lipstick lesbians done up like

runway vampires couldn't keep their hands off each other. A thir-
tyish WASPy couple in riding boots and jodhpurs waited in icy
silence with their arms crossed over their chests. Occasionally she'd
thwap his bottom with her crop, and he'd look over and briefly
smile admiringly at her. Two very pretty young men in motorcycle
jackets and jackboots bitched and moaned loudly about the delay,
making catty remarks about the bouncer, whose main duty seemed
to be to ignore everyone around him.

"Let's just leave," Vissa said, letting go of Loretta's hand. "We
won't get in. And even if we do, then what? We don't even know
that Marvelli is in there."

Loretta grabbed Vissa's hand back. "Look, I'm not exactly
comfortable with this myself," she said. "But can we at least try?
For Marvelli's sake?" She was trying to look natural, deliberately
nuzzling shoulders with Vissa. Loretta had originally decided that
she should be the femme because Vissa had the leather jacket, but
now she was wondering if maybe they should switch roles. Loretta
had to admit she had more of a butch attitude even though her
outfit was pretty blah for this crowd—a white cotton blouse, jeans,
and loafers. She looked down at Dragon. Vissa was holding him
on the leash. At least they had him. He was basically back to his
old self, which made him a good accessory for a couple of sexual
adventurers. Now and then he'd still fuzz out, but a sharp tug
usually snapped him out of it.

"I wish we had a leather outfit for Dragon," Loretta murmured. "A nice studded collar would help our chances."

"Ask if you can borrow his," Vissa said, nodding at one of
the leather boys who was wearing a spiky dog collar around his
neck.

"Think I should?" Loretta asked.

"No, I don't."

Just then the metal door opened a few inches and Mr. Rhode
Island leaned into the crack. Someone was there, but Loretta could

see only the outline of a face. The bouncer nodded, and the door closed. Finally he acknowledged the people in line right in front of him. He narrowed his eyebrowless eyes and scrutinized the first four couples.

Loretta glanced at the vampire girls who were all over each other. They were a shoo-in.

"Kiss me," Loretta whispered urgently to Vissa.

Vissa reared back. "No way."

"Come on," Loretta pleaded. "We won't get in."

"Forget about it."

"Please?"

"No."

"Just a little one?"

But the bouncer had already made his choices. "You two." He pointed to the horsey couple. "You two." He pointed to the leather boys. "And you three." He pointed to Loretta, Vissa, and Dragon.

"Hey!" the taller of the two vampire girls protested.

"Yeah, hey!" the smaller one echoed. They both made faces and whipped their jet-black manes with maximum attitude. "What about us?"

The bouncer shook his head. "You two are too into each other. If you can't share, you don't belong here."

"We can share," they whined in unison like a couple of alley cats.

"Not tonight," the bouncer said.

They both gave him the finger in unison and clicked off on their stiletto heels.

"Now what?" Vissa whispered nervously.

"Just go with the flow," Loretta said under her breath as they shuffled toward the door.

"I don't share," Vissa said through gritted teeth.

"Just be open-minded." Loretta was just saying this to get

Vissa to go in. Deep down Loretta felt the same way Vissa did. If anyone so much as touched Loretta, she'd break his—or her—or its—arm.

As they passed the bouncer, Loretta could feel the thumping beat of industrial music coming from inside. She and Vissa followed the horsey couple through a narrow entryway that was lit with black lights, which made everyone's complexion purple. Another burly character with long lilac hair down past his shoulders stood at the next doorway at the end of the hall. "Twenty-five each," he said to the horsey couple.

"You pay," Loretta whispered to Vissa.

"Why me?"

"I'm the femme, you're the butch. You have to pay."

"You'd better pay me back," Vissa grumbled.

"Put it on your expense account," Loretta said. "Julius will reimburse you."

"I doubt it," Vissa mumbled. Having left her bag in the car to complete the butch look, she dug into her front pocket for some cash and paid the lilac-haired bouncer.

He counted the bills, then shook his head. "Him, too." He was pointing down at Dragon.

"You're kidding," Vissa said.

"We're capitalist pigs here. He could get his rocks off, too." He gave Dragon a scrutinizing look. "He's a male, right? Someone will definitely want him. Count on it."

As Vissa shelled out another twenty-five dollars, Loretta cringed inside. She wasn't going to let Dragon out of her sight. That was cruelty to animals.

They went through the entryway, and it was like falling through the looking glass. The heavy bass of the music pounded against Loretta's chest. A huge dark room with a jam-packed dance floor and a bar against one wall was lit only by red and blue revolving police lights and a few strategically placed white spotlights. Several crammed hallways led off the main room where people fought to get in and out like bees in a hive.

But it was the people themselves who Loretta couldn't get over. Run-of-the-mill flamboyant gays seemed downright normal compared to some of the freaks who wandered across the dance floor. Young guys with tattooed faces. Women with body piercings in places that made Loretta queasy. People with ritual scarification on their arms, legs, and faces. There were businessmen in expensive suits who could have been Lucifer's lawyers for all Loretta knew. And there were blonde bombshells so sexy Loretta wondered if they were really women. Even the ones Loretta could identify as transvestites made her envious, they were so pretty. There was lots of black leather around the room—miniskirts, motorcycle jackets, jeans, jumpsuits, boots. A woman in a leather bustier and a beehive hairdo was leading a skinny young man in a leather thong and combat boots around the room on a leash.

"Heel," she said in a cool commanding voice as she yanked on his collar. "Heel."

He rolled his eyes to her and smiled blissfully as he followed her orders faithfully.

Loretta looked down at Dragon. "You see that?" she said. "Learn something."

The dog just looked up at her with pitiful eyes that struggled to focus. He looked pathetic. This was no place to be when coming down from the kind of high he'd been on.

Vissa leaned into Loretta's ear. "Can we do this quick and get out of here?"

"Definitely," Loretta said. "I doubt that they'd take Marvelli out on the dance floor, but Sunny and Krupnick are sick people, so just to be sure, check out the guys in masks, especially the ones who're tied up."

Vissa nodded. "I'll check the halls on this side of the room. You take that side. I'll meet you back at the bar in a half hour."

"Fine," Loretta said. "But let me have Dragon. I look too normal without him."

Vissa handed her the leash and waded into the crowd. Loretta looked away for a second when she saw an Asian woman she thought might be Sunny passing by. It turned out to be someone else, but when Loretta looked back, Vissa had disappeared into the crush.

She took a deep breath and scanned the room. *Where do I begin?* she thought. But as she studied the crowd, she noticed that there was a guy dressed in a black leather jumpsuit and a matching mask, just like the outfit that Marvelli had been wearing back at Sunny's dungeon. He was handcuffed, and a heavy chain was padlocked around his neck, the free end held by a tall, curvaceous redhead in a tight red-vinyl cocktail dress. She could have been a man, but Loretta wasn't sure. The man in black and the woman in red had just come out of one of the hallways on Loretta's side of the room.

"Come on, Dragon," she said, tugging on his leash. "Heel." Loretta worked her way through the crowd, which wasn't easy with a dog coming off a bender, and snuck up behind the man in black.

She leaned into his ear. "Marvelli," she whispered. "Is that you?"

The masked man turned around and looked at her. "No, but I'll be anyone you want me to be as long as it hurts."

"Hey!" The redhead yanked on his chain. "No talking!"

The man whimpered like a pup.

"Down!" she commanded in a husky voice.

He got down on his knees, hands flat on the floor.

"Stay that way!"

He didn't budge.

The redhead looked down at Dragon and appraised him admiringly. "Nice dog," she said, raising her eyes to Loretta. "Has he been bad, too."

"Ah . . . yes," Loretta said. "Very."

"Good. You two have fun." She jerked the man's chain. "Stand up!"

He obeyed her command, and they went on their way, blending in with the rest of the freaks.

Loretta watched them go, still trying to figure out if the redhead was a man or a woman. She crouched down next to Dragon and held his head, forcing him to look her in the eye. "Listen to me, Dragon," she said. "This is serious. Find Sunny. *Find Sunny.*"

But the dog didn't like having his face held, and he squirmed out of her grasp.

Loretta grabbed him by the jowls, desperate to make him understand. It was starting to sink in that she might never see Marvelli again—at least not alive. "Dragon," she begged, tears coming to her eyes, "please listen to me. Go find Sunny. Find your mistress."

But Dragon whipped his head away, refusing to look at her.

She grabbed him again and raised her voice. "Go and find your mistress. Do you hear me? *Find your mistress.*"

"If you can't find her, will I do?"

Loretta looked up. A giant dominatrix was staring down at her. She was NBA height without her heels. The dominatrix reached down and stroked Loretta's cheek with the coils of a bullwhip.

"Stand up," the giant ordered.

26

"I am Mistress Mona," the giant dominatrix said imperiously.

Loretta stood up from her crouch, but she was still looking up at the towering monument to flesh, leather, and hair with a torpedo bustline that could easily take out an eye. The woman was wearing thigh-high, stiletto-heeled buccaneer boots, a black leather micro-miniskirt, and a shimmery black tube top. Her fingernails were little daggers, polished black to match her lipstick. She was wearing so much dark eye shadow and mascara she looked like she was wearing a Zorro mask. Her malevolently arched brows alone could have gotten her an audition for the part of a villainess in a Disney cartoon. Her hair was pulled up tight on top of her head with snaky banana curls cascading down to the middle of her bare back. She was rubbing Loretta's bicep with the coiled bullwhip.

"I'm glad to see that you take orders well," she said.

Loretta squinted at her. "What?"

Mistress Mona smacked her arm with the whip. "Don't talk back. I told you to stand and you stood. That's the kind of behavior I like. However, I don't tolerate talking back."

"Well, too freakin' bad," Loretta said.

The dominatrix smacked her again, harder this time.

"Hey!" Loretta said, pulling her arm away. "Cool it with that thing."

Mistress Mona moved like a cat, jabbing her thumbnail up under Loretta's chin and forcing her head back. "Your attitude needs a great deal of improvement, my dear. I'm going to have to ride you very hard. Him, too." She flipped the toe of her boot under Dragon's chin and clacked his jaws shut. The dog reared back and retreated behind Loretta's leg.

Loretta was fuming. "You touch him again and I'll make you eat that whip."

"Wrong," Mistress Mona thundered, brandishing her little daggers. "I shall make *you* eat this whip. And when I'm through, you will thank me. Is that understood?"

"Screw you," Loretta said, and she turned to go. But as soon as she turned away, the braided whip came over her head and was jerked tight around her neck.

"I did not dismiss you, you pathetic lump of lard," Mistress Mona said. "Face me and make that insipid mutt lick my boot."

Loretta turned around, the whip still looped around her neck. She spoke slowly and deliberately. "I realize that you think this is some sort of sex game and that I *want* you to do this. But I really don't want any part of this. I'm not playing the game. Get it? Now let go of me."

"Or else what?" Mistress Mona grinned like the Grinch and pulled the whip tight as if it were a bolo tie.

"You won't want to find out," Loretta said, ready to take her on.

"Really." Mistress Mona's face went deadpan. "What are you going to do?" she asked. "Sic Tinkerbell on me?" She kicked Dragon in the ribs hard enough to make him yelp.

That's it, Loretta thought. She grabbed the back of Mistress

Mona's hand and manipulated it in a move she'd learned from
Marvelli. He'd said it was something he'd learned when he used
to take aikido lessons, and it worked like a dream. With just a
twist of the wrist, she was able to apply an excruciating amount
of pain. Mistress Mona let out a wail and jumped back on her
toes as soon as she felt the torque. Loretta slipped out of the noose
but kept her grip on Mistress Mona's hand.

"Ooowww!" the big dominatrix yelled. "Let go! You're hurting me!"

"I know," Loretta said calmly, but she didn't let go.

"Come on!" Mistress Mona begged. "Please!"

She was hopping up and down, her banana curls boinging
along with her, backing up and bumping into people in an attempt
to avoid the pain. But there was no escape.

"Please!" she whined. "Please, please, *please!*"

Loretta finally let go. "I thought you liked pain," she said.

"Not that much pain." Mistress Mona was cradling her wrist
as she skulked off. The dominatrix was frowning deeply, her chin
crumpled, about to start bawling.

"Wuss," Loretta called after her.

"Loretta! Loretta!"

Loretta looked all around. She could hear someone calling to
her, but it was hard to tell where it was coming from because of
the loud pulsating music combined with the undercurrent of crowd
noise.

"Loretta! I need some help over here. Like right now."

Loretta finally spotted Vissa making her way across the dance
floor trailed by a swarm of four female impersonators. As they
came closer, Loretta could see that the four men were all Judy
Garland but at different stages of her career. One was done up as
Dorothy in *The Wizard of Oz*. Another one was wearing patent-
leather tap shoes, turned-down bobby sox, a yellow gingham dress,
and a yellow satin bow in her wig to be the young Garland when

she played opposite Mickey Rooney in the Andy Hardy movies. The third Garland was in petticoats, a floor-length skirt, and a long red wig with short bangs—Garland in *Meet Me in St. Louis.* The last one wore a short dark wig and a sparkly red slit-leg cocktail dress, Garland the Vegas headliner.

"Please, please, please, please!" they buzzed in unison, all of them reaching tentatively but persistently toward Vissa's hair.

"No!" Vissa shouted, trying to shield her head. But they weren't dissuaded.

Suddenly Dragon started to bark viciously, which startled everyone, including Loretta and Vissa. He was finally back to his old self. Dragon strained at the leash, and Loretta needed both hands to hold him back. The Garlands threw up their hands and backed away. Their four mouths were little lip-glossed O's.

"It's Toto," Dorothy exclaimed in both fear and joy.

"Ooooo, you're right," the young Garland said. "A bow and a big basket and he'll be perfect."

"We're not doing *Oz,*" *Meet Me in St. Louis* Garland complained, stamping her foot. "We have to do the old Judy. Just before she died."

"Yes," Garland the lounge act agreed. "The way she was on *The Jack Paar Show.* Simple skirt, white blouse, bow at the neck, dark hose, and black pumps."

"And smoking," Dorothy interjected.

"Yes, smoking," young Garland concurred.

Loretta looked at Vissa. "What the hell are they talking about?"

But *St. Louis* Garland answered for Vissa. "Look at that hair!" she screamed in ecstasy, pointing at Vissa's do. "It's already half-way there. All we have to do is deflate it a little, change the part, and it's perfect."

"Yes," the spangly Judy chimed in. "A little pancake to make her paler, and you've got it. Judy just before she kicked the bucket.

She's absolutely perfect. You just *have* to join us, honey. We'll be the Five Judies."

Vissa growled in Loretta's ear, "Get them away from me before I kill the bunch of them."

Loretta was trying not to laugh. She let out a little of Dragon's lead and broke up the bevy of Garlands. They fluttered their hands and scattered, fleeing out of Dragon's reach.

"Oh, you're such a party pooper," Dorothy snapped at Vissa as she departed. "It would've been so much fun."

"Yeah," the other three agreed in unison.

Vissa glared at them in silence as they huffed off.

"Why don't we stay together and look?" Vissa suggested.

"That might be a good idea," Loretta said. "Come on, Dragon." Loretta started to walk, but she was abruptly halted by the leash. Dragon had planted himself like an anchor. "Come on, boy," she said, tugging on the leash, but the dog wasn't moving.

Dragon was down on his front paws, butt in the air. His lips were curled back over his gums as if he were growling, but he wasn't making a sound.

"What's the matter, boy?" Loretta asked. "The Garlands are gone. It's okay."

But then she saw what was bothering Dragon. Another man in a black leather mask and a black leather motorcycle jacket was standing a few feet away, staring at Loretta and Vissa. He had a considerable gut and gray chest hairs showed under the jacket, so Loretta knew it wasn't Marvelli. The man seemed to be unfazed by Dragon's snarl.

"What the hell's this guy's problem?" Loretta whispered to Vissa.

"I don't know," she said, her gaze locked to his.

Loretta was getting a little tired of this S&M nonsense, so she went right up to him. "Is there something you want?" she said point blank.

The man didn't answer, but he angled his head slightly, and suddenly the static features of the mask seemed to take on a curious expression.

Goose bumps crawled up Loretta's arms.

The masked man opened his black-gloved palm. "Dance?" he asked.

Loretta was flummoxed. "I . . . I don't think so."

"Dance?" he repeated. He left his palm out.

27

Marvelli had his back against the bars of the cage. Sunny was stepping inside, coming toward him with Dorie right behind her. Dorie had a vague look on her face, but Sunny's eyes were keen, her nostrils flared.

"What're you doing, Sunny?" he said. "You're making me nervous."

But Sunny didn't answer. She just kept coming closer.

"It's getting kinda crowded in here," he said. "This cage wasn't meant for three people."

"Sunny?" Dorie said. "Are you thinking what I'm thinking?"

Sunny didn't answer her, either.

"You're gonna share, aren't you, Sunny?" Dorie persisted. "You're not gonna keep him all to yourself, are you?"

"Nope," Sunny finally said, her voice a low rumble in her chest. "I'm gonna give a piece to everyone who wants one."

Marvelli clenched his fists and fought the handcuffs. "What're you talking about?"

"Think of this as your wedding day," Sunny said to him, "and you're the wedding cake. Everybody gets a piece. Starting with me." She was right in front of him now, almost nose to nose. She laid a finger on his chest and slowly ran it down his torso until she got to his crotch where she stopped to poke and prod and feel the expanding merchandise through his leather pants. "Well, I see what's on your mind," she said with a humorless grin. "And I thought you were such a good boy, so loyal to your dear Loretta."

Dorie peeked over her shoulder and gazed down at his bulging crotch, "Oh, don't take it all, Sunny. Please?"

"So tell me," Sunny said, breathing into Marvelli's face. "Have you been thinking about it all day? Imagining what it would be like to do it with me? Or with Dorie? Or maybe with both of us? See, I didn't think you were that good. No man is."

Marvelli was sweating. "Hang on, hang on, hang on," he said, trying to get his mind straight. "You're all wrong about this. It's not what you think."

"It's not what I think?" Sunny said incredulously, weighing the heft of his merchandise in her hand. "What do you mean it's not what I think? Look down. What else could it be? Men don't think about anything else."

"Stop," he said. "You're wrong. I'm not hard because of you."

"You're not?" Sunny stuck out her bottom lip, pretending to be hurt. "Then it must be Dorie you want."

"No, no, no. It's not her, either."

Sunny laughed at him. "You don't expect me to believe that you're thinking about your dear Loretta and she's the one responsible for this?"

"No," he said. "Even though it's none of your business, it's not her, either."

A smile of glee broke out on Sunny's face. "So you're just a plain old horn dog, just like the rest."

"Well, yes," he said. "And no."

"Self-serving obfuscation," Sunny said accusingly.

Dorie looked puzzled. "What's that?"

"It's typical male behavior," Sunny said. She looked Marvelli in the eye. "But I'm sure you'd disagree."

"Well, no. Not exactly," he said.

"See what I mean?" Sunny gave his jewels a squeeze.

Marvelli winced. "Easy."

"Why? You don't like it rough?"

"You know, I don't mean to pry," Marvelli said, "but someone must've hurt you bad at one time in your life. Am I right about that?"

Sunny scowled. "This is not about me."

"I don't know about that," Marvelli said. "You're the one doing all the doing. It seems to me you're working something out here, something that's bothering you, something deep-seated."

"Gosh, you think so?" Dorie asked, wide-eyed.

"Yeah, Dorie." Marvelli nodded. "I do think so."

"Quiet!" Sunny snapped. "Both of you. This is about him," she said to Dorie. "Him and his lust to have every woman who comes on his radar screen. Right, Marvelli? Say what you want, but this little guy doesn't lie." She squeezed him hard and made Marvelli flinch.

Marvelli glanced down at himself, checking for damage. "What're you picking on him for?" he asked. "He never did anything to you."

"No, but he wants to."

"Of course he wants to," Marvelli admitted. "But not really. It's just a thought. You don't act on all your thoughts, do you?"

"There you go again. Obfuscating."

"That's not obfuscating. That's just being a guy. That's the way guys are."

"Bull."

Dorie tried to shoulder her way past Sunny. "What do you mean, Marvelli? I don't understand."

Marvelli was holding his breath. "Tell Sunny to loosen her grip and I'll tell you."

"Sunny?" Dorie said with a pleading high note.

Sunny stopped squeezing, but she kept her hand on his goods. "Go ahead. Talk," she said. "I want to hear this."

Marvelli took a deep breath, then looked down at Sunny's hand. "Do you *have* to keep your hand there?" he asked her.

"Yes."

He sighed. "You don't *really* have to."

"Stop stalling," Sunny snarled. "Explain your miserable self."

"Well . . ." He looked at Dorie. She was an easier audience. "See, women think that all men think with the little guy in their pants. But that's not exactly true. It's really a circuitry problem."

"You mean, like electricity?" Dorie asked.

"Yeah, very similar," he said. "Men have weird circuitry. The little guy's connected to the brain, and the brain's connected to the heart, but the heart isn't connected to the little guy. But in women it's different. You're all wired up right. We aren't."

"You're tap dancing, Marvelli," Sunny said with a deadpan expression. "And you're no Fred Astaire."

"No, no, you think about it," he said. "Women are big on their feelings. Men aren't. Why? Because you're connected directly to your hearts, and we're not."

Sunny scowled at him. "This is bull."

"No, listen to him," Dorie said. "I think he's on to something. I don't think Barry or Arnie really feel anything for me. Marvelli, are you saying that men *can't* have real feelings for women?"

"No, that's not what I'm saying. A man can love a woman, but it has to go through his brain first. See, we can't make that direct feeling connection the way you can."

Sunny squeezed him again. "Your little guy seems to be pretty chubby right now," she said. "What kind of connection do you call this?"

"Just the normal horny guy connection. It doesn't mean anything. It's just him and the brain testing the circuits, thinking things up, imagining this and that."

Sunny smirked. "Like imagining a threesome with me and Dorie?"

"Sure, of course," Marvelli admitted. "But that doesn't mean anything."

"Oh, no. Why not?"

"Because my heart isn't involved. Sure, you can pull down my pants and seduce me, easy as pie. And the little guy'll be right there leading the charge. But that's not love. I'm not even sure if it qualifies as sex. It's just mechanics."

Sunny looked skeptical. "Are you telling me that if we seduce you, it won't mean anything?"

"Sure, it will mean *something*, but not what you think. It won't change what's in my heart because there's no connection there. Women fall in love all the time, but guys don't. They just get horny. That's why it's only a special woman who can get to a guy's heart, and it doesn't happen very often for guys. For me it only happened twice in my life. All right, maybe three times, but high-school romances don't count."

"Who were they?" Dorie asked. If she were at a movie, she would have been on the edge of her seat.

"My first wife and Loretta," he said. "That's it."

Sunny clenched her teeth. "You are so full of it, Marvelli, I'd like to slap you silly."

"Don't!" Dorie protested, getting in her way. "I've never met a man who could talk about his feelings this way. We should let him go."

"The hell we will," Sunny said. "Can't you see this is just another load of man crap? This is the kind of stuff they do all the time. They have no genuine emotions, only theories and plans. Why do you think they love computers? Why do they love to read history? It's because they're schemers, always trying to figure out how to get into some woman's pants!"

"Come on, Sunny," Dorie said. "You don't believe that. You have Thaddeus. He has feelings for you."

Sunny exploded. "Thaddeus has nothing to do with this!"

Dorie wrinkled her brow. "He didn't do it again, did he? He's not playing around with that sword swallower, is he?"

"Shut up, Dorie."

"I'm so sorry, honey. I thought you and he and Agnes had gotten things straightened out."

Sunny's face was flushed. "Enough!"

"You know, maybe Thaddeus should talk to Marvelli. He's very sensitive. He might be able to clue Thaddeus in to a few things."

Sunny screamed at the top of her lungs. "Dorie, will you please shut your goddamn mouth?"

Dorie just stared at her for a few moments. "I can do that," she said in a small voice. "If that's what you want."

"That's what I want," Sunny said.

Marvelli coughed. "I don't mean to pry, but who are these people you're talking about?"

Sunny gritted her teeth and dug her fingers into his crotch. "If you must know, Mr. Nosy, they're people who piss me off almost as much as you do. But not quite."

Marvelli doubled over in pain. "Easy, Sunny," he gasped. "Easy."

"I don't give a damn about your circuitry theories, Marvelli. All I care about is screwing up you and your friend Loretta. I am going to ride you like you've never been ridden before, and you're going to enjoy every last second of it. You'll get to know what true ecstasy is. And even if you never tell your little Loretta about it, it'll always be there in the back of your mind, throbbing away like a little lump of cancer. You'll feel guilty about it, but you'll feel denied, too. You're gonna want me in your dreams. But you'll be stuck with her, constantly wondering why she can't be more like me."

Marvelli was holding his breath against the pain. "Does that mean you're *not* gonna kill me?" he grunted.

A half smile pierced one of Sunny's cheeks. "Who knows? Death might be part of the ecstasy. But don't worry. I'll make sure that Loretta finds out that you died happy."

Marvelli sucked in a short breath. "Sunny, let's consider the consequences."

"Let's not," she said. "Dorie, pull down his pants."

Krupnick stared at Vissa and Loretta through the eye holes of his mask. It felt as if he were behind a one-way mirror or a door with a peephole. Even the throng of deviants flailing on the dance floor and the relentless pounding of the music seemed to be in another room. He could see all of them, but they couldn't see him. Not the real him.

He was grinning behind the mask, but they couldn't see that, either. The slightly dazed look on Vissa's face particularly amused him. The chemistry was still there, he thought. She didn't know it was him, but the pheromones were cooking. He just had that effect on some women. They were his to be had.

Loretta, on the other hand, was another story. She was glaring at him suspiciously. She wasn't the seducible kind.

High testosterone, he guessed. *A born alpha, too. Look at how she keeps control of Dragon. Only Sunny can make Dragon mind like that. And like Sunny, Loretta must think a little bit like a man. And that makes her dangerous,* he thought.

Loretta spoke up over the thump of the music. "So what're we supposed to do, play charades with you?" She turned to Vissa. "Come on, let's go."

"Wait a minute," Vissa said. Her eyes were fixed on him. "I want to talk to this guy."

Loretta curled her upper lip. "Why?"

"I don't know. I just have a feeling about him."

Indeed you do, Krupnick thought. *You had a feeling about me eight years ago, and I guess you still do.*

He indicated the dance floor with his open palm. "Dance?" he said again, lowering his voice.

Loretta leaned into Vissa's ear, but he could still hear her. The acoustics in here were a miracle of science. The music was loud, but it was all up on the ceiling, which made conversation possible. After all, most people had to talk in order to seduce.

"Do you think that's—? You know." Loretta was trying to be subtle.

Krupnick began to grind his molars, his anger rising steadily like mercury in a thermometer. For a brief moment he'd lost sight of the fact that both women knew that Arnie Bloomfield was Ira Krupnick. He had to get rid of them, too. With Marvelli it was going to be a big night, he thought.

Dragon looked up at him, tilting his head to one side.

How cute, Krupnick thought, gazing down at him. *You know who I am, don't you, boy? Guess I'm going to have to take care of you, too. Too bad. I always thought you were kind of a neat dog.*

"Dance? No?" he asked Vissa.

Loretta piped up before Vissa could answer. "Take your mask off first."

He shook his head, imagining how creepy the mask's expressionless features must look. "Later," he said.

"It's Krupnick," Loretta said vehemently. She was staring him straight in the eye.

A true alpha, he thought.

"I don't think so," Vissa said. "Krupnick's not that heavy."

He frowned behind the mask but then grinned. It didn't matter what he looked like now. He'd be someone else soon enough, maybe someone really cut this time. With six-pack abs. He liked that idea.

"Let me just talk to him," Vissa said to Loretta. "Alone." Vissa stepped toward him.

Krupnick's grin widened. *That's my girl.*

Loretta started to object. "But, Vissa—"

"Just stay here with the dog. I'll be right back."

Sure you will, Krupnick thought, as he backed into the crush on the dance floor, motioning Vissa forward with his curled fingers, his gaze locked on hers like a cobra.

She followed him. He lifted his arms over his head and made some minimal dance moves as he stepped backward, cutting a path through the dancers. She made some halfhearted dance moves herself. He wondered if she was scared or just cautious.

He kept stepping backward until they had crossed the dance floor and entered one of the hallways. Harsh red lights glared from the ceiling, turning Vissa into a she-devil. The booming music echoed down the hallway, bouncing off the hard surfaces. She stayed with him, but she stopped dancing. He kept on dancing, still moving backward, people squeezing sideways to let him by. When he found the door he wanted, he stopped walking but kept swinging his shoulders to the beat.

"Ira?" she asked. "Is that you?"

He loved the look on her face. It was so many things all mixed together—anger, vulnerability, curiosity, hope. "I want to talk to you," he said as he reached for the doorknob.

"Ira?"

He opened the door and stepped inside.

"Ira? Is that you? Answer me." The same mix of emotions was in her voice as she followed him in.

The room was stark—an unmade king-size bed, a pole lamp with a pleated shade, and a rust-colored area rug were the only things in it. He went over and sat on the bed.

"I thought you wanted to talk," Vissa said. She had barely come into the room.

He pulled off the mask and tossed it onto the tangle of sheets on the bed. "You guessed right," he said. "It's me."

He wiped the sweat off his face. She stared at him. He stared back.

"Close the door," he said.

"Why?"

"So we can talk."

She hesitated, but she did it. Then she just stood there as if she were afraid to approach him.

"I know what you're thinking," he said. "I'm sorry."

She stepped toward him, anger taking over the mix of emotions in her expression. "You were supposed to meet me in Cape May. What happened?"

He shrugged. "That was eight years ago, Vissa. Things happened."

"What do you mean, 'things happened'? We'd made plans, Ira. I'd arranged it so you could escape from the Jump Squad so that we could be together. You were supposed to meet me in Cape May the next week. That was the plan. What happened, Ira? I waited for you."

He shrugged.

"I . . ." She looked away, almost too embarrassed to say it. "I thought you said you loved me." She turned around and looked at him, her eyes moist.

"I did love you," he said.

"Did," she repeated in a monotone. "Meaning you don't any-more."

He rubbed his face. "Sit down, Vissa." He patted the bed.

"Why?"

"Because I don't want you so far away."

She stared at his face—searching for signs of sincerity, he assumed. Reluctantly she stepped forward and sat on the edge of the bed, her back half-turned away from him.

"This is nuts," she muttered. "I should have my head examined."

"I'm sorry," he said. "I never wanted to hurt you. Things just happened."

She whipped her head around and glared at him. "Stop saying that," she snapped, and immediately turned away again.

She wasn't looking at him. He let his hand slide off his thigh onto the rumpled top sheet. His grip closed on a fistful of material.

"I guess there's not much I can say." He sounded contrite as he took the sheet in both hands, twisting it.

Even though he couldn't see her face, he could tell from the bend of her neck that she was crying. "I really loved you, Ira," she said, almost in a whisper.

"Well . . ." He paused, twisting the sheet tighter. "I didn't."

He whipped the sheet across his body like a cape and threw the twisted end over Vissa's head, yanking it tight and hauling her backward. The unfurled part covered her head and one of his shoulders.

"Ira—!" She tried to plead with him, but he pulled harder, cutting off her voice. She struggled, but she was almost on her back, and she couldn't get her fingers under the sheet to get it off her windpipe. She tried to throw her legs over her head and kick him, but he stood up and rode over her, clenching his arms and pulling until his fingers ached.

His arms started to shake. He held her like that for what seemed like a very long time, afraid to let up, afraid that she'd still be alive. His fingers were cramped and aching, but he still hung on. He'd never done this before, so he didn't know when to stop. What if he screwed it up?

Finally he decided it was enough. He let go, and her body toppled to the floor in a contorted heap. The sheet was still covering her head.

Krupnick stared down at her, his face as immobile as the mask, his heart pounding.

Well, that's done, he thought.

Loretta tried to make it across the dance floor, but once again the leash abruptly stopped her. Dragon wasn't cooperating. He was sitting on his haunches, refusing to move.

"Come on, Dragon. Let's go. Come on, boy. You can do it." But her enthusiastic tone didn't sway him. He stayed where he was, planted like a rock.

She yanked on the leash, but it didn't seem to have any effect on him. He wasn't going to move.

"What is it?" she said. "The people dancing? Don't mind them. They're just a bunch of perverts. I'll protect you."

But when she tugged on the leash, he didn't respond at all. He was like a cast-iron statue of a dog.

She pressed her lips together and stared down at him sternly. "Listen to me, pal. You're not gonna win this. I can out-stubborn any dog any day."

Dragon wasn't even looking at her.

She hunkered down and got on his level. Gyrating hips and dancing feet were all around her. "Hey," she said, "look at me. *Look at me.*" She grabbed his jowls with both hands and forced him to look at her. "I don't have time for your little moods. Do you understand me? Vissa's out here with some nut in a mask who can't say more than one word at a time. She shouldn't be alone with him."

Dragon flailed his head to get out of her grip. He didn't want to listen.

She grabbed his jowls again. "Listen to me, mister. Either you start cooperating or I'll leave you here. The Garland girls will find you, and they'll put a bow around your neck, stick you in a basket, and make you sing show tunes."

But Dragon couldn't be threatened. He kept struggling to get loose.

Loretta frowned at him. She was worried about Vissa, but she didn't have the heart to abandon Dragon. He was a pain in the butt, but she'd come to like him. She glanced up at the dancers, looking for Vissa and the masked man, but she didn't see them. She stood up to get a better look, scanning the pulsating mass of bodies. Heads were bobbing, sweaty hair was flying, bare breasts were jiggling, arms were pumping, but there was no sign of Vissa.

Dragon still sat on his haunches. His wrinkly face was inscrutable.

"Dragon, please," she begged. "For once just do what I ask you. Trust me."

"Have you tried Vaseline?" a man within earshot asked. His words were a little garbled because he had a bit in his mouth that was attached to a bridle. He was down on all fours and naked, wearing a small brown leather saddle on his bare back. A snooty-looking blonde in riding boots and jodhpurs but nothing on top was sitting in the saddle. It took a moment for Loretta to realize that this was the WASPy couple who'd been in line with her and Vissa. "I know exactly how he feels," the horse man confided to Loretta.

The blonde clicked her tongue and dug her heels into her mount's naked thighs. He neighed and reared, then obediently rode

on. The couple had already disappeared into the crowd by the time
Loretta realized what the horse man had been suggesting she do
with the Vaseline.

"Oh, yuck," she said to Dragon, squatting down and petting
him. "These people are sicker than I thought."

"Dance?"

She looked up. The masked man was standing over her, but
Vissa wasn't with him.

"Where's my friend?" Loretta asked, standing up to face him.

"Dance?" he asked again.

"Where did my friend go?" Loretta wanted an answer.

"Dance?" He was indicating the dance floor with his open
hand. His head was tipped to one side, his eyes glinting through
the holes in the mask.

Loretta stared at him. "Where's my friend?" she demanded.

"Dance?" The static features of the leather face seemed to
mock her.

"Take me to my friend right now, or I'll sic the dog on you."

He pitched his head the other way as if he were considering
her request. "Then dance?" he asked.

The masked man started to wade into the crowd on the dance floor, but Loretta hung back. Oddly Dragon, who wouldn't budge before, was curious about the man, walking toward him and stretching out to sniff him.

"Sit," Loretta commanded, but Dragon didn't listen.

The masked man came back and bent down to let Dragon sniff the back of his gloved hand. He knew not to approach the dog palm down, and he was patient enough to wait for Dragon to come to him. When Dragon started licking his hand, the man scratched under the dog's chin.

Loretta watched all this, wanting to stay suspicious but finding it difficult now that she saw how good he was with Dragon.

How bad could this guy be? she thought. *He likes dogs.*

But then she remembered the WASPy man's Vaseline comment.

Dragon jumped up on the masked man's thigh, and he ruffled the dog's ears.

"No!" Loretta said, pulling the leash to get Dragon down. "Look, would you just tell me where my friend Vissa is?"

"You looking for the same person she is?" he asked.

Loretta narrowed her eyes. "Did she tell you that?"

"Yeah." He presented the back of his hand to Dragon, and the dog came right to him.

"We're looking for the woman who owns this dog," Loretta said. "An Asian woman."

"I know her," the man said matter-of-factly.

"Really?" *Or was he just saying this?* she thought.

"Really. I do."

"What's her name?" Loretta asked.

"I dunno."

"I thought you said you knew her."

"I don't know her name."

Loretta shook her head in frustration. "Save the bull for somebody else. Okay?" She started to walk away.

"I know the dog's name," he offered, and that stopped her.

"Oh, yeah? What is it?"

"Dragon," he said.

Loretta thought back, trying to remember if she'd called Dragon by name in the man's presence, but she wasn't sure.

"Why don't you take off the mask so we can talk?" she said.

"We can talk this way."

"But I can't see your face."

"So."

"How do I know you're being straight with me?"

"How will you know if you see my face? Either way I could be lying."

"True," she admitted.

"Anyway, I'm shy," he said.

"Get out."

"Because I'm ugly."

Loretta looked at him, trying to imagine what could be behind the mask. A burn victim? A gross deformity? Maybe he was really handsome, and he just thought he was hideous. "Is this like a Beauty and the Beast thing?" she asked.

"I'm not sure I know what you mean."

"Never mind," she said. "Would you just take me to Vissa?"

"Only if you dance with me first."

"Come on. I don't have time for this."

"That's the deal," he said. "I come here for fun."

She concentrated on his unzipped mouth hole, looking for signs of a smarmy grin, but the hole wasn't big enough to reveal the shape of his mouth. But his comment got her to thinking. He was here for fun. And so was she, supposedly. If she got too huffy with him, she might draw attention to herself. Several bouncers in black muscle shirts patrolled the outskirts of the dance floor, plowing paths through the crowd as wide as their huge shoulders. They hardly looked human, and she had a feeling they didn't hesitate to eject troublemakers and frauds.

"All right," she said to the masked man. "One dance, then you take me to Vissa."

"Deal," he said, and immediately he started to move to the music.

Loretta had no choice but to do the same, hanging on to the leash and keeping her arm movements minimal so as not to upset Dragon too much. They edged their way toward the middle of the dance floor where a couple in drag—the guy dressed like Ginger Rogers, the woman like a Nazi SS officer—were taking up more than their share of space, doing a graceless fascist tango.

Loretta avoided making eye contact with the masked man as they danced—why encourage him? she figured—but she did notice how he moved. For a big man, he danced very well—not wild and frantic like a lot of the people here. He was very rhythmic, especially in the hips. Most men dance with their shoulders and arms, but the masked man danced mostly from the waist down with his arms suspended over his head. He didn't move his feet a whole lot, but those hips—they just kept on going. After a while she realized she was staring at him below the belt, so she looked away self-consciously.

He closed the distance between them and leaned into her face. "I like the way you dance," he said.

She didn't know how to take that. It was definitely a come-on, but she wasn't sure how strong a come-on it was, so she didn't answer him. Instead she just flashed a little grin of recognition and hoped that he didn't take it as anything more. All she wanted was for him to take her to Vissa, then get lost.

Dragon leaped up on her thigh, upset by the commotion going on around him. He let out a pitiful whine, begging Loretta to stop dancing and pay attention to him. She looked at the masked man, raised her palms, and shrugged. "He's getting crazy," she said, implying that she wanted to stop.

"The deal is a dance," he said. "A *whole* dance."

She didn't want to argue with him. *Just give him his damn dance,* she thought. She scratched Dragon's head as she swayed to the music, hoping to placate the dog until the song was over.

But the song went on and on, and Loretta thought that maybe one song had segued into another and she hadn't realized it. The music was techno, and it was so repetitious and heavy on the bass and drum machines, it was hard to tell where any song started or ended. She gave it a few more minutes, then she waved her hand in front of the man's mask.

"That was more than a song's worth," she said. "Let's go find Vissa."

"Okay," he said without an argument. "This way." He squeezed through the crush, clearing a way for Loretta and a very skittish Dragon.

Awfully cooperative for a pervert, Loretta thought. *Though it makes sense for a masochist.*

He led the way to a hallway on the far side of the room. The corridor was lit with red lightbulbs, which made it hard for Loretta to see what was down there. When the masked man stepped in, he instantly turned red. Loretta went to follow him, but Dragon balked and tried to tow her back.

"Come on, Dragon," she said encouragingly. "It's okay, boy. They're just lights." But her sweet urgings had no effect on him, and she had to yank on his leash and drag him in. He jumped and fought like a marlin with a hook in its mouth, biting the leash and thrashing his head, but Loretta was determined. A strong jerk on the leash plunged Dragon into the red wash. The dog's legs stiffened. Like all dogs, he was probably color-blind, but he could definitely see that something wasn't right. He looked down at his feet, then turned his head and inspected his flanks. He was shocked and baffled by his appearance.

"This way," the masked man called to her. He was down at the other end of the hallway.

Loretta pulled on the leash and followed him. The red lights were so glaring it was like walking in a fog. Dragon didn't fight her this time. He was so spooked by the lights he walked right up against her leg, afraid to lose contact with her.

The masked man turned a corner and disappeared.

"Hey, wait up," Loretta called to him, but he didn't respond.

She picked up her pace to catch up with him. But when she turned the corner, there he was, just a few feet away, standing in front of an open doorway.

"In here," he said.

Loretta walked up to the doorway and peered inside. It looked like a bedroom, sparsely furnished with just a bed, a lamp, and a rug. She squinted to get a better look through the red glare, but finally she had to step inside so she could see.

"So where's Vissa?" she asked the man.

"I'll be right back," he said as he abruptly slammed the door shut in her face.

She reached for the doorknob, but she could hear the dead bolt turning before she could twist it. She tried the knob anyway, but it was no use.

"Crap," she cursed.

Dragon looked up at her and emitted a hopeless little whine.

"It's okay, boy," she said, getting down on one knee and putting her arm around his neck. "We'll get out of here. He's just an old weirdo. Don't worry about him."

She led Dragon to the bed and sat down on the edge. "Never gonna find Marvelli," she muttered, letting out a long sigh. Tears welled in her eyes.

She sniffed and looked around the room. One wall had floor-to-ceiling glass panels, which she'd initially thought were mirrors. It was solid black on the other side of the glass. She ruffled Dragon's ears. "So what kind of place is this?" she said. "Huh, boy?"

Suddenly a horrendous clanking sound rattled the room, startling the two of them. It sounded like metal riot gates being lifted from a storefront. As it turned out, the glass panels were backed by rolling steel gates that slowly lifted up and out of sight. Loretta ventured over to the glass and cupped her hands to look out. A crowd of men, most of them young, were gathered on the other side, staring in at her.

A pasty-faced young guy with a crooked Charlie Chaplin mustache poked his buddy in the ribs. "Hey, hey, hey! Look at this. Doggie style."

"Haven't seen that in a while," his lanky, completely bald friend commented. "They usually use big dogs, though. He looks a little small for her."

"You never know with dogs," the pasty-faced guy said. "Anyway, it ain't the meat, it's the motion."

Loretta could hear everything they were saying through a speaker mounted on the wall. She pointed her finger in the pasty-faced guy's face. "That's not funny, pal. I'm in trouble in here. We're locked in. Somebody help us. Come on."

"Ah, damsel-in-distress action," another young guy said. He was wearing a porkpie hat pulled down low over his brow. "I like it. Tell us more, sweetie."

"This isn't a show," she yelled. "I'm in real trouble here."

"Yeah, I know. Keep talking." The guy in the hat was practically salivating.

An old guy with a nose like a hot pepper piped up. "Why don't you ask Rin Tin Tin to help you out?" The whole crowd burst out laughing.

"I'm not kidding around," she said. "I really need help. I'm locked in."

The men grinned and nodded. They thought this was an act, that she and Dragon were their live peepshow.

"Come on," she wailed in frustration. "I have to get out of here. Someone's in trouble. He needs my help. Get me out of here."

"Hey," the tall bald guy said. "I thought this was supposed to be S&M. That's what it said on the door. This sounds like a freakin' soap opera."

"Stay tuned, my friend," the old guy said. "Ecstasy comes in the waiting."

"You are all disgusting. Every one of you!" Loretta shouted at the top of her lungs. "I hope your things all shrivel up and fall off. It'll serve you right."

"Oh, I like this one. I like her a lot," the old guy said, his eyes sparkling with glee. "She'll be good. I can tell. She's got spunk."

"Hey, spunk this!" Loretta yelled, shaking her fist at him.

The men howled. They were having a ball.

Dragon was hiding under the bed.

"Honey's I'm home!" Krupnick slammed the door behind him as he strode into the dungeon, pulling his mask off as he went. "Oh, that feels good," he said with relief. His beard was drenched with sweat.

Then he noticed what was going on inside the cage. "Hey!" he shouted, glaring at the three of them. "What the hell's going on in there?"

Dorie and Sunny were in with Marvelli. The top of Marvelli's jumpsuit was peeled down, his bare chest exposed. Dorie's blouse was open, and as usual, she wasn't wearing a bra. Sunny was dressed, but she had her hand on Marvelli's crotch.

Krupnick stomped over to the cage. "What the hell do you think you're doing?" he yelled.

Sunny lobbed a bored look at him. "What does it look like we're doing?"

"We're trying to seduce Marvelli," Dorie announced cheerily. "But he's *so* good, I can't believe it. It's like he's saving himself for Loretta. Isn't that incredible?"

Yeah, freakin' incredible, Krupnick thought as he stared in at the three of them.

"I thought I told you to wait until I got back," he said to Sunny.

Sunny shrugged, totally unconcerned.

"I have something else I want you to do," he said, forcing himself to calm down. "Come out of there and I'll tell you. You, too, Dorie."

Sunny bristled. "I *give* orders. I don't take them."

"You'll like this," he said, arching a mischievous eyebrow.

The women ducked their heads as they filed out of the cage, Sunny taking her sweet time. Marvelli tried to follow them, but Krupnick shut the door in his face.

"Chill, my friend," Krupnick said. "I'll get to you in a minute." He led Sunny away from the cage, Dorie trailing behind.

"Listen," he said to Sunny, lowering his voice. "I have something I want you to do. I've got Marvelli's chubby girlfriend locked up in the peep room down the hall, the one on the left. Why don't you go down and bruise her a little? Maybe shed a little blood. There's an audience waiting. I think they'd really get into a snuff ending."

"Snuff?" Dorie dove into the space between them. "As in snuff films? That's when someone actually gets killed, isn't it? You can't do that. Loretta's—"

Krupnick's anger suddenly got loose, and he backhanded Dorie across the mouth. Rage clanged through his brain like a gong. He'd been trying to stay cool, but it just got away from him. He'd hit Dorie so hard she stumbled back and fell, landing flat on her butt. She clutched her jaw and stared up at him in horror, momentarily torn between emotional pain and physical pain, unable to respond to either.

He glared down at her, ready to explode again. But he knew he had to calm down and keep a lid on it, at least for the time being. He intended to kill Dorie along with the others, but he couldn't do it now. First he had to take care of Loretta and Marvelli, then Sunny, then Dorie, then the dog. Maybe Dragon before Dorie and Sunny. Dragon listened to them so he might try to protect them, and Krupnick didn't want to get into dealing with a mad dog. That could mess up the crime scene. What he had to do was make it look like a great big rough sex party, right here in the dungeon. There would be witnesses to Loretta's murder in the peep show, of course, and Sunny's rep for violence and cruelty was well-known in certain circles, so there would be no problem making it look like she did Dorie and Marvelli, too. The way Krupnick imagined it, things would get out of hand at the orgy. Sunny would go berserk. Marvelli would put up a fight, of course, but Sunny would make him bleed. He'd retaliate, bash her over the head with something, beat her brains out, but then he'd die of his own wounds. As for the dog, well, he was just an innocent bystander, a victim of the sex-fueled frenzy. Vissa, too. Krupnick would throw her body on top of the pile for good measure. By the time the bodies were found and all sorted out, Krupnick would be long gone and well on his way to Reincarnation City.

He smiled to himself. He liked this plan.

"I'm sorry," he said to Dorie, offering his hand to help her up. He was calm now. His plan was good.

Dorie wouldn't look at him, and she got up on her own. She stormed off into a corner and slid down the wall into a crouch, burying her face in her arms.

"I said I'm sorry, Dorie," he called to her. He didn't want her walking out. He didn't want to have to go out and chase her down. She had to stay put so he could kill her with the others. "Dorie?" he said.

But she wouldn't even lift her head. Her shoulders were bobbing up and down with her sobs.

"Bet you feel like a real piece of shit now," Marvelli said. He

didn't say it nasty, but he was staring at Krupnick from behind
the bars, looking all righteous and moral. Stripped down to the
waist with his hands cuffed behind him, he looked like some kind
of Christian martyr. Saint Marvelli.

Krupnick merely looked at him until his anger simmered
down. "You never lose your temper?" he asked.

"Sure, everybody does," Marvelli said. "I just don't act on it."

Krupnick ambled toward the cage, nodding thoughtfully.
"Never took a swing at your girlfriend?"

"Never."

"Not once? I mean, she's a big target. Maybe you figured, hell,
she can take it."

"Never even thought about it," Marvelli said.

"Then you must be quite a guy. I can see that Dorie's impressed with you. Aren't you, Dor?"

Dorie didn't answer. Her face was still hidden in her arms.

Krupnick circled the cage, his eyes locked on Marvelli's.

"So," Marvelli said, "what now?"

Krupnick shrugged.

Dorie's muffled voice echoed through the quiet room. "He just
sent Sunny to kill Loretta."

Marvelli's face dropped. All of a sudden his analytical cool
vaporized. *Poor guy,* Krupnick thought. *He's worried about his
sweetie pie.*

"Hey, how about this?" Marvelli said excitedly. "Call off
Sunny, and you take me on. One on one. Just the two of us."

"What're we, knights of the Round Table?"

"Seriously. You can even leave the cuffs on."

"Be real, Marvelli."

Marvelli paced around the cage, keeping up with Krupnick as
he circled. "Do anything you want to me," he said. "Just leave
Loretta and Vissa alone."

Krupnick grinned and shrugged apologetically. "Too late."

"What do you mean, 'too late'?" Marvelli said. "Sunny just left."

Too late for Vissa, Krupnick thought.

Marvelli kicked the cage repeatedly, making a racket. "Come on, dammit! I'll fight you cuffed. That's the kind of sick crap you love. It's what you get off on. Or do you need Sunny to do it for you?"

Krupnick could feel his temper starting to swell, like dough rising inside him, cramming his head and pushing out his eyeballs. *What the hell does Marvelli know?* he thought angrily. *He's a nothing parole officer from New Jersey, a nobody.*

But that comment about getting Sunny to do it for him ate at him. It was bothering him that he'd been so nervous doing Vissa. But it was true, he did always seem to get other people to do his dirty work for him. Maybe all his elaborate schemes were just his way of avoiding direct confrontation. After all, why didn't he just sell all that heroin way back then and disappear with the profits? Because he was afraid of what Batman Jessup would do if he caught him, that's why. Maybe he really was a chicken shit and had been his whole life.

"What're you, sleeping?" Marvelli shouted. "People go to sleep to avoid reality. Did you know that, Krupnick?"

Krupnick's gaze happened to fall on the propane hibachi where the scarification pokers were sitting in hot lava rocks. The hiss of the propane tank was barely audible. He could feel a little of the heat on his face, even from this distance. There were six iron pokers in the fire, red hot and ready to go. A pair of heavy black gloves rested on top of the tank.

Do it, he thought to himself. *Don't be nervous. Show Marvelli that you can do it good.*

"Don't fall asleep on me," Marvelli yelled, frantically trying to provoke him. "Wake up! Do something!"

Krupnick slowly turned toward the hibachi. "Oh, I'm awake," he said. His eyes reflected the glowing pokers.

Loretta sat on the bed with her back to the glass panels, trying to ignore the gang of pigs on the other side. They kept coaxing and cajoling her, trying to get her to strip, to dance, to play with herself, to do something with Dragon. But these scumbuckets weren't even worth telling where to go, she thought. Even Dragon didn't want anything to do with them. He was under the bed with his chin on his paws.

"Come on, honey buns," one of the old guys shouted. "The tease does nothing for me, not at my age. You gotta heat it up a little. Do the hoochie-coochie."

Loretta glared at him over her shoulder. *Hoochie-coochie this,* she thought.

"This is great," the tall geek said. "It's all in the anticipation, the build-up. She's the best one I've ever seen."

"Yeah," his drooling buddy agreed. "I mean, she could clean out her ears with a Q-tip, and I'd wet my pants."

Sick, Loretta thought. *Sick, sick, sick, sick, sick.*

But not all of them liked the waiting game, and the majority raised the volume in protest, getting rowdier and raunchier. Loretta crossed her arms and shifted her position, trying to get them out of her peripheral vision. She wondered if Marvelli was trapped in a similar fish tank somewhere else in this place, having to put up with a bunch of horny women. She sighed forlornly. If that were the worst he had to put up with, that wouldn't be so bad. But she knew that if she started imagining worst-case scenarios, she'd lose it, and she didn't want to cry in front of these animals. They'd probably get off on it.

All of a sudden she heard the door being unlocked. She whipped her head up. The doorknob turned, and the door swung open. When she saw the black leather pants, she immediately assumed that it was the masked man, but then she saw the face and noticed the size of the body. It was Sunny. She was holding a cat-o'-nine-tails down by her side.

"Whoa!" one of the pigs wailed. "This is gonna be good!"

They all squealed in agreement. They were so loud the speaker on the wall started to distort. Sunny stepped inside and raised a warning finger at the glass. Instantly the hogs quieted down. Sunny slammed the door shut.

She tapped the side of her leg with the cat-o'-nine-tails as she moved closer to Loretta. It made an odd rattling sound. Loretta stared up at her, not moving from the bed but ready to rip Sunny's lungs out with her bare hands if the witch tried anything.

"Where's Marvelli?" she demanded.

Sunny said nothing, but her gaze didn't waver. She stepped closer to Loretta until she was just out of arm's reach, perfect whipping distance. But Loretta didn't care. If Sunny got cute with that thing, Loretta would ram it down her throat and pull it out the other end.

Sunny planted her feet, standing tall and mean in her jackboots.

"I can't take it! I can't take it!" one of the pigs gasped.

"So," Sunny said to Loretta in a malevolent purr, "what makes you so special?"

Loretta's eyes narrowed. "I don't know what you're talking about."

"I want to know," Sunny said. "What makes you so special?"

Loretta didn't answer.

"I'm talking about Marvelli," Sunny said. "He thinks you're a goddess. All he does is talk about you."

"Is he all right?" Loretta asked, still glaring at her. "Where is he?"

"I don't want to talk about him," Sunny snapped. "I want to know about you. I want to know what you have that makes him so dedicated to you. I'm jealous."

"Well, I'm not a freaking weirdo," Loretta said. "That's one thing."

"Oh, is that it? I'm a freaking weirdo? That's why I don't deserve someone like him? Is that what you think?" Sunny kept smacking her leg with the cat-o'-nine-tails, harder and harder. She seemed genuinely upset.

Loretta was baffled. Was Sunny really envious of her relationship with Marvelli? Loretta didn't get it.

"That man is absolutely crazy about you," Sunny said. Her teeth were gritted, and her statement sounded like an accusation. "Do you realize that? Do you *appreciate* that?"

"Of course, I appreciate it. But what's it to you?"

Sunny started to say something when Dragon suddenly popped his head out from under the ruffle around the bottom of the bed.

"Dragon!" Sunny said, dropping the dom voice. Her hard-ass witch face softened. "Come here, boy. I was worried about you. Come on. Come to Sunny."

Sunny squatted down and spread her arms, but the dog

wouldn't go to her. He seemed wary of her. He stayed under the dust ruffle and crawled on his belly until he was behind Loretta's leg. Loretta reached down and scratched his head.

"It's okay, boy," Loretta said. "It's all right."

"He's my goddamn dog!" Sunny shrieked.

The silent pigs rustled, and Sunny glared at them through the glass.

"What did you do to him?" Sunny screamed at Loretta. "What is it with you? Why does everyone love you?"

Loretta wasn't about to be cowed by a screeching pervert. "Dragon trusts me," she said. "Why shouldn't he? I took care of him after he ate all that spiked ice cream. You just left him. He could have died."

Dragon scooted around until he was completely behind Loretta's legs. He rubbed his head against Loretta's hand, begging to be scratched some more.

Sunny tipped her head back and suddenly let out a hideous scream that shook the glass panels. "I hate you!" she raged. Tears sprung from her eyes like little bombs. "First, you get the kind of person every woman wants and almost none of us ever gets, then you mesmerize my dog. You are the witch of all witches. You are evil!" Sunny was whipping herself with the cat-o'-nine-tails, first on the leg, then across the back. She didn't seem to be fully aware of what she was doing. It was as if she were in a rhythmic trance.

Loretta didn't know how to respond to all this. Dragon was freaked out, too. He ducked farther behind the ruffle until only his eyes and his muzzle stuck out.

"I'm wasting my entire life," Sunny screamed as she beat herself. "Thaddeus is only interested in his own orifices, and Agnes is emotionally unavailable, unleasable, and unrentable, and the two of them hate each other anyway, so why do I even try? It was stupid to think that the three of us could ever live together. Stupid!

Stupid! Stupid!" She whipped herself across the back in rhythm to the *stupid*s.

"I should be in my crone phase," she continued, "living alone in the woods. I should be growing freaking herbs. I should be taking Dragon on long walks through the redwoods, touching very old trees, empowering my inner goddess."

"What is this, *Oprah?*" one of the pigs said with obvious disapproval.

"You know, this self-confessional stuff does nothing for me," another pig said. "It's just not sexy."

Sunny turned on the crowd like a tiger. "Shut up! All of you! Shut up!" she screamed, whipping the glass furiously, the metal beads strung through the leather strips of the cat-o'-nine-tails clacking dangerously, threatening to shatter the glass. "Shut up! Shut up!"

"This may be real," the old pig said matter-of-factly, "but it's boring."

Sunny exploded. "Screw you, you old fart!"

"I wish you would," he yelled back. "Though frankly I'd rather have your friend." He winked at Loretta.

Loretta gave him a dirty look. "You wouldn't make it past foreplay," she grumbled.

"That's good enough for me," he said.

Sunny kept whipping the glass, harder and harder, and Loretta feared for everyone's safety if that thing shattered. Dragon was whining under the bed. Loretta had to do something.

She stood up and got behind Sunny, careful not to get in the way of the cat-o'-nine-tails. "Easy, Sunny," she said, trying to sound soothing. "Easy. It's gonna be all right. Just take it easy."

But the dominatrix wasn't listening, and Loretta felt like an idiot trying to console a nut job like Sunny. She wasn't good at consoling normal people—why would it work on Sunny? *Better to take a direct approach,* Loretta thought.

She watched Sunny whipping the glass a few more times to get her rhythm down, then as Sunny swung her arm back to deliver another blow, Loretta grabbed the shaft of the cat-o'-nine-tails and snatched it out of the woman's hand.

"Hey!" Sunny shouted in fury, turning on Loretta.

But Loretta got in her face and threw her arms around Sunny, pinning Sunny's arms to her sides. Loretta held on tight, keeping her knees together and her lips clamped shut, expecting Sunny to put up one hell of a fight. But Sunny's struggle was brief, and halfhearted at that. After a few attempts at breaking loose, she collapsed against Loretta, sobbing into her shoulder.

"It's okay," Loretta said. "Go ahead and cry it out." But she felt awkward and phony saying this. She wished Marvelli were here. He was better with this kind of thing.

She led Sunny over to the bed and made her sit down. Sunny was clinging to her desperately and wouldn't let go. Loretta didn't know what to do.

"You know, this show pretty much sucks," one of the pigs said. "You think it'll get any better?"

"It might," another said. "A lot of these girls are into performance art. They have to be really boring first before they get down and dirty."

"I really hope they do something with that dog," a third one said. "It would be a shame to waste him."

"Yeah, he's my favorite," a chubby-cheeked pig said.

Loretta was sick of hearing from them. "Will you guys just shut the hell up?" she snapped. "Jeez! All you do is talk, talk, talk. No wonder you have to go to peep shows."

The pigpen was suddenly dead silent. She'd hit them where it hurt.

"I'm outta here," the old pig said. "This is for the birds." He walked out, and all the other pigs followed after him. In ten seconds no one was left on the other side of the glass.

"I thought they'd never leave," Loretta grumbled.

Sunny was still blubbering into Loretta's shoulder. Now that the commotion had died down, Loretta could hear Dragon clearly. He was under the bed, whimpering pathetically.

"Sunny," she said, prying herself loose from the woman's sticky grasp. "Hang on. I just want to check on Dragon. I'll be right with you."

When Loretta finally extricated herself from Sunny, she got down on her hands and knees and peered under the bed. At first glance Loretta didn't know what she was looking at. Dragon's eyes were shining in the dark. He was cowering next to a big lumpy shape, and at first Loretta thought it was an under-the-bed storage bag—the clear plastic ones that were sort of like body bags for stuff you had no other place for. But when she lifted the dust ruffle to get more light under there, she saw that it wasn't a storage bag at all. It was a body.

"Oh, my God, now what?" she breathed. She reached underneath the bed, grabbed a handful of clothing, and pulled. She found an arm with her other hand and pulled harder. It was dead weight, but she finally managed to get the top half of the torso out from under the bed. But when she saw who it was, her stomach flipped over. It was Vissa.

Vissa's face was bone white. She wasn't moving, and there was an angry red mark around her neck. Loretta recognized it immediately as a ligature mark. Vissa had been strangled.

"Vissa!" she shouted, fearing the worst. "Vissa!"

But Loretta felt that she had to do something. She pressed her fingers to the side of Vissa's neck and felt around for a pulse, and to her astonishment she found one. It was faint, but it was there. She put her ear to Vissa's chest, wedging her head in between the woman's breasts. Loretta wasn't sure, but she thought she heard a heartbeat. Vissa was alive, but just barely.

"Vissa!" she shouted. "Wake up! Vissa!"

Vissa's head rolled to the side, but it was impossible to tell whether this was a voluntary motion or just gravity.

"Vissa!"

Her head rolled to the other side.

That *wasn't gravity,* Loretta thought. She started slapping Vissa's cheeks. "Vissa?" she said loudly. "Can you hear me? Vissa?"

Vissa moaned softly, but she didn't open her eyes, and she didn't seem to feel the slaps.

"Look out." Sunny slid off the bed and onto the floor, shouldering Loretta out of the way. Her face was puffy and tear-streaked, but she was in control now. "I know CPR," she said to Loretta. "All good dominatrices do."

"Really?"

"How else do you think we get repeat business?"

Vissa's eyelids fluttered. Her eyes opened halfway, but they were bleary and unfocused. Sunny put her hand behind Vissa's neck and tilted the head back, then stuck her fingers into Vissa's mouth to check for foreign objects. "I'm going to give her mouth-to-mouth," Sunny said. But when she opened Vissa's mouth and leaned forward to start, Vissa's eyes suddenly shot open.

"I'm fine!" she gasped. "I'm fine!" She pushed Sunny away. "I'm okay. Really. Just give me some room to breathe."

Vissa coughed as she tried to get more air into her lungs, keeping a wary eye on Sunny.

Sunny sat back on her heels and made a sour face. "I wasn't going to enjoy it," she said.

In the meantime Loretta had gone to the door and tried the knob, but it was locked tight. "Sunny," she called out. "Do you have the key?"

"No."

"It must've locked behind you when you came in," Loretta said.

"Don't worry," Sunny said. "Ira will come for us when he's through with your boyfriend." The horrified look on Loretta's face changed Sunny's smarmy tune. "Ira doesn't want any witnesses left behind. . . ." she added in a quieter voice.

"Marvelli . . ." Loretta whispered, staring at the locked door. Fear filled her chest like rising floodwaters. The blood drained out of her face. She looked out through the glass, but there wasn't a single pig left to ask for help. She tried the door again, but it didn't budge. She looked at Vissa. Her expression was as hopeless and panicky as Loretta felt.

Loretta hammered the door with her fist. "Help!" she yelled. "Help us in here. Let us out!"

But she only heard her own voice reverberating off the glass panels.

Out of frustration she slapped the door with the flat of her hand and dragged it along the painted metal surface, her moist skin squeaking as it went. *"Marvelli!"* she screamed. *"Marvelli!"* But her screams disintegrated into sobs.

Back in the dungeon Krupnick moseyed over to the hibachi and found the heavy canvas gloves on top of the propane tank. He put them on, then grabbed one of the pokers. A thin trail of smoke rose from the red-hot end, which was blunt and rounded, sort of like a big fat bullet. He brought it closer to his face and examined it carefully.

"What're you gonna do with that thing?" Marvelli called from his cage. "Pick your teeth?"

"I was thinking of killing you with it," Krupnick said evenly. "What do you think?"

"You want me to be honest?"

"Of course."

"Then I think you should get off your big fat ass and do something, you lazy sob." He wanted Krupnick to do something, anything, because this waiting was driving him nuts. Locked in this cage, Marvelli was useless. But if Krupnick stopped messing around and actually did something, like come into the cage and attack him, then Marvelli might stand a chance of escaping. But unfortunately Krupnick wasn't doing anything. He was just strutting around the dungeon, playing with the S&M toys.

I know how women feel, Marvelli thought in frustration. *Goddamn men never commit.*

"Come on, Krupnick," he yelled. "Shit or get off the pot."

Krupnick shook his head and grinned. "Do you really think you can bait me?"

Dorie was sitting on the floor with her back to the wall, her face in a tight grimace. She was trying to contain her sobs, but they leaked out anyway in pathetic high-pitched squeaks.

"Why the tears, Dorie?" Krupnick asked. "You're not having a good time?" Her face crumpled, and her emotions finally spilled out. Krupnick laughed. "Don't be so serious, Dorie. We're gonna have some fun here."

"When?" Marvelli demanded. "I don't have all day."

Krupnick nodded. "You're absolutely right about that." The poker wasn't glowing anymore, so he put it back into the hibachi and picked out another one. He examined the end carefully. It was a glowing orange X.

Marvelli was about ready to jump out of his skin. He had to get Krupnick focused. The man wasn't sufficiently motivated.

"I think I know what your problem is," Marvelli said.

"What's that?" Krupnick kept his eye on the hot X.

"You've never done a murder before. It's one of those things you've always wanted to do, but you're not so sure."

Krupnick turned around and faced him. "Excuse me?"

"Most of the people who do murders are young guys. Hotheads in their teens and twenties. You never did it when you were young, but you sort of wish you had. For the experience."

Krupnick walked toward the cage, waving the smoldering poker in the air like a conductor waving a baton. "Keep talking," he said. "I want to hear what you have to say."

Marvelli flashed a knowing half-grin. "You know what I'm

talking about, Krupnick. You've committed just about every felony a bad guy can—*except* murder. In the back of your mind, it's the one thing you've always wanted to do."

Krupnick was chuckling softly. "Why?"

"I told you why. Because you've never done it. You feel cheated. It's like guys who never went to war. Some of them feel left out. They feel inadequate, like they're lesser men."

"So you're a shrink now?"

"It's just like guys who worry that they haven't had enough women. No matter how many they've had, they think they should have more before they die."

Krupnick stepped closer to the cage.

"There're always a few who got away," Marvelli continued. "You know what I'm talking about? Cute girls in high school you wish you had done. Beautiful unattainable women, the ones who look like models. Then there are the hip ones who wouldn't look twice at you. All guys have a few Moby Dicks in their pasts, but some guys get obsessed by it. They don't want to be short-changed. They don't want to die until they've racked up a nice long list of scores. Good ones."

Krupnick was standing right on the other side of the bars. He wasn't smiling.

"What do you think?" Marvelli asked. "Am I right?"

The hot poker crashed onto the top of the cage with a jarring clang. The fiery end spit embers inside, making Marvelli turn away. Krupnick laid the poker on one of the crossbars as if he intended to thrust it at Marvelli's face. Marvelli backed away, but Krupnick didn't do anything. He was watching Marvelli's eyes.

"I get what I want, Marvelli," he said. "I always have."

Marvelli locked eyes with him. "Not everything," he said, shaking his head. "No one gets everything. So what if you don't get to do a murder? It's no big deal. You'll live."

"But you won't." Krupnick removed the poker from the bars and walked around to the door of the cage. He threw the bolt and opened it. "Come on out," he said. "Take it like a man."

Marvelli didn't move.

"You gonna make me go in there and get you?"

"You're just gonna slaughter me like a dog? I don't get a fighting chance? It won't be very satisfying for you when you think back on it. Sort of like a dentist who has to put his patient under before he can have sex with her. It doesn't really count as a score."

"Do you ever stop talking, Marvelli?" Krupnick asked wearily. "Stop trying to analyze *me* and look at yourself. Are you gonna just cower in there like a little veal? Come on out and take it like a freakin' man. You're the one who's gonna be chewing on this in his grave. 'I shouldn't have been such a goddamn coward,' you're gonna be thinking as the maggots eat your skin. 'I should've just faced the music.' "

"No, *you're* the one who's gonna be chewing on this because it won't count. It'll be too easy. You'll always know you really didn't take me down."

"Just keep talking," Krupnick said. He swiped the air with the poker a few times to stoke up the glow, then he bent his head and went into the cage, leading with the hot tip. "Any last words, Marvelli?"

"Forget it. You say I talk too much as it is."

"No, no, make your peace." Krupnick moved closer. Marvelli could see the glowing orange X as clearly as the big *E* on an eye exam chart. But he was trying not to stare at it. He wanted to keep his focus on Krupnick's entire body. "What's the problem, Marvelli? I've never seen you so quiet. You must be nervous."

"Yeah, a little."

"Well, at least you're honest."

"I try to be."

Krupnick waved the poker in slow figure eights. Marvelli could feel the heat on his bare chest. "Follow it with your eye," Krupnick said. "It's hypnotizing, isn't it? Like a cobra's stare."

Marvelli looked at it for a second, then looked away, forcing himself to zero in on Krupnick's stare instead. Unfortunately, one was as bad as the other.

A sick grin uncoiled under Krupnick's mustache. "It's wienie-roast time," he said. He was looking down at Marvelli's crotch.

Suddenly Krupnick lunged, thrusting the poker, going for a direct strike to Marvelli's jewels. But Marvelli saw it coming, and he rolled to Krupnick's side, getting shoulder-to-shoulder with him, then kept rolling until he was back-to-back with Krupnick. He turned around fast and kneed Krupnick in the butt, which knocked him down onto his hands and knees. While he was down, Marvelli stepped out of the cage and kicked the door closed. But without the use of his hands, he couldn't throw the bolt, so put his foot up against the door to hold it closed.

Krupnick climbed to his feet. A thin line of blood ran down his forehead and into his eyebrow. He'd cut his head. "Pretty slick," he said, seemingly unfazed. "That some kind of martial art move?"

"Yeah. Something I learned a long time ago," Marvelli said.

"Well, it worked." Krupnick picked up the poker and waved it as much as the space in the cage would allow. The tip, which had lost its color, started to glow again. He moved slowly toward the door. He seemed to be in a daze until he struck, jamming the poker through the bars, aiming low for Marvelli's foot.

Marvelli moved his foot out of the way, and Krupnick immediately kicked the door. It flew open all the way with a vibrating clang.

"Are you *trying* to get me mad?" Krupnick asked as he stepped out of the cage.

"Me?" Marvelli said, backing away. He looked over his shoulder to make sure he didn't trip over anything. He caught a glimpse of Dorie. She was clutching her knees, sobbing into her arms. "Dorie?" he called out, but she didn't answer. It didn't look like she was going to be much help.

Krupnick was laughing through his nose. "You didn't really think *she'd* do anything, did you?"

"I don't know. I was hoping."

"Not her," Krupnick whispered, as if he cared about hurting her feelings. "Not against me."

"Hey, I have faith in everybody."

"You're such a positive guy, Marvelli. Maybe that's why I envy you so much." Krupnick raised the poker over his head and brought it down hard, aiming for Marvelli's skull.

But Marvelli stepped aside and avoided the blow. The poker missed and hit the wood floor, leaving a brown scorch mark. Marvelli moved away quickly, opening up some distance between them, but Krupnick was undaunted. He faced Marvelli squarely and continued to stalk him.

"Know any good jokes, Marvelli?"

"Nah, I'm bad at jokes. I never tell them right."

"Good reason to kill you then." Krupnick raised the poker and took another swing at Marvelli, aiming for the side of his head this time.

Marvelli ducked and moved forward, slipping behind Krupnick. He got his foot in the small of Krupnick's back and gave him a good shove. Krupnick hurtled forward and went down hard on one knee. He came right back up, though, and faced Marvelli, shaking his head disapprovingly.

"Bad move, Marvelli. Didn't your mother ever tell you never to piss off the guy with the hot poker?"

Marvelli glanced at the door on the other side of the room. It appeared to be the only way out. But even if he could get past Krupnick, he'd have a hell of a time trying to turn the knob with the handcuffs on. If only Dorie would just snap out of it.

"Dorie—" he started to say, but Krupnick was coming at him with the poker again. He was aiming to bash Marvelli over the head.

Marvelli moved fast, stepping into Krupnick and dropping to a crouch as the poker came crashing down. The force of the blow, having missing its target, took Krupnick's balance. Marvelli stood up with his back against Krupnick's gut and lifted the big man off his feet, flipping him over onto the hard floor.

"Shit!" Krupnick hissed. The poker had somehow gotten under him, and he'd burned himself. Cursing and groaning, he scrambled to his knees. The smell of burning leather traveled over to Marvelli. He could see a small irregular burn hole in Krupnick's pants behind his thigh.

Krupnick covered his wound and reached for the poker at the same time. "Bad, bad, bad, Marvelli. Now I'm mad. I was trying to keep my emotions out of this, but you ruined it."

"My apologies," Marvelli said as he made a run for the door. He knew he had to give it a try, but as he ran, he noticed Dorie, and he realized that he couldn't leave her here with this maniac. She'd seen too much. Krupnick probably planned to kill her, too. Marvelli stopped short and turned around.

Krupnick was standing over by the hibachi. He'd thrown his old poker back in and pulled out two fresh ones, holding them up high to show Marvelli. "Do you think if I pressed one of these things into each side of you, I could burn a hole right through?"

Marvelli shrugged. "Beats me."

"Let's try it." Krupnick hobbled forward like a pirate on a peg leg, holding the pokers like hooks.

Marvelli was looking all around, searching for an idea. They could keep this up for a little while longer, but without the use of his hands, he was bound to lose. He looked to Dorie, who was still inconsolable.

"Dorie?" he said gently. "Dorie, listen to me."

But Dorie wasn't responding to anything, not even his impending shish kebabing.

Krupnick was lumbering closer. Marvelli stepped backward, keeping his distance from the hot pokers. Suddenly he stumbled over a misplaced pair of thigh-high, stiletto-heeled boots, but he caught himself before he fell.

"Watch it," Krupnick said. "Don't want you hurting yourself."

"Wouldn't want that."

"No, no, no," Krupnick said. "I want to do the hurting. All of it."

Without warning the door opened, and Dragon rushed in, followed by Loretta, Sunny, and Vissa.

Krupnick's Jolly Roger mood instantly turned foul. He glared at Loretta and Vissa. "You're supposed to be dead," he yelled at Vissa. He shifted his gaze to Loretta. "And who the hell let *you* out?"

"I did," Sunny said defiantly.

"And she had to throw the bed frame through a plate-glass window to do it," Loretta said, echoing Sunny's attitude.

Dorie was on her feet. "He's trying to kill Marvelli," she said to the other women.

"Well, duh," Sunny said caustically. "He wants to kill us all."

"Oh, Sunny honey," Krupnick said in mock shock and disappointment. "Would *I* do that?"

"I never thought you had it in you," Sunny said, "but you might."

Krupnick's face contorted in barely concealed fury. "What do you mean, you never thought I had it in me?"

"You're a crook and a son of a bitch," Sunny said, "but believe me, you're no killer. Look." She pointed at Vissa. "You botched her, didn't you?"

Vissa was rubbing her neck. "Yeah, thanks for nothing. Is this what I get for old times' sake? A sheet around the neck? I don't know what I ever saw in you."

"Me neither," Dorie said.

"Same here," Sunny concurred.

Loretta paused and looked at the other women, then looked at Krupnick. "Well, if I had slept with you, I'd feel the same way."

Even Dragon was snarling silently at Krupnick.

He turned to Marvelli. "So do you have anything to add?"

"No," he said. "I think they've just about covered everything."

"Good," Krupnick said. "Excellent. I'm glad for all of you." He was moving slowly, stepping toward Marvelli, who was between him and the women. Krupnick's face was flushed, and his eyebrows had taken on a wicked arch. "You know what else makes me glad? That you all think I'm incapable of murder. Somehow you all got the idea that I'm inadequate. Impotent, even. Well . . . you're wrong." He raised the poker in his right hand and lunged toward Marvelli.

Marvelli started to move out of the way, but he was startled by Loretta, Sunny, and Vissa all yelling in one voice. *"Dragon! Sic him!"*

"Yeah, sic him!" Dorie chimed in.

Dragon was already in the air, sailing past Marvelli with teeth bared. Everyone except for Sunny was stunned. They'd never seen Dragon move like that before. The dog landed on his feet between Marvelli and Krupnick, who now had to shift his attention to the new nuisance. He lifted one of the heavy pokers across his shoulder, about to backhand Dragon with it.

"No!" Loretta shouted.

But Dragon moved like lightning. Before Krupnick could bring down the poker, Dragon leaped up and latched on to Krupnick's codpiece.

Krupnick's eyes shot open, his brows disappearing in the accordion wrinkles in his forehead.

"Half and half!" Sunny called out, and the dog obeyed, applying just enough pressure with his jaws to keep hold of the codpiece.

Krupnick didn't seem to be in pain, but he was white with fear. "Sunny! Please!" he begged. Frozen where he stood, he held the poker up over his head. He didn't dare move a muscle.

"Drop the pokers," Sunny said.

"But, Sunny honey—"

Sunny shook her head. "Dragon only knows two jaw commands. 'Half and half' means just hold it. The other command means bite it off. All I have to do is say the word, and you'll be half the man you are right now."

"Sunny, please," Krupnick sputtered. "You know I never intended to hurt you. You're different."

Vissa rolled her eyes and looked at the other women. "How many times have we heard that before?"

"Plenty," Dorie said.

"Come on now," Krupnick pleaded, pointing with his eyes at the dog attached to his crotch. "Have a heart." Dog saliva dribbled down the inseam of his leather pants.

"Did I ever tell you that Dragon has a little pit bull in him, too?" Sunny said to Krupnick.

"Sunny, call him off. Please!"

"Drop the pokers first," Loretta said, raising her voice.

"But the noise might upset Dragon," Krupnick said. "I don't want him getting upset." Sweat was dripping off his nose.

"He won't get upset," Sunny assured him. "Not that way. To do that he has to hear me say—"

"Don't," Krupnick blurted. "Here. Look. I'm putting them down. See?" He laid the pokers down as gently as he could. Dragon held his position like a gargoyle, keeping his teeth clamped on Krupnick.

"Good boy," Sunny said to her dog. "Isn't he a good boy, Arnie? Come on, praise him. Say 'good boy.' "

"Good boy," Krupnick murmured.

"Louder. And you have to sound happy. Tell him you're proud of him. Say, 'Arnie's proud.' Say it like that."

"Good boy," Krupnick said quickly and louder. "I'm proud of you. I am *so* proud of you."

"I trained him to hang on like that," Sunny said. "One of my clients asked for it specifically. See, what he's doing now is his soft mouth, which is for flesh. But he also has a hard mouth, which I always demonstrate to my clients to show them how much damage he can really do."

"Just out of curiosity," Marvelli asked, "how do you demonstrate hard mouth?"

"With a broomstick. He can bite one in half without even trying."

Krupnick was turning green.

"And all he needs is to hear your command?" Marvelli asked.

"That's right. Two little words."

Loretta turned to Sunny. "So what are they?"

"No!" Krupnick begged. "No! Don't say it!"

Sunny motioned for the other women to come closer. They huddled together, and she whispered in each of their ears. One by one they came up nodding and grinning after they'd heard it.

"Now we all know the command," Sunny announced. "So if you misbehave, any one of us can punish you."

"Severely," Vissa said.

"Horribly," Dorie said.

"Irreversibly," Loretta said.

Krupnick winced.

Marvelli watched him with intense interest and maybe even a little sympathy.

Loretta went over to Marvelli and stroked his cheek. "Are you all right?" she asked.

"Yeah, I'm okay. How about you?"

"I'm fine." She threw her arms around him and hugged him tight.

"I wish I could hug you back," Marvelli said. "Think you could persuade Sunny to take the cuffs off?"

"Sunny?" Loretta said.

But Sunny already had the keys out of her pocket. "Here." She tossed them to Loretta, who immediately picked out the smallest one on the chain and unlocked the cuffs.

"Oh, that feels good," Marvelli said, massaging his raw wrists as he hugged Loretta.

"Sunny, please!" Krupnick hissed. He and Dragon were perfectly still, the dog up on his hind legs, his front paws on Krupnick's thighs, the codpiece clamped in his jaws. The only thing that moved was the sweat trickling down Krupnick's face.

"Better than handcuffs," Marvelli said.

"Depends on your point of view," Krupnick muttered.

"Can I borrow these?" Vissa asked as she took the handcuffs from Loretta and went over to Krupnick. "Hands behind your back, Ira. You know the drill."

"But, Vissa, let's discuss—"

"Sssshhh! Don't talk. I know the command."

Krupnick immediately buttoned his lip, though it was clear from his face that it was killing him.

Loretta was laughing softly to herself. "A con artist who can't talk is like a man without a . . ."

The other women howled with laughter as Vissa secured the cuffs.

But Marvelli was still curious about that command. He took Loretta aside and whispered to her. "So what is it?" he asked. "What's the command?"

Loretta's eyes sparkled as she raised her eyebrows. She flashed a mock innocent grin and shrugged. "Sorry. It's a woman thing."

Marvelli looked sideways at Krupnick's crotch. "Just as long as it's not *my* thing," he murmured.

Loretta took his face in her hands. "I don't think you have to worry about that."

The next day Loretta, Marvelli, and Dorie were in Krupnick's living room in Haight-Ashbury. It was early in the afternoon, and they'd just arrived. Dorie had offered to let them in so that Marvelli could collect his clothes from the dungeon.

"Can I get anybody anything to drink?" Dorie asked as they came in from the front hallway.

"No, thanks," Marvelli said.

"Not for me," Loretta said. "Anyway we don't have much time. From here we have to go pick up Vissa and Krupnick at the county jail, then get to the airport. We're flying Krupnick back to New Jersey this afternoon."

Dorie threw her a sly look. "With or without Dragon attached?"

"I suggested that," Loretta said, "but Sunny didn't want to part with him, even temporarily. She said she was going to take him up north and let him run through the redwoods. She said she owed it to him."

"But not until the police talk to her," Marvelli pointed out.

"They're gonna want to know what she knew about all that heroin back at the Arnie and Barry's plant."

"But I already told them," Dorie said. "None of us knew anything about it. Except for Barry, I guess."

"Yeah, the police picked him up late last night," Marvelli said. "They must be grilling him right now."

Dorie sighed wistfully. "I'm gonna miss those two. We had a some good times together."

Marvelli sat down on one of the striped sofas. "You think it's all over between you and Barry?"

"It was all over a long time ago."

"Hey," Loretta said, "you can do better than them, Dorie. A lot better."

"I know." Dorie sighed again and struck a pose like a sad willow tree, her hair cascading along her face. "Marvelli?" she said. "Can I ask you something?"

"Sure. What?"

"Remember what you said to Arnie when you were in the cage last night about men never feeling that they've ever had enough women? Is that really true?"

"Well . . ." He glanced at Loretta to check her expression. She seemed curious but not angry curious—not yet. "Well . . . yeah, I think that's basically true. With most guys."

"Really?" Loretta said.

He resisted the urge to stall with a phony cough. "Yeah, on a certain level I think that's true. But only some guys act on that urge. The rest of us try to—you know—mature. Or something."

Loretta tilted her head to one side. "And where exactly do you fall in the general population?"

"Oh, I dunno." He shrugged. "I'm like most guys, I guess. Just trying to cope with my inner struggle."

Loretta narrowed her eyes. "And are you succeeding?"

"Yeah. For the most part."

"For the most part," she repeated.

"You know what they say, Loretta. Perfection is unattainable."

"God forbid. Wouldn't want you to be perfect, Marvelli."

"I'd be hell to live with."

"Well, you're kind of like purgatory now."

"Yeah, but with purgatory at least there's hope for salvation."

"Amen."

Loretta was smiling, and secretly Marvelli was relieved. *A man may think he knows a woman, but he should never get too cocky,* he thought. *Women are like volcanoes. They may look calm, but deep down they're always active, and they can blow at any second.*

"Dorie, where is the bathroom?" Loretta asked.

"Upstairs," Dorie said.

"I'll show you. I'll get your clothes, too, Marvelli. I washed them for you."

"Oh, thanks," Marvelli said. He watched the women climb the wide oak staircase. Mostly he was looking at Loretta, thinking.

He scanned the coffee table and spotted an artsy photography book called *Strip.* The black-and-white photo on the cover was of a topless dancer up on stage, holding on to a pole, her face lost in thought. He was tempted to flip through it, but then he thought better of it. In the past two days he'd had more than his fill of sexual perversion. Sexual perversion without any real sex.

He got up and wandered through the living room and into the kitchen. When in doubt, eat—that was his motto. The kitchen was gleaming white with natural wood cabinets. The refrigerator was big enough to hold a cow, and the double doors matched the wood on the cabinets. He opened the door on the left, which was the freezer. Dozens of pints of Arnie and Barry's Elmer Fudge Whirl were stacked on the shelves, each one marked *Private Stock* in a hasty handwriting with a black felt-tip pen.

Extra heroin, Marvelli thought.

His first impulse was to chuck it all, throw it in the sink and run hot water over it. But then he realized that it was evidence. The state of California would definitely want to try Krupnick on illegal distribution of narcotics as well as a few other things, like food poisoning and fraud. When Krupnick finished serving his time in Jersey, he'd be sent back here, and with any luck at all he'd spend the rest of his days in a California penitentiary. For him, the thought of rehabilitation would be a joke. Ira Krupnick was the kind of criminal who never changes his ways. *People like Krupnick are like fine wine in reverse*, Marvelli thought. *They get worse with age.*

Marvelli shut the freezer door and left the kitchen. He decided he wasn't really hungry after all. But on his way out, he noticed a doorway next to the walk-in pantry. He wondered if it led down to the basement.

He leaned into the living room and listened for Loretta and Dorie, but it was quiet in there. He assumed they were still upstairs. The door next to the pantry was locked, but Marvelli threw the bolt and opened it. He was looking down a dark staircase. He flipped on the light switch at the top of the stairs, and fluorescents down below fluttered to life. He walked down the steps, knowing instinctively what was down there. He could smell it.

He stopped at the bottom of the steps, bent his head, and looked in. It was Sunny's dungeon, of course—the rack, the iron maiden, the costumes, the wigs, the whips. He stepped into the room and noticed a small cage in the far corner. It was smaller than the one at Deep, about the size of a phone booth. He hadn't noticed it before.

As he looked around, it seemed like years had passed since he'd been here, but in fact it was just yesterday. He went over to the narrow table where Sunny had strapped him down and ran his fingertips along the textured leather. It was still sticky from the sundae toppings Sunny had put on him. A cool breeze wafted in from the broken basement door.

He remembered all the fears that had gone through his mind when he thought he was going to die. Most of them revolved around Loretta—his fear that he wouldn't be able to save her from them, that he wouldn't ever see her again, that the two of them would never be together again.

He remembered some of the things he'd thought about the women he'd been with the past few days. He couldn't help but compare and contrast. Of course, every woman who came into his consciousness was assessed. He did it all the time. Friends, acquaintances, coworkers, clients, actresses in movies, models in magazines, perfect strangers walking down the street. He never had any intention of actually having these women. He just liked to test-drive them—in his mind.

Dorie was a dream, he thought, a blonde vision. But she was about as substantial as a dream. A nice person but a real ditz.

Sunny was definitely intriguing, despite the weirdness, but she was definitely more woman—and man—than he could ever handle.

Vissa? Yeah, he had to admit Vissa was nice. Basically a very good person and sexier than any ten women put together. But she was also kind of sad. Always looking for love in all the wrong places. And she probably always would. Poor Vissa had spent eight years chasing down Ira Krupnick. And for what? Nothing.

And then there was Loretta. He grinned to himself when he thought about her. *What can you say about Loretta?* he thought. *What can't you say about her? She's certainly different and totally unique. Solid. Dependable. Tender. A real ballbuster. All woman. The kind of woman you want for the long haul.*

"This stuff turn you on?"

He turned around, startled. Loretta was standing on the bottom step. He laughed and shook his head.

"You sure you're not getting kinky on me?" she asked.

"No."

"You're awfully quiet. You feel all right?"

"I was just thinking."

"About what?" She got off the step and walked toward him.

"I saw the cage over there, and it reminded me of the lockup back at the Jump Squad. Where Julius caught us making out?"

"I remember," she said.

They were both quiet for a few moments.

Marvelli nodded at the cage. "So you want to get in?"

She couldn't suppress her smile. "You're reading my mind."

They ambled toward the cage. She got in first, and he squeezed in beside her. There was enough room for two people to stand about a foot apart, but they'd already been apart for too long. Marvelli put his arms around her waist. She rested her forearms on his shoulders.

"I was worried about you," he said.

"I was worried about *you*," she said.

"So I guess we can stop worrying now."

She shrugged. "Guess so."

They were both grinning. Then they were both kissing. But in the middle of their kiss, Marvelli suddenly found himself halfway between laughing and crying. His emotions were like Elmer Fudge Whirl, chocolate and vanilla swirled together. *This must be male menopause*, he thought.

Or love.

When they finally disengaged, his face was flushed. He was thinking about asking her, but he didn't know if he should. Not that he had any doubts about it—it was just that he didn't know if he should do it now. Maybe he should wait until they got back home. Then again, maybe he shouldn't wait at all.

"Loretta, I have a question."

"What?"

"Well, actually, I have two questions."

"Okay. What?"

"Well, maybe I should start with the second question because the second one is more important."

"Whatever. Just go ahead and ask."

"Okay, here it is." He cleared his throat.

Do it, he thought. *Just do it.*

"Marvelli?" she said, giving him a sly look. "You're not bashful, are you?"

"No, retarded. But that's neither here nor there."

"So ask."

"Okay, here goes." He took a deep breath. "Loretta—" He cleared his throat again—"I want to get married. To you. Us. Together. You know what I mean?"

A smile lit up her face like the sun. "Oh, Marvelli . . ." She hugged him and ground her lips into his.

He held on tight and didn't want to let go of her. But through the swirling clouds of joy overtaking his brain, something suddenly occurred to him. *Does this mean yes?* he thought. *She didn't say yes.*

"I love you, Marvelli," she said in a dreamy exhale.

"I love you, too, but this means yes, right? You do want to get married?"

"Of course I do, you big mo."

"Phew! I was worried there for a minute."

"Stop talking, Marvelli."

She kissed him again, and now he was light-headed. He was leaving the atmosphere, about to experience weightlessness.

She said yes, he shouted in his head. *Yes!*

But then the kiss suddenly stopped. She abruptly pulled her head back and looked him in the eye. "So what was the other question?"

"Huh?"

"You said there were *two* questions."

"Oh, yeah. I forgot about that. It's not that important." He leaned into her, hoping to pick up where they'd left off, but she resisted.

"Hang on," she said. "I want to know. What was the other question?"

"Really, it's not that important. Forget about it."

"I can't forget about it. I have to know. What was the other question?"

He looked at her for a moment. "It's nothing really. I was just curious."

"I'm getting mad now, Marvelli. Just tell me what you're curious about."

He let out a sigh of resignation. "The command," he said. "What was Dragon's command for biting off Krupnick's ding-a-ling?"

A mischievous grin squiggled across Loretta's face. "Why do you want to know?"

"I told you. I'm curious."

"What's the matter? You feel left out because only the girls know?"

"No. Well, maybe a little bit. But if you don't want to tell me, that's okay."

"No, I'll tell you," she said. "Seeing as we're going to be married and all."

"That's true," he said. "So what was it? What was the command?"

Loretta paused as if she were reconsidering.

"Okay, fine," he said. "You don't have to tell me."

"No, I'll tell you. It was 'hot fudge.' "

"Hot fudge?"

"Yes. Now can we kiss again?"

He smiled. "Like we never stopped."

But after a few moments, he did stop. "Really?" he asked.

"Really."

They continued what they'd been doing, but as their lips caressed and their tongues explored, Marvelli couldn't help thinking to himself, *hot fudge? Damn.*